Psychological Analysis

Psychological Analysis

How to Make Money,
Outsmart the Market, &
Join the Smart Money Circle

Adam Sarhan

WILEY

Published by John Wiley & Sons, Inc., Hoboken, New Jersey.
Published simultaneously in Canada.

For general information on our other products and services or for technical support,
please contact our Customer Care Department within the United States at (800)
762-2974, outside the United States at (317) 572-3993 or fax (317) 572-4002.

Wiley also publishes its books in a variety of electronic formats. Some content that
appears in print may not be available in electronic formats. For more information about
Wiley products, visit our web site at www.wiley.com.

Library of Congress Cataloging-in-Publication Data is Available:

ISBN 9781119282044 (Hardback)
ISBN 9781119282129 (ePDF)
ISBN 9781119282112 (ePub)

Cover Design: Wiley
Cover Images: © artmakerbit/Shutterstock, chart - Wiley

SKY10032078_122021

This book is dedicated to everybody I love.
Including you.

Contents

Foreword

I want to thank Leo Melamed, the man who literally created stock market futures, currency futures, and treasury futures after running his "idea" by the legendary economist Milton Friedman. Leo's story is remarkable, and his knowledge, experience, and wisdom is second to none. Leo, thank you for your friendship, guidance, and support during my "journey." Leo sent me this excerpt from his wonderful book, *Man of the Futures*, and he shares timeless wisdom about psychology and futures trading. The same underlying principles apply to trading and speculating in just about any liquid and freely traded public market in the world. The lessons outlined in this book are designed to help you thrive in all market environments.

"Do you think I can make money speculating in futures?"

I have been asked this question, in one form or another, countless times. Unfortunately, it is a question without an easy answer. I have seen seemingly well-qualified people fail in their attempts at futures trading and investments. I have seen the least likely type succeed. Consequently, I have learned never to make a definite evaluation of a person's prospects until after I have had an adequate opportunity to really get to know the person and observe his or her actions and reactions to market situations.

It would be nice if there was a simple test which one could take to determine the issue. Much of it has to do with psychology. In most respects, this is the overriding ingredient that divides winners from losers in futures trading. The type of person you are, i.e., the way you react under pressure? After you enter the market will your judgment be influenced by emotion based on profit or loss? Your philosophical approach toward money? Will other life concerns or circumstances affect your decision making? Will you be foolishly swayed by the actions of others? Conversely, will you stubbornly refuse to listen to good advice? If you find you are wrong, can you *openly* admit error in the face of defeat? Remember, you will have to admit defeat in broad daylight. Your broker will always know and, eventually, so will your family and friends.

In futures trading, one's personality and emotions are stripped of customary buffers and aids that offer comfort and assistance in most other stresses of life. Moreover, in trading, emotional problems are enormously magnified because you are dealing with money—your money! Here, your personality, your emotions, your character are tested as nowhere else. The normal tranquilizers or accepted diversions which we consciously or unconsciously lean on in other fields of endeavor are not available in this challenging field.

Here, you cannot adjourn the meeting to think things over, you cannot temporarily turn to a different subject, you cannot postpone a decision to consult with an expert or friend. Nor can you take time out to relax. The market goes on with or without you, the moment of decision cannot wait. Your emotions and your psychological make-up must be such that they will not interfere with a prudent decision at the instant when you must make it. Your personality cannot be such that it requires some form of diversion before you can rely on your judgment at a critical moment.

These psychological elements are but a sampling of the important essentials in determining your probable chances of success or failure in futures trading—quite apart from luck and being right on the fundamentals. In futures trading, more so than in most other fields of endeavor, one's psychological make-up is critical.

Best wishes,
Leo Melamed
Chairman Emeritus, CME Group, Inc.

Prologue: You Deserve to Win and Be Rich

This book will help anyone who wants better results in their life, with their money, and in the market. Most people suffer (lose money or are frustrated with their performance) in the market and my goal is to change that by teaching you how to win (make money) by taking control of your mind, so it stops controlling you.

This book has the potential to change your life. Why? Because the stock market has the potential to change your life. Keep in mind, real wealth comes from being fulfilled, by being happy, and by winning (in whatever activity you put your mind to). This book will show you how to think like a winner and bring out the best version of yourself (even when you don't feel like being it).

This book will also show you how to think like a winner so you can help yourself, accomplish more in life, accumulate wealth, compound your returns, help others, do the right thing, and have great relationships with other people, yourself, and the world around you. When you do that, there will be nothing for money to do but to flow to you in abundance.

The first thing you should know is that you deserve to win and you deserve to be rich. Let that sink in for a moment. You deserve to win, and when you win, you will be rich. Most people focus on money and not a winning process. That's why most people do not accomplish their financial goals. If you chase money, and don't focus on a winning process, it will be very tough to accomplish your goals. This book will give you a foundation you can use to build a long-term winning process that will work in any market condition. The beautiful part of life is that you don't have to be a superhuman genius to win and get rich. You just have to learn how to control your mind so it doesn't control you. That's one of the core principles of this book.

It's possible that you're uncomfortable with the word "rich." Maybe you prefer to be wealthy. We'll get to that later, but for now, if you have chosen to read this book, I believe you have the capacity and the obvious desire to take control of your life, win more often, control your finances, get richer, and build generational wealth. You can be rich. You should be rich. You deserve to be rich. You just have to learn how to do it.

Maybe you work with a financial advisor who keeps charging you fees while your portfolio languishes and it seems like the market (and everyone else) is taking off without you. Or perhaps you like to trade and are not getting the results you want. If you find yourself watching the market all day or constantly opening up your brokerage account, hoping or praying your stocks go "up" or only get back to "even," I'm here to tell you there is a better way. The madness can end. You don't have to sweat while you watch the numbers tick up and down, making uninformed, emotionally charged trades, unsure of whether some imminent catastrophe is going to wipe you out or lead you to live in a negative state (angry, upset, frustrated, or any other negative emotion you can think of).

I believe you can beat the market. "Beating the market" means you have the ability to consistently earn more in the market than someone who simply parks money in an index fund like the S&P 500. On Wall Street, they call it "generating alpha." To consistently beat the market, you need to develop a trading strategy proven to perform well in all market states (up, down, and sideways), and you need the will and mental discipline to stick with your strategy, even when it gets difficult (during the inevitable drawdowns that happen to everyone). In this book, I'll share my trading strategy, I'll give you suggestions on how to build your own strategy, and most of all I'll help you take control of your mind and your money.

SIMPLE BUT NOT EASY

Building wealth is simple but not easy. The key to building wealth is to earn more money than you spend. That's simple. However, repeatedly making the decisions that allow you to build wealth and avoiding the common mistakes that hold people back—that's not easy.

Denying yourself the car you want, or your dream vacation, or the big house you feel your family deserves—that's hard. Putting in the work required to make more money, or finding the courage to start your own business, or making uncomfortable changes to increase your income—that's hard.

Most things in life are simple but not easy. Think about personal fitness; it is simple but not easy. Losing weight is a matter of calories in versus calories out. Eat less and exercise more. That's simple. However, just like with your financial health, fitness is about denying yourself things you desire (eating the cookie) and putting in hard work (doing the sit-ups) to meet your larger goals. You have to forgo indulgent foods and you have to engage in strenuous physical activity. For most people, that's hard to do. If you have a trained and disciplined mind, however, losing weight is a piece of cake (pun intended). The same is true with becoming financially fit.

TWO TYPES OF MONEY

Capital comes in two forms: smart money and dumb money. The decisions people make regarding how they manage, invest, and spend their money determine whether they are in the "smart money circle" or the "dumb money circle." Don't worry where you were yesterday; the key is to focus on where you want to be today and to set yourself up for a better tomorrow. Nearly everyone starts off in the dumb money circle and, sadly, most stay there forever. I'm here to change that. Over time, I've learned how to stop making dumb money mistakes, I've entered the smart money circle, and now I find tremendous joy in helping other people enjoy financial freedom and do the same thing.

Cash flows in and out of the market all day long. The same is true for cash flowing in and out of your pocket. Before I go any further, it is important that you know that there are an infinite number of ways for people to make money in capital markets, and you just have to find one that works for you and your personality.

Regardless of your approach, it boils down to one thing: successful people, people in the smart money circle, consistently take money *out* of the market, while unsuccessful people, those in the dumb money circle, consistently put money *into* the market. By the time you finish reading this book, you will learn how to join the smart money circle and consistently take more out of the market than you put in. Plus, you will learn my strategy and how you can build your own successful strategy for beating the market.

Perhaps the most important thing that will allow you to consistently make big money, achieve financial freedom, and join the smart money circle is to learn how to make great decisions—objective decisions based on information, not emotions—especially when you are under pressure. Everyone makes decisions, but making great decisions is what separates those in the smart money circle from everyone else.

I have been studying "smart money" since the 1990s, and I've managed to transform my life by moving from the dumb money circle into the smart money circle. People don't get rich by accident, just as athletes don't win championships by mistake. It's not a fluke that Michael Jordan was number one in basketball or that Tom Brady was number one in football: they both were relentless, they both made sacrifices, and they both put in the work necessary to rise to the top of their games. Likewise, it's not a fluke that Warren Buffett, William O'Neil, Paul Tudor Jones, Stanley Druckenmiller, David Tepper, and countless others have amazing track records and *win* on Wall Street decade after decade: just like elite athletes, they all make the sacrifices and put in the work necessary to become legends in their chosen profession.

In sports, you must have a certain physique to win. If someone is 5′4″, they're at a tremendous disadvantage if they play Michael Jordan in a game of one-on-one—but in the market, anyone can compete and *win* if they are willing to put in the work. Investing your money and placing thousands of trades over several decades is largely a mental sport, not a physical one. Success in this business is the result of your thoughts, decisions, and, most importantly, your actions. In order to win, you must bring out your smart money superhero (the best version of yourself) and defeat your dumb money beast (the emotional, lazy, and unproductive version of yourself).

YOUR BIGGEST OBSTACLE

The biggest obstacle that prevents most people from getting ahead is *themselves*—not the market, not the economy, nor any other external force. At the end of the day, your success in life (and in capital markets) is determined by one factor: the quality of your decisions. Most people spend their life thinking they are making great decisions, but their actions tell a different story. Talk is cheap; actions matter.

Most people live in a near-constant state of suffering, and most of the disasters that befall them are the result of self-inflicted wounds. Dumb money people sabotage themselves, often feeding personal addictions. Dumb money people have no structure, no plan, and repeat the same mistakes over and over.

There is a battle between good and evil going on inside all of us. For the purposes of this book, I will call the good side "the smart money superhero" and the evil side "The dumb money beast." I've named the beast "Shmelf." Shmelf is a concept I developed while raising my kids. It's the beast inside of them that doesn't want to take a bath, wants to eat candy, doesn't want to brush their teeth, and throws a fit before bedtime.

Shmelf is consumed by petty desires, fears the future, worries about the past, is highly emotional, is not rational, and is consumed by an endless stream of foolish thoughts. We pretend to stomp on Shmelf, squashing the beast while symbolically destroying the base instincts inside ourselves that prevent us from being successful and achieving our goals. "Squashing Shmelf" is a great exercise that can snap anyone out of a funk, change their mental state, and help them focus on winning.

Smart money people recognize the self-sabotaging forces within themselves and they make changes that allow them to convert suffering into prosperity.

To live your dream life, you have to overcome your self-destructive desires (stomp on Shmelf) and become the best version of yourself (bring out your smart money superhero). If you make a real effort to level up, showing the world your best version of yourself on a daily basis, your life will improve in ways that I can not even begin to explain with words, and you will thrive in more ways than you can imagine!

The easiest way to do that is by living life with a clear purpose, learning how to overcome the common psychological pitfalls that are holding you back, conquer the dumb money beast inside of you (your dark side), and bring out the smart money superhero (even when you don't feel like it) so you can shine!

ACTIVATING YOUR SMART MONEY SUPERHERO

In this book, I'll share with you how I developed my investment strategy, and I'll show you how you can adopt that strategy and customize it to make it your own. The strategy is simple but not easy. During the early part of my trading career, I struggled with some catastrophic losses. Even after I refined my investment strategy, I didn't always follow my own trading rules and continued to suffer losses. That's when I realized that success in the market is 1% mechanics and 99% psychology. Likewise, this book is a little bit about mechanics, but it is mostly dedicated to helping you achieve the psychological mental state to be able to successfully execute your own winning strategy.

THE FOCUS IS ON WALL STREET

The strategies presented in this book pertain to all publicly traded markets but the discussion focuses primarily on stocks, options, currencies, bonds, and commodities. While this book mainly focuses on U.S. stocks, please keep in mind that the lessons, techniques, and truths are also applicable for any of the aforementioned markets.

Throughout this writing you will see me use many of these words interchangeably: stock, market, commodity, currency, bond, and plenty more. To avoid confusion, simply understand that these are all asset classes and that speculators can, and do, thrive in all of these environments. It is your choice where you focus your attention.

Back in the old days, not long after the Civil War, the first stock tickers appeared. They used the power of the telegraph to transmit the moving prices of stocks during the trading day, which were printed out on a seemingly endless ribbon of paper called ticker tape. Smart traders could follow the market trends they saw hammered out on the tape and they learned not to bet against it.

I'll end by saying: always keep your losses small and never fight the tape. Trade wisely,

Adam Sarhan

PS: *Before we go any further, I want to share an important disclaimer with you: Please remember, everything in this book is general in nature and at no time is any specific investment advice given (it can't be because I do not know you personally). My lawyers want to make sure it is very clear that past performance is not indicative of future results; investing involves risk; leverage can be used for you, and against you; and everything I share is for educational, illustrative, and informational purposes only. Additionally, I want you to know that it is of the utmost importance that you take full responsibility for every decision you make. That is one of my main goals of this book: to help you make smarter decisions so you can join the smart money circle!*

Acknowledgments

Welcome to the smart money community. I want to start by thanking you for reading this book. When you're done, I invite you to share your feedback and to let me know if you were able to put the lessons in this book to work. I want to hear the story of how you joined the smart money circle.

Before we get started, I want to give a sincere, heartfelt, over-the-top THANK YOU to God—and also to a few key people who have made a huge impact on my life:

I want to thank my family with every fiber of my being. The journey we have enjoyed (so far) is by far my greatest pleasure in life. The love, support, trust, openness, honesty, priceless memories, precious moments, and the joy we have savored over the years mean more to me than anything else I have ever experienced. I also want to deeply thank my extended family for believing in me and supporting me—even when I had nothing. Especially when I had nothing.

Next, I want to thank a few people for their friendship, love, support, guidance, and for being all-around great people who have helped me on my journey thus far (to protect their privacy I will use their initials; they know who they are): WON, SEK, FS, JR, GK, MC, KG, SS, SS, DS, AO, MO, RT, SS, MR, DS, AS, MK, AH, CL, AD, MB, RS, ML, MM, LM, CM, BI, NH, TB, FB, and RI.

I want to thank all of my clients, members, work colleagues, business partners, friends in the media, and the millions of readers who have read my articles on Forbes.com. I also want to thank everyone who listens to and supports my SmartMoneyCircle.com podcast.

I want to thank the wonderful team at Wiley for all of their support and patience over the many years it took me to write this book.

Finally, I have a very special, huge, from-the-heart *thank you* to my good friend Shawn Vincent, who turned this book into what it is today. Some people enter your life at the right time for the right reason. Shawn is truly one of those people.

Years before this book was published, we did some work together (in the legal field) and stayed in touch. Then, years later, I hit a "wall" with this book, and thanks to the stars aligning, he showed up and wowed me once again!

Without his help, this book would not be published in its current form. Shawn rose to the occasion, pushed himself, and went above and beyond at every turn as he brought out his smart money superhero, made time to work on this book, sacrificed other important demands on his time, and got the job done.

Shawn, thank you, and hats off to you; here's to many more great decades of bliss together, my friend!

About the Author

Adam Sarhan started from scratch and is living proof that anyone can make it on Wall Street. He opened his investment firm in his dorm room as a graduate student, overcame many personal and professional obstacles, and has since advised numerous multibillion-dollar firms, some of the largest celebrity billionaire investors in modern history, several of the country's largest banks, a slew of hedge funds, exchange-traded funds, and mutual fund managers. He also works with countless businesses, institutional investors, and a large number of individual investors. Adam has been quoted in every major financial media outlet, is the host of the successful SmartMoneyCircle.com podcast, and is a contributor to *Forbes*, with millions of readers.

Adam is passionate about helping people join the smart money circle by destroying their mental walls (overcoming their internal obstacles) and making smart decisions (especially with their money). Adam developed two powerful concepts that are outlined in this book: psychological analysis (for trading and investing) and mental walls. Psychological analysis was developed after he discovered that the traditional approaches to the market—fundamental and technical analysis—are only two pieces of the puzzle, and they are not enough to allow a trader or investor to consistently beat the market. The term "mental walls" describes the psychological barriers that stop people from accomplishing their goals. In this book, Adam shows you how to identify your mental walls and how to destroy them.

Adam is an investor and a trader. He runs several businesses, including but not limited to a family office, a consulting practice, FindLeadingStocks.com, and several other stock market membership sites, just to name a few. You are invited to visit Adam's FindLeadingStocks.com and his SmartMoneyCircle.com site for more information.

Disclaimer

This book is not a source of investment advice. All the information and any opinions expressed are intended for general informational and educational purposes only. The information, opinions, or any other content provided herein should *not be* interpreted as specific investment advice or a call for engagement in any transaction involving the purchase or sale of any security or investment product or service. You are solely responsible for any decision you make. All the information comes from resources believed to be reliable but are not guaranteed as to accuracy or wholeness as of the date of this publication. Past performance is not necessarily indicative of future results. There is always a risk of loss in trading and investing. Opinions articulated are subject to change without notice. The risk of loss in investing and/or trading can be substantial, and traders/investors should carefully consider the inherent risks of such an investment in light of their specific financial condition and consult a qualified professional. The author, firm, associates, or the author/firm's clients may have a position in any of the investments mentioned and their positions are subject to change without notice. Any reproduction or retransmission of any portion of this book without the express written consent of 50 Park Investments is strictly prohibited.

Psychological Analysis

Dumb money puts money into the market; smart money takes money out.

CHAPTER 1

How to Think Like the Top 1%

One of the big goals of this book is to help you bring out the best version of yourself (your smart money superhero) and join the smart money circle. I will call that the alpha version of yourself. On Wall Street, alpha means above-average returns, so the alpha version of you is the best version of yourself. Everyone starts out in the dumb money circle—even the children of wealthy families that are in the smart money circle. That's why most family businesses do not last past the first or second generation. The good news is that anyone can learn the skills necessary to bring out the best version of themselves, learn from their mistakes, live their "dream life," and join the smart money circle. Once you do that you will accomplish more than you ever dreamed of and enjoy life at a completely different level!

I started out in the dumb money circle. I began my professional life saddled with student loan debt and not having a clue about how to make money or how the market actually worked. For years, I toiled at thankless jobs for lousy wages. Some of my first forays in the market resulted in spectacular, soul-crushing losses.

I was in the dumb money circle, but I had an overriding need to break out; eventually, I did, and you can, too. It started when I had my first realization that there is an endless battle raging inside all of us between (what I call) the smart money superhero (your good side) and your dumb money beast—a.k.a. Shmelf (your bad side).

ENTREPRENEURIAL SPIRIT

In order for you to properly understand the timeless concepts I discuss in this book, I give you some context by sharing some important stories with you.

I was born in New York City. My mother taught elementary school, then later ran her own logistics business, and my father, an immigrant, ran a small business selling men's suits a few blocks from Wall Street. I remember seeing "Wall Street" guys come in and buy dozens of suits, shirts, and ties, and from a young age, deep in my subconscious, I felt the allure. My parents taught me the value of education, they taught me the value of a dollar, and they instilled in me a work ethic that propelled me through college, graduate school, and into my working life.

I inherited my parent's entrepreneurial spirit, and even as a kid, I envisioned myself as a "businessman." I loved the idea of buying and selling things, and I was intellectually fascinated with the idea of solving a problem, adding value, and making a profit. I loved using my mind to make money. While in middle school, before Costco and Sam's Club were "a thing," I found a local source where I could buy candy at wholesale prices, and I sold the treats at school between classes. Blow Pops were my number-one seller.

Eventually, I was forced to shut down because the "business" grew and attracted the attention of the principal, who told me that I had to stop. He called my parents, and I was terrified that I would be in big trouble. In the meeting, my parents asked him, "What did Adam do wrong?" He stumbled and couldn't find something to say (because, technically, I did not break any rules), and he finally proclaimed, "He's competing with the cafeteria!" To my surprise, after we left, instead of being in trouble, my parents said the incident offered a very important lesson about monopoly and power. "Next time," my parents said, "don't get caught."

For my next "business," I sold fireworks but stopped when I realized that, in the wrong hands, they were really dangerous. I knew that if someone got hurt I would really be in big trouble. Unbeknownst to me at the time, the big timeless lesson there was *always respect risk*.

AN INVESTOR IS BORN

I had saved some of the profits from my early businesses, and by high school, I had taken an interest in the stock market. I looked around and asked a lot of people: "What is the biggest business in the world?" What did the top 1% of people do with their money? Some invested in real estate, I discovered, but the most common answer always led me straight to Wall Street.

Back in the 1990s, the crash of 1987 was still fresh in people's minds. But the market and the economy were on fire, the flames fanned by dot-com stocks and the rise of the internet. The U.S. economy seemed unstoppable. Cell phones were becoming widely used and telecommunications companies were hot. I consolidated my little horde of candy and fireworks money and bought my first stock: SprintPCS.

For a period of time, the stock did great, but then it collapsed, and I didn't sell it until it was too late. Years later, as fate would have it, my first "real" job during college was working for SprintPCS, selling cell phones at the now-defunct Circuit City.

After my freshman year at Pace University in Manhattan, I transferred to Florida to escape the high cost of living in New York City. As luck would have it, and thanks to grace from above, that turned out to be a very good move because, back in New York, I would literally walk through the World Trade Center every morning to get to school. I transferred in the summer of 1999 and, had I stayed, I would have been there on 9/11.

To get by, I worked five days a week and I went to school five days a week. I tell people I work with (and my kids) that makes 10 days in a seven-day week! At first, most people do not believe it, but for most of my 20s, I never had a weekend off, and that's what I did to get ahead.

One day, about a week after I moved to Florida, I was standing at the bank at 4:00 p.m. waiting for a friend to pick me up. The lobby had just closed, so I was forced to wait outside in the hot Florida sun (and I mean hot). A red Corvette pulled up and a beautiful lady hopped out.

"The lobby is closed," I said.

"I know," she said, but walked up anyway and knocked on the door. The door opened, she went inside for five minutes, and when she came out she asked me what I did for a living.

I told her I had just moved to Florida and I was studying political science. I asked her what she did and she said she was an executive at Sprint-PCS. I said, "Wow! What a small world. I own your stock." She was not expecting that from some random kid waiting for a ride outside a bank.

We talked for a little while, and then she asked if I wanted a job at the corporate office. I said sure, we met the following week, and she offered me a position: I was to help increase sales at Circuit City in South Florida. I worked there for the next few years, helped open the first Circuit City in Boca Raton (which later became Barnes & Noble), and my stores became the most profitable in South Florida.

MARKET TUITION

The late 1990s was the era of the dot-com craze. I pumped money into the market speculating on the euphoria that drove stock prices for internet start-ups ever higher. They had no earnings, no sales, but all you needed at the time was a ".com" in your name, and people would buy the stock! At one point, on a golden afternoon around the turn of the century, I felt invincible while staring at my brokerage account, proud to have doubled my tiny fortune at such a young age. I've learned that money is all relative. To me, a kid who started with less than nothing, $500 was a lot of money, $5,000 was crazy, and $5,000,000 was a dream. It is amazing how your perspective changes over time.

Then, in March 2000, the dot-com bubble burst; the market crashed, and I was in a state of shock and disbelief as it imploded over the next two years. I made every mistake under the sun. I did not have a plan to sell if the stock went down, I did not have a clue about risk management or position-sizing—and thanks to my naivete, I couldn't imagine that stocks could go down so far for so long. I also had no idea that it was possible to actually make money in a bear market. Looking back, I realize I was clueless.

My investment portfolio was bankrupt. But to me, it wasn't just money that I had lost. It was deeper. I lost my Blow Pop profits, my fireworks sales, my cell phone commissions—all the fruits of my early entrepreneurship had evaporated. Essentially, my life's work had disappeared. Gone. All my sacrificed college weekends spent selling cell phones while my friends partied—vanished. It was a gut punch like no other. It was personal. It was emotionally devastating.

On The Street (Wall Street, that is), they call that kind of experience "market tuition"—provided you walk away with some lessons. I knew I wanted to win. I also knew I had no idea what I was doing so I had one job: to learn. Knowing what I don't know became (and still is) one of my biggest strengths.

THE ALLURE OF SPECULATION

Around the same time, my childhood friend Stephen Klein (my business partner in my candy and fireworks ventures) scored a great six-figure job working at a huge commodities desk in midtown Manhattan as a futures broker.
Within a few weeks, he turned $5,000 of his own personal money into over
$100,000. As you would imagine, I told him I wanted in. The timing seemed
perfect because Stephen's bosses had realized he was conducting personal
trades, and they wanted him to stop and focus his attention on his "day job."

To get around his bosses, we concocted a plan: I would open an account in
my name, he would trade it (the same way he had been trading his account),
and we would split everything right down the middle, 50/50. My only problem was that I was wiped out from the dot-com crash, so to ante up, I had
to scrape together some dough. I managed to borrow $5,000 from my father,
and then I held my breath and jumped in with both feet. I wish I could tell
you that I took that $5,000 and turned it into $5 billion, but this story has a
completely different ending.

In an ominous sign of things to come, the day before I opened the
account, Klein lost $25,000 of his own money in one day—not fun. Our trad-
ing account number ended with the digits "69," so with all the maturity of a
couple of recent college graduates, we dubbed it "the infamous 69 account,"
and as a testament to our friendship (considering what was about to occur)
we still, every now and then, look back on this adventure and laugh.

We filled out the paperwork (at the time we still had to open accounts
with paper), and we funded the account on a cold Monday in January. The
plan was that Klein would do everything—buy, sell, handle the position siz-
ing, and so on; he'd make all the decisions. Back then, I didn't have access to
real-time quotes, and I could not log in like today and see my statement in
real time. Everything was delayed. Essentially, I was flying blind.

At the end of that first day, I called him to ask how we did. Without skip-
ping a beat, he said it was a good day. I asked him how much we made. A
little over $8,000 on a $10,000 account, which he added, constituted an 80%
return in just one day. "How much do you think we'll make by the end of the
year?" I asked. To this day, I can still hear Stephen's voice in my ear, crack-
ling on the other end of my SprintPCS cell phone. It was one of those pivotal
moments in my life—one that you just simply never forget. He responded,
very casually: "One million dollars."

I was overcome with joy. Remember, I started with nothing but an insatiable hunger to learn, and for me, at the time, a million dollars was more

money than I could fathom making, and it was all happening without me having to lift a finger.

Blinded by emotion, my naive and flawed logic went something like this: Stephen just turned $5,000 into $100,000. Why wouldn't he be able to do it again and then grow $100,000 into $1,000,000? If he could multiply his portfolio 20-fold in just a few weeks, why wouldn't he be able to multiply it by a measly 10-fold in a year?

This, by the way, is dumb money thinking. Anyone who knows anything about trading, risk management, or returns knows that while periods of rapid, exponential growth are not unheard of, in the long term such gains are simply not sustainable. The best traders in the world average 20–30% annual returns; realizing 80% gains in one day is not sustainable. I suspect you've guessed where this story is headed.

On Tuesday, the very next day, the market corrected, we lost all our profit, and we were left with our initial investment: the original $10,000, which included the $5,000 I had borrowed from my father. We both wrote it off as "just a bad day," and didn't think anything of it. On Wednesday, day three of our misadventure, the market gobbled up our principal. The account was bankrupt. Not only had we lost everything—we had a margin call, which meant we owed the firm money!

Fueled by Klein's early success—the promise of one million dollars resounding in our ears—we decided that our failure was just bad luck, and we kept on trucking. I "borrowed" $5,000 from my credit cards and wired money over on Wednesday afternoon to restore the account before the end of the day. *Boom!* Just like that, we were back in business!

By Thursday morning, the infamous "69" account had doubled (if we ignored the money we had already lost—which we did), and we now had around $20,000 in liquid cash. I was immediately reminded of the line, "Mortimer, we are back!" from the classic movie *Coming to America*, which was a reference to the legendary trading movie *Trading Places*.

By Friday, the account was bankrupt . . . again! Emotional roller coaster? Sure. Fun? Not really. Devastating? Painful? Borderline soul-crushing? You bet. Broke and 10 grand in debt, I was forced to shut down the account. Back in the "real world," I wasn't making any significant money at my "day job," so it took me what felt like forever to pay back the money I owed. Plus I had to tell my father that I failed, which stung more than losing his money.

As traders, we count our wins and our losses—our "W"s and "L"s. At face value, the infamous 69 account looked and felt like an L, but thankfully, we both turned that experience into a major W. I chalk it up to more "market tuition" because that week's experience was the proverbial seed that was planted that sparked my entire career.

TAKING CONTROL

Now that I'm a husband and a father, I am thankful to have survived that kind of devastating setback early in my life—at a time when I had time to recover from the loss, and the consequences were mine alone to bear. That Friday night, I felt stunned and beyond shell shocked, but the very next day, I woke up with a drive that I had never felt before. I made a decision that changed my life forever; I decided to ***take control***, to figure out how to trade successfully, and most importantly how to go from the dumb money circle into the smart money circle (and stay there). Everything I did from that point forward was to accomplish that one goal: learn how to win. In order to do that, I had to rewire my mind, conquer my (former) self, bring out the smart money superhero inside me, and learn the laws of the smart money circle!

I was at my lowest point financially, and I decided I only had one place to go: *up*! Thankfully, I knew at the time that I didn't know how to join the smart money circle. I had tried a couple of times and failed, so instead of repeating my mistakes (which is what the dumb money circle does), I went on a quest for information and knowledge—and the wisdom to use them properly. I read just about every investing and trading book I could get my hands on. I attended seminars all over the country and did my best to meet some of the greatest financial minds I know of.

Years later, I learned the phrase "I know that I know nothing." It comes from ancient Greek philosophy, and the saying is derived from Plato's account of the oral legal defense Socrates made for himself during his trial in 399 BC for impiety and corruption. Socrates himself appeared wiser than he actually was, he argued, because he "does not imagine he knows what he does not know."

It is the foundation for intellectual curiosity because, if you think you know everything, then why would you spend any time learning something new?

Intellectual curiosity is the spirit of just about everyone who is self-made in the smart money circle (the top 1%), and it is the spirit I want you to adopt as you move through the pages of this book. If what you've been doing hasn't been working for you, challenge yourself to approach the subject anew—with the spirit of a beginner. Live your life to the fullest, become intellectually curious, learn more, do more, and achieve more!

The American Tailwind

CHAPTER 2

Why You Aren't Beating the Market

HOW I ACCIDENTLY STUMBLED ON MY SECRET WEAPON: PSYCHOLOGY

Early on, I learned that your psychology (a.k.a. your mental capital) and your psychology alone will determine your success in life and in the market. Life, and the market, are filled with endless opportunities, more opportunities than any one person can possibly enjoy. Trust me, there is more than enough to go around a few trillion times. Your job is to be open-minded, train your mind to recognize opportunities, and act on them whenever you can—because if you don't, someone else will. Even if you don't act on one opportunity, just like an elevator or the proverbial bus, there will always be another along shortly, guaranteed. It's illegal for anyone to guarantee results in the market, but I can guarantee you that there are what feels like an infinite number of ways to make money in the market, and your job is to find one that works for you and run with it.

Throughout this book, I will share with you what I've learned, but the key is for you to think differently, demand the best from yourself, and commit to doing the right thing, even if you don't feel like doing it. Your future self will thank you. Again, thanks to grace from above, here's how I stumbled across the connection between psychology and winning.

After my initial, gut-wrenching losses in the market, I dedicated myself to learning everything I could. I read every book about trading I could get my hands on. Over the next six years, I earned an undergraduate degree and a graduate degree in political science, but my "real" education was in capital markets and psychology. I stumbled upon psychology and how it impacts just about every aspect of our life when I realized how psychology was a major force that impacted both political science and capital markets.

In my early 20s, I was studying political science during the day, markets at night, and working in between, and I realized that a golden thread between political science and investing/trading was psychology. The biggest blunders in both political and market history usually came from people who lost control of themselves, threw logic out the door, made lousy emotional decisions, and/or just became intellectually lazy. The opposite is true for the biggest success stories in both worlds. The most successful leaders, traders, and investors tend to be extremely logical and very disciplined, they respect risk by making great risk-versus-reward decisions, they do the work other people do not want to do, they've mastered themselves, and they make rational (not emotional) decisions—especially when they are under pressure. So, naturally, hungry to learn more, I dove into psychology, and that ultimately became the foundation of everything I do and part of the title of this book!

PAPER TRADING

Without realizing it, I turned into a learning machine. At every waking moment, I was reading about the market and trying to apply what I learned. Because I was buried in debt and had no money, I could not actively trade in the market. Instead, I wrote a daily and weekly "newsletter," which covered my thoughts about the market, what stocks to buy and sell, where to enter and exit each trade, and how much to risk when the trade went the wrong way. Basically, I wanted to get my ideas out of my head and put them on paper so I could have accountability and actually track my ideas. I started a paper trading account—essentially a ledger of when I would have bought and sold—so I could track how I would have done if I had been working with real money. There's a benefit to trading with fake money—you're not emotionally attached to what happens; this way your emotions do not infect your decision-making process. But the downside to paper trading is that when real money is on the line, your emotions *are* involved, and *everything* changes. So your real-world results are rarely the same as your paper trading results.

During the early paper trading days, I lost a lot of fake money, but the more mistakes I made, the more I learned, and I wasn't paying the painful "market tuition" price that marked my very first experiments with the market.

Looking back, now that I'm in the smart money circle, the mistakes I made seem mind-boggling. I had no discipline. I failed to respect risk. I jumped from one shiny object to another. I did not understand portfolio management. I did not follow a time-tested strategy—or any rules at all for that matter. Basically, I made every beginner mistake you can think of and struggled for years.

After what felt like an endless, painful parade of failures, I decided I needed a well-thought-out coordinated system for researching investment ideas, developing strategies, and testing those strategies in the market with my paper trading accounts. It turns out someone had already developed that system. It's called "the scientific method."

Just in case it's been awhile since you participated in a high school science class, here's a quick refresher on the scientific method:

> ➤ Scientists ask a question about the nature of the universe;
> ➤ They conduct research to see what data exists on the subject;
> ➤ They propose a hypothesis;
> ➤ They design an experiment to test their hypothesis;
> ➤ They collect and analyze the data; and then
> ➤ They draw conclusions and share their results.

Having just rediscovered the scientific method, I began organizing my research and documenting the strategies, and I was eager to start seriously testing my ideas in the market. Because sharing results is part of the scientific process, I decided to write a stock market newsletter, where I would publish my ideas and track my results, pretending that I had $1,000,000 under management (which at the time, I mistakenly thought was all the money in the world). That number seemed inconceivably high to me at the time. If it seems inconceivably high to you right now, keep reading, because that mindset is part of what's keeping you out of the smart money circle (and you can change it!).

As time passed, I started to study which strategies tended to win and which would lose.

At first, I published the newsletter, which I titled *The Green Machine*, daily, but struggled because—another timeless lesson that I learned years later—most days are meaningless on Wall Street. Then I pivoted and started publishing the newsletter every weekend.

For me, I found that making my buy/sell decisions on a weekly basis gave me much-needed structure and it best suited my trading style. After several months of maintaining the weekly discipline, I started posting some pretty solid gains. After a few years, by 2007, I had an average annualized return of 21%, and my deepest drawdown was 9%. That wasn't bad for a kid who started out with nothing!

BEATING THE MARKET

It was more than just "not bad"; it was in fact very, very good. At the risk of seeming immodest, the best multi-million and -billion fund managers generate average annual returns of about 20%, and the real legends averaged about 30%, so I felt like I had developed the chops to compete—and win—with the "smart" money.

The big difference, of course, is that the titans of Wall Street were dealing with big money, and I was dealing with small money. Still working my way out of debt, I didn't even have the resources to profit in the market because a 20% return after one year on $10,000 is only $2,000. No one can live on $2,000 a year in the Western world. I knew that I had to keep pushing.

Stephen Klein (who had also learned from our early mistakes and was an up-and-comer on The Street) kept up with my newsletter and found value in the information I provided. One day he asked, "Why don't you sell it?" I had never considered profiting off the newsletter—not beyond eventually being able to put some real money behind the paper trades—but it made sense. I had established a decent track record that proved that I could beat the market, and I knew that most people couldn't, so there was definitely value there.

Beating the market—also known as generating alpha—refers to earning annual returns that surpass the performance of the primary indexes such as the S&P 500, the Dow Jones Industrial Average, or the Nasdaq Composite—each of which represents a broad swath of the overall market. When the market does well, most of the time the indexes do well; when the market falls, generally the indexes fall. Here's one extremely valuable fact that I want you to internalize and live by (especially if you are a pessimist or have a bearish leaning): in the United States, over the course of several decades, the market tends to go *up*!

For example, on average, the benchmark S&P 500 has returned around 8–10% per year since the early 1900s. Keep in mind that some years it is down double digits, some years are really strong and it jumps over 20%, and some years it is flat (up or down a few percentage points). But for the most part, it has averaged a steady gain of about 8–10% per year. In his letters to the shareholders of Berkshire Hathaway, the legendary investor Warren Buffett has described this phenomenon as the "American Tailwind."

Before I go any further, pause for a second and really digest this fact. The market tends to go up over time, so ask yourself how you are going to profit from the American Tailwind? However you decide to invest or trade in the market, you will be greatly rewarded if you factor in the baseline growth that has propelled the American stock market for centuries and figure out how you can profit from that incredible force, not fight it.

ONE IDEA, PROPERLY EXECUTED

With Klein's help and encouragement, my original newsletter has blossomed into FindLeadingStocks.com (FLS) and GlobalMacroResearch.com (GMR), which service investors of all sizes across the globe—from multibillion-dollar funds down to small single-person shops.

Back in 2008, during the peak of the Great Recession, Klein worked for a large multibillion-dollar family office. He was printing money (putting up big returns) when most were suffering losses. He graciously also became a client of mine, and Stephen would take my ideas and add his secret sauce, and he did a great job making money—even in a very difficult environment. On one spectacular trade, which we will never forget, he helped the firm make more than a half-billion dollars on one trade! That's more than $500 million from one idea, and in the middle of the 2008 financial crisis!

That lesson resonates with me to this day: one idea, properly executed, can truly change your life.

The revenue I generated by selling my investment ideas soon gave me enough capital to put my strategies to work for myself. Today, in addition to my other businesses, I publish a stock market newsletter at FindLeading Stocks.com where I share educational content and market research, give members a steady flow of new actionable ideas, and let them know when the service enters and exits a position.

PAIN AND PLEASURE

Now let's jump into another timeless lesson I've learned along the way and how you can use it to join the smart money circle. When I was beginning my journey, I mistakenly thought that I had to follow what someone else did to be successful in the market.

In reality, that is not a winning approach on Wall Street. In fact, the exact opposite is true; just about every legendary trader and investor in history has established their own winning approach. The strategies I have developed work for me—based on my trading style. My clients take my work, adapt it to their own trading style, and profit from my ideas. Everything I share with you in this book is designed to open your mind's eye and help you reach a higher level of thinking so you can build on my work and develop your own winning approach.

For most people (folks in the dumb money circle), even if I told them exactly what to do—when to buy, when to sell, and when to hold—they couldn't follow the plan. They might see some minor losses, get scared, and dump a position too soon. Or they might get greedy and buy more of a stock that seems like it's on the rise only to realize they've risked too much when the price suddenly plummets. This is really big with systems traders—people who create algorithms that tell them when to buy and sell. Most systems traders fail, not because the system failed, but because they do not have the discipline to take the trades and follow the system! The reason this happens is because dumb money makes decisions based on emotions rather than logic.

To be successful in life and in the market, the first step is to prepare to win by having a well-thought-out plan. The second step is to be able to execute it, even when you don't feel like it and/or when the pressure is on. Do not take my word for it; look at this timeless quote from the 1700s:

By failing to prepare, you are preparing to fail.

—Benjamin Franklin

Let's illustrate this powerful point in a different way. Lots of people have trouble losing weight, and it's not because they don't know what to do. To lose weight, you have to burn more calories than you consume. It's a simple formula: calories in versus calories out. Yet, in the real world, as of 2020, 71.6% of adults in the United States were overweight, with four out of 10 registering as obese. Despite how simple weight management is on paper, people, it turns out, don't make logical decisions.

At this point, you might be asking yourself "why?" You see, it all comes down to our association with two driving forces behind almost all our decisions: pain and pleasure. Since the beginning of time, people have been programmed to avoid pain and seek pleasure; it is how our ancestors literally survived. People look at something and they, in a microsecond, instinctively think, "Does this give me pain or pleasure right now?" In most cases, if it triggers pain, they will avoid it, and if it gives them immediate pleasure, they will keep doing it.

Smart money knows that there are short, intermediate, and long-term consequences to every decision we make. The dumb money is short-sighted and only thinks about right now (short-term consequences). The smart money takes the long view, plans ahead, and wins. In practice, something can give you pain in the short term but a tremendous amount of pleasure in the long term and vice versa. Food is the easiest way to explain this timeless lesson because it is something we can all relate to.

You see, people like to eat because it provides immediate, short-term pleasure, and they do not like to exercise because, for the untrained mind, it triggers instant short-term pain. That's why most people are overweight. People who are in shape do the exact opposite; they learn how to rewire their brains, and associate pleasure with sweating and pain with eating cookies. Why? Because they are looking at the long-term consequences of their actions, not the short-term ones. Once you are aware of this dynamic, you can change it, and, more importantly, control it. The easiest way to do that is to focus on the long-term consequences. If that activity gives you long-term pleasure, go ahead and do it.

PSYCHOLOGY OF SUCCESS

Winners win. They understand the psychology of success. They have a clear goal in their mind's eye. Then, they build a smart game plan to accomplish that goal. They are extremely disciplined. They use their pain and they do not let their pain use them. That means they look forward and embrace making mistakes. They study their mistakes, they lean into their mistakes, and most importantly they learn from their mistakes, so they don't happen again. They use their pain so their pain doesn't use them. That means they turn their (emotional) pain into a massive driving force of good. That force essentially becomes the fuel that drives them to go above and beyond, to keep pushing, and to not give up. They keep doing all of that until they win. Everyone else makes excuses or gives up. Remember, winners win.

Weight loss, just like succeeding in most things in life, is 99% psychological and 1% everything else (the mechanics or the exact knowledge about what to do). Throughout the decades, there have been many different fad diets and new exercise trends, yet Americans (and people all over the developed world) continue to get heavier because human nature never changes.

The same is true with money. Why are most people struggling financially? Building wealth is, after all, a simple formula: cash flow in versus cash flow out. The pain/pleasure dynamic is at play in our subconscious minds (where Shmelf hides) when it comes to how we spend and invest our money, and, in most cases, we are not even aware of it! When people spend money, the short-term result is pleasure, and the long-term consequence is pain when, after years of mindlessly spending, they don't have enough money to live the lifestyle they desire.

The smart money flips it; they associate pain with spending and pleasure with saving and investing. Over time, they end up with a lot more money and the retirement lifestyle they desire. Another powerful force that should be considered is that when people buy things they are buying things that typically make them feel good and then they justify that purchase with what I call "emotional" logic. As you can guess, emotional logic is usually biased and not sound. It is carefully selected to justify the emotional decision that was already made.

When I described my first big loss in the market, I told you how devastating it was for me emotionally (it generated emotional pain). I knew how hard I had worked for every dollar that evaporated during that period. I was emotionally attached to those dollars. When I started trading with fake money, I realized I didn't have the same emotional attachment to the units I was trading. It was infinitely easier to make logical, dispassionate decisions and to follow the trading strategy week in and week out—which strikingly improved results.

Armed with the realization that I had been making emotional trading decisions, I wondered how many others were letting their emotions impact their trades. I suspected I wasn't the only person making emotional and irrational decisions with their money. It triggered a new line of inquiry for me in my study of markets. At that point, I really wanted to understand human nature and the impact psychology has on the decision-making process—specifically, how it impacts our decisions about money.

During the course of my research, I came across a quote dating back to the early 1900s and that was made famous by Warren Buffett's mentor, the celebrated investor Benjamin Graham. Graham said, "The investors' chief problem, and even his worst enemy, is likely to be himself." It takes a healthy measure of intellectual humility to understand what that means, and even more to do something about it.

More research uncovered a great book titled *The Psychology of the Stock Market*, written by G. C. Selden the same year the *Titanic* sank. On Amazon .com, the description of the book reads as follows:

> When this book was originally published in 1912, Selden's idea that "movements of prices on the exchanges are dependent to a very considerable degree on the mental attitude of the investing and trading

public" was a novel notion. It is still happening today, an established fact. Though published in 1912, Selden's book could have been written today. This makes complete sense, as the main topic—human psychology—has not changed at all in the past century.

I started digging back further, finding more evidence that psychology—human nature—had been impacting markets for centuries. For a while, I became obsessed with economic and market-related bubbles, conditions in which market prices seem to become completely unhinged from reality, and the inevitable messy crash that followed. In my short life, I'd lived through and actively participated in two massive bubbles and subsequent busts: the dot-com bubble of the late 1990s and the U.S. housing bubble that crashed in 2008.

I went back and studied every major economic cycle going back to the third century and every major bubble and bust I could find. I found that history was littered with numerous bubbles and subsequent busts. There are over 50 bubbles, busts, and bear markets—from the famous Tulip Bubble in 1637 to the COVID meltdown in March of 2020. The good news is that every bear market is followed by a major bull market. Then, the market gets extended, buyers are nowhere to be found, and then a new bear market/corrective phase happens. This cycle repeats itself over and over again throughout history.

Here are a few examples: the Great Depression followed the Roaring Twenties. Before that, unbridled confidence in America's westward expansion sent railroad stocks soaring until the bottom fell out in the Panic of 1857. During the Age of Discovery, both the British and French mercantilists were propelled by wild speculative investments that left many in financial ruin. And of course, there was the seventeenth-century "tulip mania," where the futures market for tulip bulbs diverged sharply from any rational evaluation. When you study history, you can clearly see that the assets changed, people, language, century, and just about every other variable changed, but the one constant was human nature.

SMART MONEY VERSUS DUMB MONEY

It became clear to me that Selden was right. Not only did I agree that psychology had a significant impact on the "movement of prices on exchanges," I took it a step further and decided that human nature (specifically, my thoughts and behavior) is the most powerful force I could control—and the best part is human nature never changes.

Markets are counterintuitive in nature, and the main reason is that humans, all too often, are intellectually lazy and prefer immediate results, they want a shortcut, they want the easy way out, and they do not want to work. The smart money does the opposite. They focus on the goal: winning. They know the work needed to win is just an inevitable part of the process.

The dumb money loves drama; it loves being the hero of its own (usually dumb) story. Dumb money loves to play the victim card, find villains, and blame others for failure.

Smart money does the opposite on Wall Street; we play to win, take responsibility for our actions, measure our results, improve our game, and focus on the next win. The dumb money runs away from pain and is drawn to instant gratification and pleasure.

The dumb money chases shiny objects, is constantly tempted by greed, is crippled from fear, thrives on chaos, and clings to hope. It's always been this way. Human nature never changes.

Put simply, people in the smart money circle are in control of their psychology—their thoughts, their decisions, their actions, their money, and their life. The people in the dumb money circle are not.

Knowing that human nature never changes, and understanding that psychology affects the price for just about every freely traded market in the world, I began looking for evidence of human nature at play in stock charts. You see it when a price jumps on the promise of good news. It's there when institutional traders show up and support a stock that is falling. It's there when millions of traders jump to buy a hot new stock as it races impossibly upward, fueled by a fear of missing out or blind greed. You see it when the faint-hearted abandon their positions the first time a stock falls a few points and they experience pain.

Unfortunately, human nature is difficult to quantify. It's difficult to predict with an algorithm—just ask Google, as they spend unimaginable fortunes to unravel the mystery. Instead, human nature has a more intangible quality. You know it when you experience or see it. In time, with experience, the intangible qualities become obvious when you know what to look for—in yourself and in others.

THE INDESCRIBABLE QUALITY OF HUMAN NATURE

Don't believe me? Try this challenge: I will give you $1 million cash right now (in unmarked bills) if you can tell me what the color red looks like—to describe it in a way that someone who has never seen it before would instantly recognize it. Go ahead, I'll wait. How about this: describe what chocolate tastes like so that someone who has never tasted it will know it when it touches their tongue. Don't worry, I'll stop waiting. You can't because no one can. That is an example of an intangible quality in life.

There are certain qualities in life that you have to experience in order to understand. It is impossible to explain what an intangible quality is because you have to experience chocolate to know chocolate. You have to fall in love to know what it feels like to be in love with someone else. It cannot be explained in words. But once you experience it, you know it. After you eat chocolate, I cannot give you vanilla and tell you it is chocolate.

That's exactly like the intangible quality of human nature that I look for in stock charts, and although it's impossible to describe, I know it when I see it. That's one part of psychological analysis. This book is dedicated to helping you develop the ability to detect human nature in the market. We start by considering some basic questions:

> ➤ Why do you invest/trade stocks?
> ➤ Why are other people investing/trading?
> ➤ Why are you buying/selling?
> ➤ Who is on the other side of a trade?
> ➤ Why are they buying?
> ➤ What are they selling?

These aren't questions you can answer with 100% certainty, but simply asking them will start making you aware of the presence of human nature in the market. Over time, you'll develop skills and an accurate feel for the market that will help you get in and out of positions before the crowd. It will become a priceless tool in your toolbox.

To be clear, at first, most people have an inaccurate feel for the market and they should not trust their gut in the market. Why? Because their gut is not properly trained. The goal is to rewire your brain and train your gut so that it provides an accurate feel that can help you identify opportunities and avoid common pitfalls. That will come with time, experience, patience, many (hopefully small) losses, and many (hopefully big) wins.

What's more important than recognizing human nature at work in the market is recognizing human nature at work in your own trading decisions. Hope, greed, fear, pleasure, and pain are some of the emotions that affect our decision-making (and almost never to our benefit). You can learn to use psychological analysis on yourself, and in time develop a state of mind that helps you rise above your inherent shortcomings, and learn how to do what Benjamin Graham, Warren Buffett, and countless other one-percenters have done, and turn yourself into your strongest asset and not your worst enemy.

It is important for you to know that, by no means, do I recommend that people trade by that "feeling" alone—it is simply a valuable skill to develop that can help you read the tape (a.k.a. the market) and complement your overall trading strategy.

People ask me what my strategy is and I always say, "a rules-based discretionary approach." Meaning, I have strict rules for everything I do, but I use my discretion, informed by psychological analysis, when it comes to executing my trades.

In a few chapters, I'll spell out my investment strategy, and then we'll explore how psychological analysis can help you establish the smart money mindset required to execute the strategy. Just like weight loss, trading is 99% psychology and 1% knowing what to do. Once you learn how to do this, you will be ahead of the crowd and well on your way to beating the market.

First, however, I have to make sure you understand the basics of how the market works, and how traders and investors have traditionally used fundamental and technical analysis to inform their trades.

Profits are a function of time.

CHAPTER 3

The One Question You Need to Ask Before Getting Started

Markets are a meeting of the minds, and the smartest minds win.

—Adam Sarhan

ARE YOU AN INVESTOR OR A TRADER?

Many people use the terms "investor" and "trader" interchangeably, but there are very important differences. One takes a fundamental approach and is interested in the intrinsic value of an asset. The other takes a technical approach and is more concerned with the price. One thinks in the long term, the other in the short to mid term. Soon, you'll know which is which, but first, we have to explore a more basic question.

WHAT IS "THE MARKET"?

The best investors (and traders) in the world have clarity. They are focused, they know exactly where they excel, and they know what they are doing. Everyone else is confused, lost, or just dabbles in different things. In order to thrive on Wall Street, I strongly recommend that you define yourself and learn how to master one specific style, and resist the temptation to be a jack of all trades. This chapter is intended to help give you clarity, cover some basic concepts, help you define yourself, explain timeframes in the market, and give you a strong foundation to succeed.

There are many financial markets in the world, some private and some public. For the scope of this book, I will be talking about free publicly traded markets. There are free, publicly traded markets for every major type of asset class: commodities, bonds, derivatives, and currencies—and then there are equities markets, also known as stock markets. Virtually every major country in the world hosts a financial exchange (a stock market) but, for the purpose of this book, when I talk about "the stock market" or simply "the market," I will be referring to the U.S. stock market. As of this writing, the two major U.S. stock markets (the New York Stock Exchange and Nasdaq) combined represent about 46% of the global equities market.

Markets are undoubtedly complicated, and traders and investors can spend a lifetime learning all their subtle nuances. However, whether you're buying shares of Amazon on Nasdaq or selling sunflower seed futures on the South African SAFEX, all markets share some core principles.

At the most basic level, the market consists of buyers and sellers. For every trade you make, there is someone on the other side. If you're buying, someone else must be selling. If you're selling, there must be a buyer. While everyone has their own independent motivations for why they take an action in the market, you can bet that the one universal constant is that every trader hopes to make money.

At first, looking at stock charts can be confusing, but it's important to understand that there are only three ways a market can move: up, down, or sideways. That's it. It doesn't matter if you are buying shares of the hottest tech stock, real estate, crude oil—or anything else freely traded in a market; at the most basic level, every market in the world, private or public, can only move up, down, or sideways.

Armed with that knowledge, traders can take only three actions in any market: they can buy, sell, or hold. Sure, there are different mechanisms for making a trade or triggering an action, but despite all the perceived complications—the frantic action on the trading floor, the near-light-speed fervor of high-frequency computer trading—ultimately, the only actions of consequence in any market are buying, selling, or holding.

To put it all into perspective, buyers and sellers interact in a market where asset prices go either up, down, or sideways, and they either buy, sell, or hold those assets. That's it. Everything else comes second.

It is also important to remember that the market does not care about you. The market is not your mommy. The market is neutral and does not have an agenda. It is not here to cuddle you or make you feel good (or bad, for that matter). It just exists. It will open and close whether you decide to trade or stay on the sidelines. If you want a friend, get a dog. If you want to feel good, call your mother. The market is famous for humbling even the most confident traders, and it doesn't owe you anything. It doesn't know you, and it doesn't care who you are.

Also, it's important to understand that markets are counterintuitive in nature. The basic way we are programmed to operate in the world doesn't work in this business. Most people are taught to live in a box, follow rules, obey someone else, and become what I call a George Jetson (from the old cartoon, where the main character just pushed the same button over and over for eight hours and then went home). To be successful in this business, you must learn how to think and act independently. That's not easy because people are social creatures and there is a "safety" in numbers (following the herd/crowd).

People crave certainty, but markets, by definition, are uncertain. You've got to get used to this fact if you're going to be a trader. People also like to contribute or feel like they are accomplishing something or helping in some capacity. Literally, there's nothing that you can do in the market to help it. Just like the ocean, there's nothing you can do by standing on the shore hitting the waves that will impact the ocean. The same with the market. Each trade is akin to hitting a wave or tossing a stone into an ocean.

MARKET LEXICON

Traders share a common vocabulary that describes the market, and before we get into a discussion of trading philosophies and market strategies, it's a good idea to define a few key trading terms so you can become more familiar with the lingo.

Are You Long or Short?

The term "long" means that you take a position in the market that will appreciate if the market goes up. On the other hand, "short" refers to a position that will make money if the market declines. Trading options is a common way to take a position, and the existence of mechanisms for speculators to take both short and long positions means that it's possible to profit in both bull (up) and bear (down) markets.

Bull and Bear Markets

A "bull market" refers to a market that is trending higher, and a "bear market" refers to a market that is declining. Most bull markets last five to 10 years while most bear markets are shorter, lasting on average about one to three years. It is important to note that, most of the time, the U.S. stock market tends to be bullish, meaning it has a very strong upward bias—a phenomenon Warren Buffett calls the American Tailwind.

The following chart, from an article by Thomas Franck, courtesy of CNBC.com and S&P Dow Jones Indices, shows you prior bull and bear markets before March 2020.

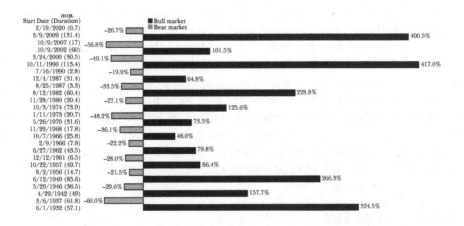

Source: Adapted from Thomas Franck, "A Look at Bear and Bull Markets Through History," CNBC, March 14, 2020, https://www.cnbc.com/2020/03/14/a-look-at-bear-and-bull-markets-through-history.html.

The following chart shows the big crashes. As you can see, most bear markets are shorter in nature and tend to last nine to 36 months or so. Now let's talk about orders.

History of Market Crashes

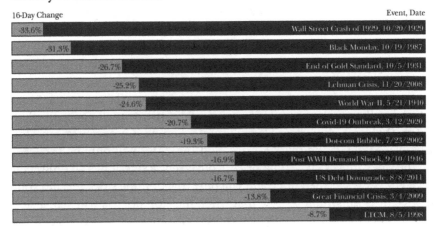

16-Day Change	Event, Date
-33.6%	Wall Street Crash of 1929, 10/20/1929
-31.3%	Black Monday, 10/19/1987
-26.7%	End of Gold Standard, 10/5/1931
-25.2%	Lehman Crisis, 11/20/2008
-24.6%	World War II, 5/21/1940
-20.7%	Covid-19 Outbreak, 3/12/2020
-19.3%	Dot-com Bubble, 7/23/2002
-16.9%	Post WWII Demand Shock, 9/10/1946
-16.7%	US Debt Downgrade, 8/8/2011
-13.8%	Great Financial Crisis, 3/4/2009
-8.7%	LTCM, 8/5/1998

Source: Adapted from Thomas Franck, "A Look at Bear and Bull Markets Through History," CNBC, March 14, 2020, https://www.cnbc.com/2020/03/14/a-look-at-bear-and-bull-markets-through-history.html.

Orders

There are many ways you can enter and exit a position. Some of the basic ways are listed here, but I strongly recommend that you ask your broker what their terminology is for placing orders and ask them to give you examples for each order before placing any trades.

Market Order: A market order means that you want to buy or sell immediately at the best available price. A note of caution: If the market is trading in large ranges, you might have a bad fill, meaning the transaction occurred at a different price than you had hoped for. Perhaps a buyer wanted to fill an order at $50 per share, but by the time the order was processed, the stock was trading at $51. The difference between where you want to get filled and where you are actually filled is called *slippage*. A *fill* refers to where your order is executed (or where it was "filled").

Limit Order: A limit order is used to buy or sell an asset at a specific price or better. Here's how it works in layman's terms: if the market price is $20 and you place a limit order to *buy* at $19, then your order will be executed at $19 or lower. Meaning, if the stock goes up and never touches $19, that order will not be filled. By definition, a buy limit order can only be filled at the limit price or lower. On the other hand, if you place a sell limit order, it can only be executed at the limit price or higher; for example, if you want to sell a stock at $55 and the stock is falling and never hits $55, your sell limit order will not be filled.

Stop Order: A stop order is very useful when used properly. A buy stop will be placed above the market price, and the order will only be triggered when the stock moves above that price. Conversely, a sell stop is an order that is placed below a specified price and will only trigger if the stock reaches your stop price. It is important to note that when the stop price is reached, a stop (buy stop and or a sell stop) order becomes a market order and is filled at the best available price, so there is no guarantee that you get filled at your stop price (meaning there could be some slippage). A buy stop order is set above the market and is used to enter a long or exit a short position if the stock rallies to your stop price. Conversely, a sell stop is placed below the market and is used to enter a short position or exit your long position if the market declines. We'll talk a lot about sell stops in this book, so this term is essential to remember.

Trailing Stops: Trailing stop orders are orders that move higher or lower based on the market action. In most cases, they are used as "trailing stop-loss orders." For example, the market may be moving higher and you set a trailing stop to exit your position if certain criteria that you define are met. This way, the stop moves higher as the market rallies (or moves lower as the market declines).

Conditional Orders: Conditional orders are advanced orders that allow you to set instructions for your broker to submit or cancel a trade if specific criteria are met. In most cases, conditional orders are considered the most basic form of automating a trade.

Day versus Good Till Canceled (GTC) Orders: When you enter a new order, you have the option of setting it so it expires at the end of the day or GTC. Most brokers set GTC orders to expire between 30 to 90 days—or until the trader manually cancels the order. Hence, the name GTC.

THE (GREAT) AMERICAN TAILWIND

I want to continue to reiterate this point about the Great American Tailwind. For most people, especially people who are not beating the market, it is in their best interest to go along with the market and ride the Great American

Tailwind, which you can do buying an exchange-traded fund—a.k.a. ETF—that gives you exposure to the major indices. They are very liquid and can be bought in just about any trading account.

For more than two centuries, the U.S. stock market has enjoyed a very strong upward bias. Warren Buffett calls this phenomenon the American Tailwind. I call it the Great American Tailwind. The legendary investor coined the term in his 2018 Berkshire Hathaway annual letter where, reflecting on his 77-year trading career, he noted that if his first trade of $114.75, made in 1942, "had been invested in a no-fee S&P 500 index fund, and all dividends had been reinvested," his pretax stake would have been worth $606,811 on January 31, 2019. His point is that America, born in revolution, a survivor of the Civil War and the Great Depression, has experienced an "almost unbelievable prosperity" that is so persistent that a child could invest a sum in an unmanaged American equities market during the darkest days of a global war and achieve a gain of "$5,288 for 1."

Now, a note of caution: the American Tailwind does not apply to other markets such as currencies or commodities, or to other stock markets around the world. Over the past few centuries, neither the price of the greenback (the U.S. dollar), nor commodities such as oil, corn, sugar, or gold have enjoyed the same explosive run as U.S. equities. In fact, as of this writing, just about no other liquid publicly traded market in the world that has been around as long as the U.S. stock market has matched its long-term success. In the future, that may change, but for now, it establishes the baseline for American investors—a persistent upward trend that can create life-changing wealth for you and your family.

MAKE THE TREND YOUR FRIEND

There is an old adage on Wall Street: "the trend is your friend." I like to say, "make the trend your friend." Any seasoned investor and/or speculator can tell you that it is a lot easier (and a lot more profitable) to align yourself with the intermediate- and long-term trend than to try and fight it. Remember, the market and the economy are larger than you. The market does not know you, it is not out to get you, or to do anything to you. It is neutral; it is going to do whatever it wants to do without thinking about your personal situation. It doesn't matter how much money you manage, or even if you are running a major global pension fund; the market is larger than any single participant. This seems like simple advice, but I've seen too many investors in the dumb money circle simply fail to acknowledge market trends, bail out of good positions too early, and try to fight the market, opting to listen to bad advice (instead of listening to the market) or to follow misplaced emotions.

Extending that concept of making the trend your friend, I find that the biggest returns come from aligning yourself with major market movements. That is why, for most casual investors, a long-term buy-and-hold strategy is the way to go. Barring some major unforeseen disruptive global economic, military, or political shock (perhaps even more disruptive and unforeseen than the Civil War, World War I, the Great Depression, and World War II, each of which the economy survived, then thrived after each event was over), the global economy is constantly growing and will most likely continue to do so. As the economy grows, corporate profits grow, and both factors translate into higher equity markets. As we progress deeper into the twenty-first century, the global economy becomes more integrated, and I take Buffett's American Tailwind concept a step further: there is a powerful Great American Tailwind and a Great Global Tailwind that investors need to recognize and capitalize on.

INVESTING VERSUS TRADING

For the scope of this book, I define "investing" as the act of taking long-term positions in assets, and "trading" refers to taking short-term positions. For tax purposes, the government considers long-term (which I refer to as investing) as anything over one year and short-term (which I refer to as trading) as anything less than a year. So, for the sake of consistency, I'll use the same definitions. Keep in mind, some people make better investors, and others find more success as traders.

To be clear, I regard trading as speculating. Short-term traders want to enter and exit stocks for a profit. Plain and simple. On the other hand, investors who buy and hold for years are considered long-term investors.

Most people confuse "investing" and "trading," and that confusion leads to subpar performance. I know that speculating has a negative connotation and many people do not like it. I strongly disagree, and I believe that speculating is a healthy and necessary component of a prosperous free-market society. Think about it for a second: How much wealth has the stock market created over the decades? Wealth for our society, hundreds of millions of people (directly or indirectly), public companies, entrepreneurs, founders, private companies, retirees, pension funds, venture capital firms—the list goes on and on; the market is the engine for the entire economy. Without speculators, the daily volume would be so low that markets would not function the same way they do now, and they would not be as big as they are now. Speculators are a necessary component of healthy markets and healthy economies.

TYPES OF INVESTORS

You'll hear this repeated often throughout this book: there are many ways to make money trading. The important thing is to find a strategy and style that works for you. Next are some of the popular types of investing styles you may encounter.

Value

Value investors are the most common type of investors, and they tend to seek out "undervalued" companies and/or other investments; they avoid overvalued assets. A value investor is interested in the fundamental financial position of a company, and they view their investments as buying a piece of the company. An important side note: value, like beauty, is very subjective and each person is free to determine the value of something however they want.

Disruption

Some investors love to buy stocks that fundamentally disrupt and change the way people behave. Two great examples of disruptive companies are Amazon and Apple Inc. Amazon revolutionized the online shopping experience, and Apple's technology and design radically changed computers, tablets, mobile phones, and the music industry—just to name a few. Those who saw potential in these companies (and countless other disruptive companies) and bought shares early saw explosive growth. That said, many potential disruptors fail, and speculators who move early take the risk of potentially big losses in exchange for the opportunity of a big score.

Growth

Growth investors love to buy stocks that exhibit strong earnings and sales growth on both a quarterly and annual basis. On average, these people are more inclined to focus on growth and not on typical valuation metrics. These may be companies like Netflix, which, as of this writing, has grown beyond its initial disruption phase and continues to grow its top line (another way of saying revenue or total sales) and bottom line (another way of saying earnings or net profit after you subtract expenses from revenue).

Hypergrowth

A stock doesn't necessarily have to be a disruptor to have explosive success. Some businesses, with the right products, at the right time, with the right leadership, can experience spectacular expansion. Think of the rise of Starbucks since the late 1990s. Wouldn't you have liked to own Starbucks shares before there was a store on practically every corner? Hypergrowth investors seek out companies that are poised to experience rapid expansion.

Growth at a Reasonable Price

Growth at a reasonable price (GARP) is another common category that people look for. If you see a stock that has strong earnings growth but is reasonably valued (remember, valuation is largely subjective), there will be a segment of the investing population that is happy to buy those stocks with the hope of relatively steady, although not always stellar, returns.

SPECULATORS

Speculators are traders who look for stocks experiencing strong price movement in the market in one direction (either up or down). On average, these traders will likely take a long position in stocks that are moving up and short stocks that are moving down, and they will have a strategic exit point planned for when they sense the ride is over. Stocks seldom experience sustained price movement for long periods of time, so by nature, most speculators tend to take short-term positions.

At the end of the day, speculators take a view on an opportunity, risk their capital, expect a positive outcome, and manage their risk accordingly. Some trades are profitable, but—and this is important—most are not. That is the reality of this business. The trick is to win big when things go your way and keep your losses small when the market moves against you.

I believe that both investing and speculating are good and healthy for global capital markets. I consider myself both an investor and a speculator, but when I identify opportunities, I make a very clear distinction between investment opportunities and trading opportunities. I apply a different strategy for each and, perhaps more importantly, I don't confuse the two as I execute my strategy. A big part of knowing what mode to operate under (trader or investor) is to understand the time frame during which I'll be trading a particular asset. Another tactic I use is to have different accounts for different strategies. This way I know that one account will be used for trading and another will be used for investing.

PROFITS ARE A FUNCTION OF TIME

When Warren Buffett describes his first investment—the $144.75 he put in the market in 1942—he provides two key details: the price he paid, and the time the investment was held. To make money in any market, anywhere in the world, you need two basic components: time and price. Put simply, profits are a function of time.

Time is a necessary and critical component of any successful market strategy, even for short-term traders. To realize profits in the market, you need to learn how to allow time to pass. That means you have to work patience into the hard rules you develop for your trading strategy so you don't overreact to temporary market fluctuations (a.k.a. wiggles and jiggles).

The second component in our profit equation is price. You need the price to move in your favor. When you take a long position in a stock, you want it to go up, and if it does, your strategy should have rules in place to determine when you will sell. If the price fails to rise, you should also have rules for determining when to sell and cut your losses.

OPERATIONAL TIME FRAMES

Some people choose to operate on an intraday basis—day trading. It is very tempting to day trade, and it may work at times, but I would be remiss not to note that since I started trading in the 1990s, I have yet to meet a day trader who is successful over multiple market cycles in the long term. Swing traders prefer to make their decisions and hold a stock for a few days to a few months. Position traders prefer to make their decisions on a weekly or monthly basis. Longer-term investors prefer to make decisions quarterly or annually.

Many financial advisors meet with their clients quarterly or annually to execute long-term investment strategies. When I developed my first trading newsletter, I found that publishing weekly made the most sense, and I began looking at market trends on a weekly basis, making my buy, sell, and hold decisions mostly on the weekends when the market was closed. That worked best for me and my strengths. I am very good at analyzing the macro landscape—the "big picture"—and very bad at micro details. On Wall Street, I've learned (and it took me many years to learn this) that I do very well interpreting weekly charts, and do very poorly at trying to make a decision based on a one-minute intraday chart.

The good news is that there is no right or wrong when it comes to the investment rhythm you choose; you can make money in any time frame. The key is to find the trading strategy that works well for you.

PICK YOUR TIME FRAME: SHORT, INTERMEDIATE, OR LONG TERM

There are three primary time frames that matter: short, intermediate, and long. From a trading standpoint, "short" is anything under one month, "intermediate" covers strategies spanning one to 12 months, and "long" describes investments that will take longer than 12 months to be realized.

Short-Term: Scalping

Short-term trading ranges from high-frequency traders—people who use computer algorithms that are built to capitalize on extremely short-term price movements—to short-term discretionary traders—day traders—who sit in front of their screen watching every tick. "Every tick" is market jargon, and it means "every time the market moves."

People who use high-frequency trading (HFT) tend to trade faster than you can read this sentence. They are a relatively newer force in the market and they place trades based on computer algorithms that can process information faster than the human eye can read it. Just like every other trading system, some HFT algorithms work, and some do not. If you decide to focus on day trading or very-short-term strategies, just be aware that the odds of success are stacked against you. Just about every credible piece of research shows that super-active short-term discretionary traders underperform the market. Research also shows that there is an inverse relationship between the number of trades you make and your performance.

That means that most people will do much better if they get out of their own way and let their money work for them. That may seem counterintuitive because we are taught to work hard for our money, but on Wall Street, you want to learn to step back and be okay with your money working hard for you.

Intermediate-Term: Swing and Position Trading

As previously mentioned, the intermediate term is where I find the most success. Meaningful trends in any major market tend to last, on the short side, a few months, and most last up to a few years. To identify these trends, a trader has to step back from the noise of the daily fluctuations of an asset price and instead focus on the weekly and/or monthly action. A trader working in the intermediate term will most likely miss the absolute low and high of a stock's move, but I find that it is virtually impossible for anyone to consistently capture the absolute low and high of any move. That's why I'm more interested in capturing the bulk of the move and profiting broadly from the larger trend, and not trying to pick the exact top or bottom (which almost no one can consistently do).

Long-Term: Buy-and-Hold Investors

Buy-and-hold investors are long-term investors. Their goal is to buy undervalued assets, hold them for the long run, and profit over time. In most cases, they hold on to the underlying asset as long as their underlying fundamental thesis remains healthy. Warren Buffett is the king of long-term value investing. He often seeks out businesses with strong fundamentals that are undervalued—that is, they are trading below their intrinsic values—and he buys a stake that he plans to hold for years. Most people will do better with this approach because they will be able to ride the Great American Tailwind.

FUNDAMENTAL AND TECHNICAL ANALYSIS

As I write this book, there are two prevailing schools of thought when it comes to analyzing markets for the purpose of making informed investment and trading decisions: fundamental analysis and technical analysis. All things being equal, fundamental analysis is used to study the company and technical analysis is used to study the stock. I hope that people will build on my work and that psychological analysis, as introduced in this book, will become the third major school of thought.

Fundamental analysis focuses on the core measurements used to determine the health of a company: sales, earnings, the price-to-earnings ratio, return on equity, and many other factors. Fundamental analysis also considers the overall health of the economy, including external factors (like politics) that could have an impact on the performance of the stock in the long term. In short, fundamental analysis is a process investors use to measure the health of a company and assess the state of the economy, to identify under- (and over-) valued assets.

Technical analysis uses historic price patterns, measures of market volatility, volume, and other technical indicators as means of interpreting price movements for particular assets. Technicians acknowledge that the price of a stock does not always reflect the financial realities documented in a company's annual report nor the existing economic climate. Good traders can use this data to make money even when dealing with troubled assets in volatile markets. Whereas long-term investors rely on fundamental analysis to inform their market strategies, short- and intermediate-term speculators use technical analysis to guide their trading decisions.

It doesn't matter what type of analysis you use to inform your market strategy as long as it works for you and returns a profit. Personally, I have realized extraordinary success by building a market strategy born out of the principles of technical analysis. While I have long-term investments in my broader portfolio, most of my profits come from short- and intermediate-term trades that take advantage of sustained price movements in the market. At my core, I am a speculator who likes to ride trends and capitalize on abnormal price and volume action.

That said, being a speculator is not for the faint of heart. I lost a lot of money before I developed a strategy that could beat the market, and I lost even more money before I developed the discipline and the smart money mindset required to stick to my strategy and realize actual profits. Trading is not for everyone. Thanks to the Great American Tailwind, despite the daily ups and downs, the long-term trend of the U.S. stock market is upward; that's why most long-term investors tend to outperform active short-term traders. However, for those of us who can excel at the art of trading, the results can be magnificent.

THE ANATOMY OF A TRADER

A trader creates a market strategy based on technical analysis of price patterns and looks for assets that are poised to make a significant movement in one direction or another. They can take a long position when they think a stock will go up, and they can take a short position if they think a stock will go down. Either way, if they are right, they are poised to make a tidy profit.

A trader will invest most of their time poring over stock charts looking for patterns that may indicate that a particular asset is poised to make a move. Good traders are agnostic with respect to the direction; they will profit whether the stock goes up and or down. To be clear, discretionary trading is more of an art than a science.

Stocks that are ready to move often present some telltale signs (I'll share some of them with you when I reveal my A.M.P.D. strategy), but at first, you'll likely find these signifiers difficult to spot on your own; they have a quality that is very difficult to describe. Just as I can't accurately describe what the color red looks like or what chocolate tastes like, I also can't accurately describe the quality of a stock that's ready to take off. I can, however, point you in the right direction so, as you explore stock charts on your own, you can begin to develop a sense for detecting this important quality yourself. The best traders use several characteristics, but irrespective of their exact method, it will usually revolve around price as a primary component and volume—or some other technical indicator—as a secondary component.

One goal of this book is to help you determine whether you are an investor or a trader (then bring out the smart money superhero out to play). If you decide that a long-term investment strategy best suits your personality, style, and appetite for risk, then my hope is that as you read on, you understand why you feel that way, and you'll avoid the temptation of dabbling in trading and instead commit to a strategy that works for you. If you decide that you are a speculator, this book will provide you with a great risk-adjusted and time-tested trading strategy. More importantly, we'll explore the psychology required to develop the smart money mindset needed to avoid the common pitfalls traders face so you can win.

I am looking forward to sharing my A.M.P.D. trading strategy with you and telling you about psychological analysis, but first I need to make sure you know the basics of fundamental and technical analysis. Once we get through that homework, you will have the tools you need to benefit from the rest of this book.

Price is what you pay; value is what you get.

CHAPTER 4

How to Use Fundamental Analysis Like a Pro

Price is what you pay; value is what you get.

—*Warren Buffett*

FUNDAMENTAL ANALYSIS 101

Fundamental analysis is, perhaps, the most common tool people use to analyze the market. It is very powerful when used properly. It is especially popular with long-term, value investors. At the most basic level, fundamental analysis uses intrinsic factors relating to the underlying health of a company, the underlying business, economy, or market, to inform an investor's buy and sell decisions.

Fundamental analysts concern themselves with annual reports, sales reports, corporate earnings, cash flow, pretax margin, price-to-earnings ratios (a.k.a. P/E ratios), margins, return on equity—the list goes on and on. A fundamental analyst is not concerned with price patterns on a chart; that's the domain of technical analysts. To further help explain the difference, fundamental analysis tends to be extremely important for long-term investors while technical analysis is more useful for shorter-term traders.

Fundamental analysis is not limited to studying just one single business. Many other factors, such as macro and microeconomic data, financial, political, and other qualitative and quantitative factors, are analyzed to determine the possible ramifications on the market, sector, industry, company, bond, commodity, or any other asset you can think of.

Many investors like fundamental analysis because it works, plain and simple. It is tangible. It is intuitive, and it reflects documented financial realities. Warren Buffett and many other ultrasuccessful investors use fundamental analysis to inform their value-investing decisions. They want to identify undervalued assets, buy them early, and hold them for an extended period of time as the market price of an asset grows to match its intrinsic value. I do not know anyone with a similar winning track record who wants to argue with the Oracle of Omaha—especially when it has to do with the market. I have also never met a person who is not happy when they get a good deal on anything they buy, especially if it makes them money later. When used properly, fundamental analysis is extremely powerful.

Caution: just because something is cheap doesn't mean it can't get a lot cheaper. The opposite is also true: just because something is expensive on Wall Street doesn't mean it can't become a lot more expensive. In fact, most of the time, that is what happens. Remember, markets trend, and you will do infinitely better over the years if you live by this mantra: Respect the Trend.

VALUE VERSUS PRICE

Warren Buffett once said, "Price is what you pay; value is what you get." Pause for a minute and really try to understand the deep meaning behind what he said. It reflects the reality that the market price for an asset doesn't always match the underlying fundamental value. Fortunes are made and lost on Wall Street because of that extremely important difference.

Ideally, a value investor will calculate the value of a company, compare it to the market price, and when they find an undervalued asset, make a strategic investment. The challenge for the investor, however, is that beauty is in the eye of the beholder, and there is no single concrete method for determining the value of an asset. Value, like beauty, is very subjective, and where one person may find value, another may not.

If you want to learn this lesson, just look at the clouds in the sky. One day when my kids were preschoolers, we had a pool party; a few of the kids' friends came over with their parents and everyone played and we had a great time. At one point, while we were eating, I asked everyone to look up at a very big cloud in the sky and tell me what they saw. As you might expect, just about every person (adults and children) saw something completely different. Even though it was the exact same cloud!

The same is true in the market. The market is the sky and each stock is a different cloud—and each participant sees something completely different. Your job is to learn to anticipate what most people will see, take a position once that trend develops, and get in as early as possible.

A note of caution: when getting in early, you want to make sure there is a preexisting trend before you enter. This way, you are aligned with the market and it agrees with your thesis. The last thing you want to do is tie your money up for years because you believe something even though the market disagrees with you. Remember, all that matters is what the market believes. It is also important to keep in mind that there is a major opportunity cost in owning a stock that is not performing well, especially when your money can be used to buy a leading stock that is performing exceptionally well!

FUNDAMENTAL INDICATORS OF VALUE

Although value is subjective, there are a few key fundamental indicators that value investors use to begin their assessment of an asset. Every quarter, publicly traded companies publish earnings reports which show how the company fared in the prior quarter. Buried in those reports investors will find several key metrics to help them better understand the company's fundamentals. Here are a few key indicators that fundamental analysts like to focus on: a company's price-to-earnings ratio, their sales and earnings growth, return on equity, and cash flow, to name just a few. There are many others, but knowing how these four indicators work will give you a broad understanding of how to evaluate a publicly traded company's value.

Price-to-Earnings (P/E) Ratio

A company's P/E ratio, or PER, measures the relationship between its actual earnings and price per share. By this measure, the "earnings" part of the ratio connects to the net income reported by a company—a real number that correlates to real money. The "price" part of the ratio comes from the current market price of a company. To calculate the ratio, divide the current stock price by the earnings per share (EPS). If the price of the stock is low compared to the earnings, it's a sign that the asset may be undervalued. If the share price is comparatively high, it suggests the asset may be overvalued. If you can pay a low price for a company that reports high earnings, someone like Warren Buffett might call that a value.

Sales and Earnings Growth

Long-term investors want to see the companies they bet on experience increased sales and rising earnings over time. They look at the top and bottom lines on a company's profit and loss statement looking for sales and earnings on a quarterly and annual basis. The top line is revenue; the bottom line is earnings. Market history shows us that some of the strongest-performing stocks (on a percent change basis) have enjoyed both robust sales and earnings growth.

Return on Equity

The return on equity (ROE) ratio is typically used to determine profitability based on the shareholders' equity in the company. Put simply, the return on equity ratio shows how much profit each dollar of common stockholders' equity generates. To determine ROE, simply divide the net income by the shareholders' equity. The resulting number, especially when compared to the ROEs of other companies in the same industry, can help an investor understand how well a company's management can turn available cash into profits.

Cash Flow

Cash flow is a very important tool that most investors misunderstand and most traders don't even look at. In the simplest sense, cash flow refers to the total money that comes into a company versus the total money going out. All things being equal, positive free cash flow is one healthy characteristic nearly all successful businesses share. A strong cash flow helps a company stay liquid; it allows it to remain solvent during difficult periods, and it gives a company the opportunity to capitalize on emergent opportunities.

THE TROUBLE WITH FUNDAMENTAL INDICATORS

So, if you were to pore through volumes of corporate reports, you could perhaps eventually find a company with a strong cash flow, a strong return on equity, a consistent pattern of steady sales and earnings growth, and a low profit to earnings growth—then you could take a position and in a few years, reap a big reward, right?

If you're skeptical, you'd be right to feel that way.

The truth is, there is a spurious correlation between a company's value as indicated by any of these fundamental indicators and the way the stock actually trades at any given moment in time.

IMPORTANT:

A company and a stock are completely different. Treat them as two completely separate entities.

Remember, you can have a great company and a lousy stock and vice versa. Think of the company as one entity and the stock as a separate entity. The reason is simple: price is a function of perception, nothing more and nothing less. The price of a stock will move based on how most buyers and sellers perceive the value to be at any given time. Since we all see "different clouds," not all buyers and sellers make decisions based on the fundamentals. In fact, most buyers and sellers don't read the fundamentals in the exact same way, especially when the market is moving fast, and there is a large number of people who do not even use fundamentals at all to inform their trading decisions.

New data, headlines, technological developments, political events, scandals, global pandemics—lots of things can influence the price of an asset. The fact that perception is constantly changing and buyers and sellers are entering and leaving all the time means stock prices are frequently untethered from basic valuations.

Prices are determined exclusively by how much one party is willing to pay for something and how much another party is willing to sell it for at a specific moment in time. It is that simple. Everything else is secondary. And, as you know by now, dumb money is around us all the time, and, you guessed it, dumb money people do dumb things—such as overpaying for stocks, not selling a "great company" even though the stock is tanking, and making emotional, not rational, decisions with their money. All of that impacts the price of a stock. My experience has taught me that the two most powerful forces that impact market prices are perception and emotions.

There's a famous quote by an extremely influential economist John Maynard Keynes. Keynes famously said, "The stock market can remain irrational longer than you can remain solvent." What he means is that the market is more emotional than it is logical. That said, it is very important to react promptly when the underlying conditions change and always respect risk.

CONFUSING NUMBERS AND CREATIVE ACCOUNTING

Some of the core fundamentals value investors use to evaluate a stock aren't as rock-solid as they might hope. Two key fundamental indicators, the price-to-earnings ratio and sales and earnings growth, rely on an accurate accounting of a company's earnings. Calculating earnings, however, isn't always a straightforward process.

Two Types of Earnings per Share

When we're looking at the earnings of a publicly traded stock—especially if we're trying to work out the PER—we are focusing on the earnings per share (EPS). In the simplest form, EPS is the portion of a company's profit for each outstanding share of common stock. EPS is calculated using the following formula:

$$EPS = (\text{Net income} - \text{Dividends on preferred stock})$$
$$\text{divided by Outstanding shares}$$

Here's an example of the equation in action (we'll keep it easy by imagining a stock that doesn't pay dividends):

Stock	Earnings (Net Income)	Preferred Dividends	Average Shares Outstanding	Basic EPS
XYZ	13.64 billion	0	3.1 billion	13.64/3.1 = $4.40

The most common types of EPS are "basic" and "diluted." The equation just shown is used to calculate the basic EPS, and it is the standard method. The problem with basic EPS is that it is based solely on the shares outstanding and does not incorporate the dilutive impact of convertible securities such as stock options, restricted stock units (RSUs), warrants, and other more esoteric investment instruments. These additional securities, if exercised, could significantly change the number of average shares outstanding and adversely impact EPS. Typically, when a company reports its earnings, it reports both basic and dilutive EPS because the dilutive EPS represents the worst-case scenario, but it takes a savvy investor to know the difference.

Two Types of Accounting

Just as there are two common ways to report earnings per share, companies also use two popular methods to calculate overall earnings: GAAP and non-GAAP.

GAAP is an acronym for "generally accepted accounting principles." GAAP accounting standards are designed to offer uniformity in how companies report their financial numbers each quarter. The problem with GAAP earnings is that income statements reported based on GAAP do not always accurately reflect the ongoing performance of a company's underlying operations. For example, a company can create a one-time nonrecurring adjustment such as a purchase or write-down of an asset, and that could substantially distort earnings.

Because the GAAP earnings could be distorted, a company will also provide an adjusted (non-GAAP) earnings number that excludes these nonrecurring items. The benefit of analyzing non-GAAP earnings is that it will show what the earnings are minus the nonrecurring one-time adjustment. Are your eyes glazing over yet? Don't worry, you're almost done with this part.

Beware of Manipulated Reporting

All these different reporting conventions provide some room for creative accounting. Accountants can shift items around on their balance sheets to benefit one key indicator or another. There are countless ways companies can massage the numbers, but one of the most common tactics is to add, remove, or defer expenses in order to change the way the earnings look at any given point. Some unscrupulous companies manipulate their earnings reporting enough that it qualifies as fraud. Some famous frauds have made headlines in the past: Enron, Tyco, HealthSouth, and Lehman Brothers are just a few. Be careful when you analyze the data and always check to see how the company calculates earnings and whether there are any accounting adjustments or irregularities that are taking place.

STRONG FUNDAMENTALS? SO WHAT?

Just because a company demonstrates strong fundamental metrics doesn't mean the market will reward investors with a high stock price. Warren Buffett famously owned Coca-Cola, loved it, and drank it for decades and the stock barely moved in 20 years. In 1998, the stock hit a high of $44.47 and in Q1 2018, the stock was trading at $43 and change. Granted, during that time the stock fell down to $18 and charged back up to the low $40s—but from 1998 to 2018, the stock price was virtually unchanged. Meanwhile, both revenue and earnings were substantially higher in 2018 than in 1998. This is just one of many countless examples. Remember, price is a function of perception, and the market perceived that the price was a proper reflection of the company's value during that time.

It's possible that Coca-Cola's stagnant stock price is a factor of the company's maturity. How much growth potential is there for a soft drink that can be found practically anywhere on the planet? Most investors would prefer to post big gains quickly, and when they look forward with Coca-Cola, they don't see that hypergrowth potential, regardless of how good the company's quarterly reports look.

Conversely, some companies post objectively terrible numbers while their stock prices soar. Famously, Amazon posted huge losses for years while its stock price climbed higher and higher. During that time, Amazon's founder, Jeff Bezos, was reinvesting the vast majority of the company's revenue into innovations that would eventually transform the upstart online bookseller into a global e-commerce juggernaut while concurrently reinventing the entire supply chain. Many investors believed in Bezos's vision, they saw the potential, and despite the fact that Amazon in the early days wasn't a profitable enterprise, they bet it would be wildly successful in the future. They bet right.

Any investor who relied too heavily on Amazon's price-to-earnings ratio during its hypergrowth phase would have dismissed the opportunity. A growth investor might have ignored the P/E ratio and focused more on sales and earnings growth figures—but there again, the Coca-Cola example has shown the potential problems with making decisions based on those figures alone. Let me be clear: fundamentals are important, but they do not tell us everything we need to know to be successful on Wall Street.

THE MARKET IS A FORWARD-LOOKING APPARATUS

The market looks forward but most investors look backward. This illustrates a key problem: financial reports do a great job of revealing where a company has been but not what's going to happen in the future—although they sometimes try.

Undervalued assets are often overlooked because most people lack the imagination to see the future potential. The value investor's job is to look forward to the future when most people are looking backward into the past. Economic and earnings data can do nothing more than tell us what already happened. It's history. The market, however, is a forward-thinking apparatus. When you shift your focus and start looking at what a company can do (not just what it has done), then you can start to assess whether the market will properly price an asset in the future. I call that "navigating to the right of the chart." I discuss some indicators that are used to look to the future next.

Leading Earnings

Most of the financial websites publish a price-to-earnings ratio based on the "trailing twelve-month earnings per share," or the P/E TTM. It's a backward-looking number. Each quarter, most companies publish future guidance when they report earnings, allowing analysts, investors, and speculators to calculate a "forward P/E." The problem with forward earnings, as I'm sure you can imagine, is that they are projections and have not happened yet. Unforeseen events can very easily change the actual results from the initial guidance months earlier. Secondly, some companies purposely lower guidance so they can "beat" expectations in future quarters. So, while guidance is important, it is always good to take it with a grain of trading salt.

Sales Growth as a Leading Indicator

For those looking to the future, sales growth may provide a better metric. The beauty about sales, or revenue, is that accountants can't really play around with that number. For example, if a company sold 10 widgets at $2 each, the company has $20 in revenue. Revenue is also referred to as the "top line number" because it is the first number on an income statement. After that, you remove expenses, and then you are left with net profit or loss. Revenue is the starting point and everything else follows that number. Accountants can manipulate the bottom line, but the top line is more concrete. That said, just because a company has posted steadily increasing sales in the past quarters doesn't guarantee that the trendline will keep going up—and even if it does, there's no guarantee that the market will reward sales growth with a rising stock price.

Cash Flow as a Leading Indicator

When it comes to trying to divine the future health of a company, you can't do much better than cash flow. Many people don't understand the difference between cash flow and earnings so here's a quick primer: it is possible for your business to be profitable but to have no cash. Profitability is an accounting concept and has nothing to do with the amount of cash you have in the bank. Many companies operate on an accrual accounting basis, meaning they record revenue when they send out an invoice, rather than when the check is cashed. A company's accounts receivable ledger is an asset that counts toward profit, even when the money is not in the bank.

There are many other circumstances where a company can run low or run out of cash, and that is why total free positive cash flow is an important piece of the value investor's puzzle. But it's just one piece, and if a company is sitting on too much cash, it means they are not reinvesting it into future earnings.

THE VALUE INVESTOR'S LONG-TERM BET

Value investors understand that the market price of a stock doesn't always match the intrinsic value of a company. They understand that a positive cash flow or steady earnings cannot guarantee that a company's stock price will rally today or tomorrow. Value investors do, however, believe that, in the long term, a company that consistently makes a profit, shows potential for steady growth, and reports strong fundamentals will ultimately be recognized by the market and be rewarded with a stock price that matches the company's value.

Traders and speculators, on the other hand, know that there is money to be made in the market in short term, and they know that the price of a stock on any given day has a spurious correlation with the fundamental indicators that value investors use to make their trading decisions. That means there are other forces at play in the market driving prices up and down, and traders become obsessed with identifying and studying those drivers.

ANOTHER WAY OF DEFINING PRICE

George Soros says that price is based on the perception of value. His reflexivity theory suggests that actions that people take based on their perception of reality have a tangible impact on the market. This principle is extremely powerful. Your perception and emotion control your decisions. Market prices are determined by the perception of value and that depends on where market participants perceive value to be at any given time. Remember, there is no concrete formula for determining value, so prices are constantly moving based on incoming data and how market participants think, feel, and behave. Once we start looking at markets from this perspective, we are venturing into the domain of technical analysis.

What's happening is more important than why it's happening.

CHAPTER 5

How to Use Technical Analysis Like a Pro

What happens on Wall Street is a lot more important than why you think something happened. Don't get lost in the "why"; focus and align yourself with what is happening right now.

—Adam Sarhan

WHAT IS TECHNICAL ANALYSIS?

Fundamental analysis does a great job of telling you *what* to buy/sell, but not *when* to buy/sell. Technical analysis solves that problem because it tells you what to buy/sell *and* when to buy/sell.

Before we dive in, it is important for you to know that technical analysis is, perhaps, one of the most powerful and misunderstood trading approaches on Wall Street. In its purest form, technical analysis helps traders make "buy" and "sell" decisions based on the objective study of price action.

Technicians analyze historic price patterns, volume, market volatility, open interest, and a slew of other technical indicators as a means of interpreting price movements. To a person who only focuses on very strict technical analysis, price is primary; everything else is secondary.

What that means in plain English is that technicians make their entry and exit (buy and sell) decisions solely by what is happening with the price of the asset. The easiest way of doing that is by looking at a chart. They do not make their buy and sell decisions based on other external factors (inflation, deflation, earnings, economic growth, news, or any other variable you can think of); they are based strictly on price and recurring patterns, many of which will be discussed in this book. The best low-risk entry points tend to come as the stock breaks out of a digestion area (a.k.a. a base) or it bounces after a dip in an uptrend. I'll expand on these two powerful concepts several times in this book.

Since most people do not understand this approach, they often dismiss it and say that it is mumbo-jumbo or a bunch of nonsense. Just like fundamental analysis, technical analysis has both strengths and weaknesses.

To be clear, technical analysis primarily serves short- and intermediate-term traders, and it is less useful for long-term investors. Technical analysis helps people stay in harmony with the market by following cycles and analyzing patterns—which is a great tool for an active trader. Meanwhile, long-term investors tend to hold an investment for years so they are less concerned with what the market is doing at any given day, week, or even month in some cases.

Technical analysis helps you make decisions based on the stock price, not the company's fundamentals. It helps you with timing, and it allows you to fine-tune your skill for knowing when to enter and exit a trade.

Before we continue, it is important for you to know that no one can time the market 100% perfectly every single time. That is impossible. Technical analysis stacks the odds of success in your favor because it requires you to stay aligned with what is happening (facts) on Wall Street, not what you think will happen (opinions). Dealing with facts is a much better way to navigate the market than dealing with opinions, even if those opinions are your own. Another way of explaining this is to tell you that technical analysis helps you understand what something "is" worth right now while fundamental analysis helps you determine what you think something "should" be worth in the future. Again, both approaches have strengths and weaknesses; I just want you to be aware of—and harness—the power involved with properly reading the tape (the market).

NAVIGATING THE AMERICAN TAILWIND

We've already established that fundamental analysis relies, in part, on Warren Buffett's American Tailwind, which drives the American equities market up over time. But we've also learned that price doesn't always match value, and speculators know that there are fortunes to be made by capitalizing on the inevitable market turbulence that drives prices up and down along the way.

Aircraft making long-distance voyages require a navigator and a pilot. The navigator plots the course, and is concerned with headings, bearings, and waypoints. The navigator calculates the effect of a headwind or tailwind. The pilot, however, flies the plane, and is concerned with speed, altitude, pitch, and yaw. The pilot is less concerned about the headwind and tailwind and more concerned with the immediate effect of possible turbulence and storms. The navigator uses a compass and a map (and a GPS, these days). The pilot relies on the throttle, yoke, and pedals.

If I'm taking a trip, I'd like to know that the aircraft I'm on has a navigator and a pilot, but to extend the metaphor, trading in the stock market without technical analysis is akin to boarding an aircraft without a pilot or flying without the proper instruments. It's no wonder so many people crash and burn on Wall Street.

BRIEF HISTORY OF TECHNICAL ANALYSIS

Technical analysis has been used in many different forms for hundreds of years. Some of the first counts occurred in Europe back in the 1600s. Joseph de la Vega began analyzing price action to predict Dutch markets in the seventeenth century (that's what happens when a diamond merchant is also a philosopher-poet). If you find learning all the intricacies of the stock market perplexing, you're in good company: Vega entitled his book on the subject *Confusion of Confusions*.

Around the same time, on the other side of the word, in Japan, a man named Homma developed candlestick charts for determining the price of rice. Homma discovered that there was a link between the price and the supply and demand of rice; his charts are still used today in technical analysis. Homma also discovered that the markets were strongly influenced by the emotions of traders. Clearly, he was way ahead of his time!

More recently, in the 1900s, technical analysis gained acceptance thanks, in part, to famous traders who published their work on markets. Charles Dow pioneered the use of averages and trendlines in market analysis—perhaps you've heard of the Dow Jones Industrial Average. Robert Rhea built on Dow's work and used it to help identify the tops and bottoms of price trends, the subject of his 1932 book *The Dow Theory*. William P. Hamilton used technical analysis to sound the alarm ahead of the Great Depression, although not enough people listened. John Magee was the first to identify common shapes in stock charts that indicated potential future moves.

Other prominent voices include Robert D. Edwards, Jesse Livermore, Edson Gould, Richard Donchian, William O'Neil, John Murphy, Nicolas

Darvas, and Stan Weinstein, just to name a few. These innovators shared what they learned and discovered with the world, which helped shape our current understanding of technical analysis.

DISCRETIONARY VERSUS SYSTEMATIC TRADING

There are two main types of technical traders: discretionary and systematic. Systematic traders make buy and sell decisions based on a hard set of rules that are often automated via a computer program. Discretionary traders also develop rules, but they recognize that the systems they work with don't incorporate all the data available, and they exercise their discretion rather than blindly following an investment algorithm.

For discretionary traders, I've learned that technical analysis is more of an art than an exact science, and each person is free to create, and follow, a process that works for them. So, be flexible with your interpretation and how you, personally, use technical analysis. Meanwhile, if you decide to become a systems trader, then you will want to view markets more as a science and you will create rules that are more of a science than an art.

When you step back and study the legendary traders and investors in our history, there is a good mix of both, so feel free to find an approach that works for you. The overwhelming majority of them tend to be discretionary traders and view trading as an art, not an exact science. The rest of this book is dedicated to helping you become a good discretionary trader.

READING CHARTS

A technical trader makes decisions based on price, and a stock chart paints a picture of a stock's price over time. Knowing how to read and interpret charts is a fundamental skill that all technical traders must master, and there are different types of charts designed to convey different types of information.

Line Charts

If you've ever looked up a stock price using a search engine on the internet, you've likely encountered a line chart of the stock's price history. Each point on the graph represents the stock's closing price at the end of a trading day. The resulting chart will generally have sharp angles as the stock price moves up and down from day to day, and it can resemble a mountain range. In fact, a line chart with the area below the line filled in with color is called a "mountain chart." Line charts and mountain charts are a great way to see a stock's performance over a long period, but for a technical trader, these charts are missing key information.

OHLC Bar Charts

OHLC stands for "open, high, low, and close." Whereas a line chart only shows the stock price at the close of a trading day, the OHLC has vertical bars that represent the high and low range of prices at which the stock traded during the day. A little peg on the left of the bar shows where a stock opened, and a little peg on the right shows where a stock closed. Moreover, an OHLC chart can be configured to represent any period a trader desires. A long-term investor may choose for each bar to represent a week or month. A shorter-term speculator may want to see bars that represent one day at a time.

Candlestick Charts

Thanks to Homma's work in the seventeenth century, candlestick charts became popular and were used by Japanese merchants to discover trends and detect trading patterns for their rice harvests. Like OHLC bars, the candlesticks show the price range at which the stock traded during a period along with the open and close prices; however, the "candle" portion of the candlestick demonstrates the difference between the open and the close, while the "wicks" on the top and bottom represent the high and low trading ranges. While candlesticks represent the same fundamental information as OHLCs, the visual difference makes it easier to spot certain types of patterns. Savvy practitioners can use candlesticks to detect the Doji and the engulfing pattern, or they may be able to predict a bearish reversal.

There are other types of charts that help identify other kinds of patterns. The important thing is that you find the chart that speaks to your individual trading style. I personally prefer OHLC charts, but I still use candlesticks from time to time, depending on what information I'm looking for in my analysis.

FINDING PATTERNS IN STOCK CHARTS

In its purest form, technical analysis studies price action. The idea is that all pertinent information is available in the price of the stock, and technicians try to find price patterns that they can capitalize on. Some of the most popular patterns are double bottoms, double tops, head and shoulders, cup with handle, rounded top/bottom, u-shaped base, flat/rectangle base (Darvas box), and triangles.

These patterns occur in all three market states—uptrends, downtrends, and sideways patterns. Moreover, these patterns appear at different scales;

a technical analyst can see the same type of pattern form over the course of a couple of minutes, over the course of a few days, or over weeks and months. Some patterns mark the top of a price movement at the end of a big uptrend; others mark the bottoms of downtrends. Other patterns may signal the continuation of a prevailing trend. Remember, the market is constantly moving and patterns emerge in multiple time frames. The key is for you to remain consistent in your analysis and focus on the prevailing trend in your desired time frame.

Each one of the common patterns in Figures 5.1 and 5.2 can be used as continuation patterns within a broader trend or as standalone tops or bottoms (there are countless others, but these are some of my favorites and the most common setups).

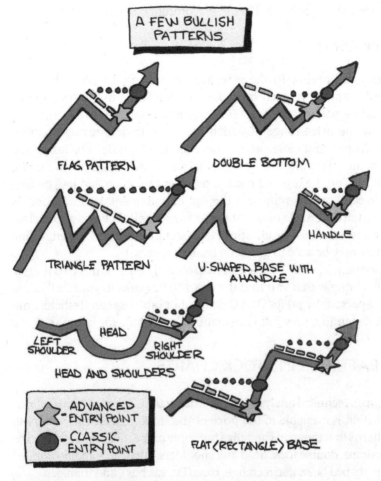

FIGURE 5.1 Bullish patterns in technical analysis.

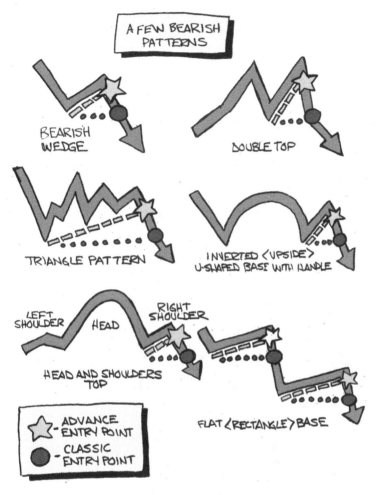

FIGURE 5.2 Bearish patterns in technical analysis.

I provide simple sketches of these patterns because, in the live market, these shapes rarely appear perfectly. Real life is sloppy, and it takes some practice to learn to identify these patterns on a real chart. Again, technical analysis is more of an art than an exact science.

STAGE ANALYSIS: FOUR STAGES

Legendary trader Stan Weinstein taught me the importance of stage analysis. In his book, titled *Stan Weinstein's Secrets for Profiting in Bull and Bear*

Markets, he discusses four timeless stages that you will see on a chart. His concept is simple and very powerful and basically gives you a road map for diving deeper and studying a stock's movements.

> Stage 1: Base
> Stage 2: Uptrend
> Stage 3: Top
> Stage 4: Downtrend

Here's what it looks like:

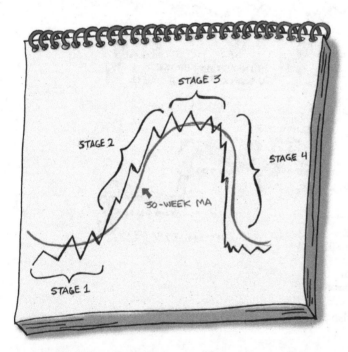

Source: Adapted from Stan Weinstein, *Stan Weinstein's Secrets for Profiting in Bull and Bear Markets* (McGraw-Hill, 1988).

Stage 1 occurs when a stock is trading near a 52-week low and is building its first base (sideways trading range). The top of that base is known as resistance and the bottom is known as support.

Stage 2 occurs when the stock breaks out above resistance of that base and begins a new uptrend.

Stage 3 happens after a big uptrend and the stock tops out.

Stage 4 happens when a stock breaks down below support of its top and begins a new downtrend.

My two additions to Weinstein's excellent and timeless work are that charts evolve/morph, and stage 2 and stage 4 can tend to last for months and years—so there are many times you will have smaller bases develop within a bigger stage 2 uptrend or stage 4 decline. Those are two important elements that most traders do not properly understand.

Allow me to explain further. It is important to note that during stage 2 and stage 4 you can have many bases (sideways trading ranges) form as the trend pauses and then resumes again. It is also common for patterns to morph. There are countless times that you see a stage 3 top form but instead of breaking down it breaks out and the uptrend continues. The same is true in a long downtrend. You might think the downtrend is over and that a new stage 1 base is forming but instead, the stock breaks down and the downtrend continues. The key lesson is that you want to understand stage analysis and make sure you are buying *early*, not late. By the end of this book, you will learn how to buy early and listen to the market like a pro.

TRENDLINES—CONNECTING DOTS

Charles Dow pioneered the use of trendlines. At the most basic level, a trendline occurs when you connect the highs or lows of recently emergent price patterns. Some investors use the daily closing prices to draw their lines. However, when you chart a trendline, the big idea is to visually represent an ongoing market trend. While the peaks and valleys of a daily price chart might look like the jagged crest of a mountain range, the trendlines seem more like rolling hills—which offer more stable projections into the near future. William P. Hamilton, the technical analyst who foresaw the Great Depression, might have referred to trendlines as swells, the undulating waves of the ocean, as compared to the meaningless splashes and chop that might represent price fluctuations on any given trading day.

The market is constantly moving, and trendlines can be used in just about any time frame. Like with patterns, there is no right or wrong way to draw a trendline. In the simplest form, you want to connect at least two points (the more the better) on a chart, then extend the line out to the right and the left.

The idea of a trendline is that it helps you see potential patterns so you can anticipate what might happen in the future when the market comes near a potential trendline. Some people like to draw trendlines based on prior chart highs or lows and other people prefer to draw them based on prior closing prices. Again, there is no right or wrong way to draw it as long as the trendline works for your strategy—and by "works," I mean that the process you employ produces results in real-world applications and that it earns you money in the long term.

MOVING AVERAGES—SMOOTHING OUT PRICE ACTION

Like most other technical indicators, moving averages come in different shapes and sizes. The key is to find the ones that work best for your style of trading. At the most basic level, a moving average smooths out price action by adding the closing prices over a certain number of trading periods, then dividing the sum by that number. The two most widely used moving averages on daily charts are the simple 50- and 200-day moving average (DMA) lines. Some traders prefer different time frames: 9 DMA, 10 DMA, 21 DMA, 50 DMA, 100 DMA, and 150 DMA are all in common use.

Most charting software defaults to the 50- and 200-day moving average. The 50 DMA line takes the closing price over the past 50 days, then divides that number by 50. A 200 DMA line takes the closing price over the past 200 days and divides it by 200. Then, a line is drawn on the chart every time a new bar emerges. These lines smooth out the price action and are used to help traders see past the daily volatility and gain a sense of whether the market is moving up, down, or sideways, and how quickly it's moving. My studies show that, in strong uptrends, leading stocks tend to react when the price meets the 10 DMA, the 21 DMA, then the 50 DMA. In sideways markets, prices fluctuate between the 21 and 70 DMAs.

FAST- AND SLOW-MOVING AVERAGES

Since moving averages come in all different shapes and sizes, it is important to understand that some move fast, and some move slow. Think about that concept and understand what that means for your money. Which is faster, a 1-day moving average or a 200-day moving average? The answer should be clear—a 1-day moving average is a lot faster because the line will move based on every day's close while the 200-day moving average moves much slower because it is the average of the past 200 days. So, when you plot your moving averages, try to find ones that work well for your style of trading and keep in mind that faster moving averages tell a completely different story from their slower counterparts.

SLOPE

The slope refers to how steep the moving average line is. Is the moving average line moving sideways? Is it moving up? If so, how quickly is it moving up? Is it moving down? The steepness of the line will tell you how fast it's falling. All things being equal, in a bull market, most moving averages will slope higher; in sideways markets, they will flatten out; and in downtrends, they will decline. That is a general rule of thumb and tends to work well for moving averages that are shorter than 200 days. Longer than that, the data varies significantly because it takes so long for those averages to adjust.

Another point to remain cognizant of is that market prices are constantly in flux and trends change depending on the time frame you are looking at. The 150-day moving average for a stock may be sloping upward, but if the line is sloping down on a shorter moving average, you might be witnessing the start of a longer downtrend. Different DMAs will provide you with different snapshots of the market action, so it's important not to rely on just one.

It's possible to look at more than one moving average on the same chart. On a chart that shows both the 50- and 200-day moving averages, it's not uncommon for one line to be sloping upward and the other to be sloping downward. Occasionally, the two trendlines will meet in what's called a crossover. If the 50-day breaks above the 200, it could be a sign that a downward trend may soon be reversed. If the 200 breaks above the 50, it could signal the end of a recent rally.

VOLUME

Volume refers to the number of shares that are traded in a given period. Volume refers to the number of shares that are traded in a given period. From where I sit, after price, volume is the second most important characteristic to look for. I love finding unusually large price and volume moves as a stock moves out of a digestion area. That is by far my favorite setup.

When a stock experiences a high volume day, it's usually because of some big news or because some large institutional investors are making some big moves. In the "old days"—that is, before 2000, when modern-day computer analysis became mainstream—volume mattered more in technical analysis.

Back then, a high volume seemed to suggest that a large number of investors, particularly institutional investors, supported whatever price move the stock made that day. If we look at buying or selling a stock in terms of voting on that stock's future, more votes reinforced the market's perception of whether the move went in the right direction. Some traders would go so far as to include volume as a critical component necessary before making a decision to buy or sell. I used to follow that rule, but it cost me more money than I care to mention.

Back in the early 2000s, I was watching the price of BIDU (China's Google) after it went public. Eventually, it broke out and triggered a buy signal, but the volume was not as high as I was told it should be on the day it broke out, so I followed the conventional wisdom, and I waited. That was when I was blindly following someone else's rules. The stock turned out to be a huge winner and, of course, I did not buy it because I still thought volume was a critical component of technical analysis.

I missed several other opportunities before I realized that volume is secondary and should not interfere with my decision to enter or exit a trade. Part of the reason for the change in volume's role in technical analysis is that, in the past, when most people still got stock prices from their newspapers, institutional investors could make big moves all at once. Now that buying and selling can be automated, and because information moves with lightning speed, big investors have adapted, and they slowly enter and exit their positions so as not to make waves that will affect their trades. To be clear, I still love to see monstrous volume behind a big move, the more volume the better. But my experience has taught me that price is primary and everything else, including volume, is secondary.

TIGHT ACTION

Tight trading ranges are great for both the long and the short side. Tight action occurs when volatility dries up just below resistance or just above support. Typically, you want to see volume dry up during these tight consolidations and expand when it breaks out or moves higher. For example, if a stock is trading between $45 and $50 for six months, that's a $5 range. Then all of a sudden over a few weeks it tightens up and trades between $48.50 and $50 and volume dries up. Then one day it blasts off and rips above $50 and volume explodes. That's a great example of a breakout from tight action.

IDENTIFYING TOPS AND BOTTOMS

The most timeless stock market advice anyone can give is to buy low and sell high. Using the terms of a technical analyst, a trader wants to buy at the bottom and sell at the top. Ostensibly, the big goal of technical analysis is to identify patterns that indicate that the price of a stock is ready to trend (up or down) and give you a favorable risk-versus-reward entry point. (Traders can also make money by shorting stocks that fall, but to keep the conversation simple, we'll talk about upward trends.) If a trader can buy at the bottom of one trading pattern and sell at the top of the next pattern, they can stand to make a tidy profit. If they can do it over and over again, they can earn a tremendous amount of wealth. Another timeless piece of advice is to learn how to buy high and sell higher. Meaning, buy strength and ride the trend for as long as the uptrend remains intact. Again, there is no one universal right or wrong way to trade, the key is to find an approach that works for you and stick to it.

This is not easy. It takes time to get used to reading stock charts. It takes longer to learn the common patterns that signal movement in the market, and it takes longer still to recognize patterns in their various shapes and forms, in real time, so that you can make informed buy and sell decisions.

EXPECT PULLBACKS AND CORRECTIONS; DON'T FEAR THEM

It is extremely important for you to understand and learn to expect that the market is going to pull back and correct several times a year. Occasionally, you will get a violent bear market where the market falls hard. Most people fear these pullbacks, corrections, and bear markets. Smart money loves them. Why? Because they get out of the way when things are not acting well and load up the truck (buy) after the selling has ended. Some of the biggest moves in history have occurred in the early stages of a bull market, which happens right after a bear market ends. Also, keep in mind that in an average year, the S&P 500 will pull back 5% three separate times. It will also fall around 10% once or twice every 12 to 24 months. These moves are normal and healthy. Keep in mind that most of the time the market is going *up*, not down, and these short-term pullbacks and rolling corrections are perfectly normal and healthy for the longer-term uptrend. When they happen, you may feel scared but when you train your mind to expect them, they become a fantastic buying opportunity. Remember, I always respect my stops and I have done very well buying the bounce after the dip.

TECHNICAL ANALYSIS IS MORE OF AN ART THAN A SCIENCE

My experiences have taught me that technical analysis is more of an art than a science. Additionally, I have found that most people get caught up in the minutiae and miss the big picture. These people—and early in my journey, I was one of them—have a strong, almost blinding need to follow hard rules and obsess about things that simply do not matter. In the process, they end up beating themselves up and they miss the *big moves*. The idea is to capture the spirit of the rule and not the letter of the rule.

Many people who trade based on technical analysis fail. Even some of the pioneers of technical analysis lost the fortunes they had accumulated. If you want a relatively safe bet, you can avoid all the hard work and park your cash in a low-fee index fund and ride the American Tailwind, as Warren Buffett mentioned in his famous letter to Berkshire Hathaway shareholders. Of course, Buffett himself is not simply content to ride the tailwind. He wants to outperform the market, and he almost always does. If you're still reading this book, I assume it's because you also want to beat the market, but you recognize that value investing isn't the only way to do it.

If that's the case, perhaps it's time to take the best from what you've learned so far and build your own trading strategy . . . which will be discussed in the next chapter.

Legendary traders from top to bottom: The smart money superhero inside you, John W. Rogers, Jr., Geraldine Weiss, William O'Neil, Warren Buffett, Muriel Siebert, Jesse Livermore, Benjamin Graham, Charles Dow, and J.P. Morgan.

CHAPTER 6

How to Develop a Winning Strategy That Beats the Market

The market is speaking. Are you listening?

—*Adam Sarhan*

DEVELOP YOUR STRATEGY

As you know by now, all the best traders in the world have built their own trading strategy, but they didn't just conjure them out of thin air. Most of them simply modeled what other people have done and customized the strategy to make it their own. Again, there is no one universal "right" or "wrong" way to trade. There is an infinite number of ways to be successful in the market (and in life), and your job is to find one that works for you. I want to help you build your own successful trading strategy, but in order for me to do that, it is important that you know how markets work and that you are familiar with some timeless concepts. Additionally, I will share the logic I use and my actual trading strategy with you—all with the intention to help you get ahead and thrive.

THREE DIRECTIONS

First, it is really important for you to understand that there are only three things that can happen after you enter a position. It can go:

1. Up;
2. Down; or
3. Sideways.

That's it! It doesn't matter whether you are buying shares of Apple, bitcoin, sugar, coffee, gold, silver, crude oil, Microsoft, the U.S. dollar, the euro, the S&P 500, or Nike. The same is true after you buy (or sell) just about anything in life. Keep that simple, yet extremely important, fact in mind for every trade you make.

THREE ACTIONS

As complicated as the market may seem, when it comes right down to it, there are only three actions you can take: buy, sell, or hold. Some people may not consider holding to be a decision, but back in the 1990s, I bought shares of SprintPCS and then I chose to hold that stock as the price tanked. I was making a clear decision not to sell, and, at the time, it cost me dearly. The art of trading starts to get complicated when you have to decide *what* to buy, sell, or hold—and it gets even more complicated when you have to decide *when* (and what) to buy, sell, or hold. This may sound complicated but the best traders learn how to keep it simple.

WHAT TO BUY

As of this writing, there are about 2,800 companies traded on the New York Stock Exchange and about 3,300 listed on the Nasdaq—not to mention thousands of other stocks that are listed on other exchanges—and that's only the United States. The U.S. stock market represents about half the value of all publicly traded companies in the world. I don't know about you, but I have trouble deciding what to order at restaurants with more than three things on the menu, and the U.S. stock market alone has a menu of thousands of stocks to choose from. It is physically impossible for one person to properly analyze every stock, every week. The good news is that you don't have to.

The first step to building my edge is to develop a set of parameters to narrow my options. Warren Buffett calls this your circle of competence. When looking for a new idea (I call trading opportunities "ideas" or "candy"), I like to start with leading stocks. Assuming I'm in a bull market, I define a leading stock as one of the strongest-performing stocks in the market at any given time. An easy way to find a leading stock is to run a scan for the strongest percent change stocks on a year-to-date (YTD) basis. You can also scan for just about any other time frame you want. The big idea is that the market is speaking; it is telling you that these stocks are leading the pack. My job is to listen and make sure I own those stocks.

A good leading stock may be trading at or near a 52-week high, likely outperforming its peers in the marketplace, and/or faring better than the S&P 500 (that outperformance is also known as relative strength). Again, there are times where a stock is a clear leader but, for whatever reason, it has been lagging the market recently and is exhibiting poor relative strength. Stan Weinstein, a brilliant trader (and author of a great trading book titled *Stan Weinstein's Secrets for Profiting in Bull and Bear Markets*) taught me to look at the weight of the Evidence, and not only one indicator.

For my process, price is primary and everything else is secondary—although I really like to see a stock have strong fundamentals, especially strong sales, earnings, and cash flow. I'm looking for a stock that is buoyant, unencumbered, and able to rise to the top of an upward market trend.

In sports, the coach will put his best-performing players on the field and bench the ones who are not performing as well. It's nothing personal; it's just business. The same is true with my portfolio. I want to be vigilant and make sure only the strongest-performing stocks are in my portfolio at any given time. Otherwise, what's the point?

Now to be clear, I will hold my longer-term positions even if they are not going up or are briefly underperforming over a short period of time. Additionally, I do not just buy a leading stock because it hit a new 52-week high; in fact, I rarely do that. Instead, I wait for a leading stock to pull back and then buy the bounce after the dip (which I will explain in more detail later when I talk about my early entry points).

The good news is that there is no one "right" or "wrong" way of making money on Wall Street. The idea is to find an approach that works for you. This way you can build a watchlist and then be ready to buy when the stock triggers a buy signal. The idea is to prepare to win before the market opens on Monday and avoid scrambling when the market is open. Once you have a plan, your edge is to get out of your own way and trade your plan. Like just about everything in this book, it applies to all areas of your life, not just the market.

SUPPORT AND RESISTANCE

Before you can learn to spot a stock that may be poised to move, you need to understand two important concepts: support and resistance. Think of support as the floor in a room and resistance as the ceiling. Stocks, over certain periods of time, tend to develop a trading range. From day to day or week to week—or even month to month—the price will fluctuate between two areas until that consolidation is over and it either breaks out above resistance or breaks down below support. Imagine a stock that has been trading for a couple of weeks at between $45 and $40; $45 is the ceiling and $40 is the floor during that trading range. The market is supporting the stock from falling below $40 and resisting it from trading above $45. In this example, $40 is support and $45 is resistance.

Why does this happen? There are lots of factors that contribute to the tug-of-war that sets this pattern in motion, but on a basic level, you must remember that the market is made of buyers and sellers who are all hoping to make money. As a stock price trends higher, some shareholders may see an opportunity to cash out and realize a profit, so they sell. Very likely, there are many others who also decide to sell, and the existence of more sellers may cause the price to drop. As a stock price trends back downward, it often becomes more attractive to buyers looking for a bargain, and if there are enough buyers, the competition might start pushing the stock price higher again. It is helpful to think of support and resistance as general areas, not exact price levels that can be narrowed down to an exact penny.

Think of this pattern as a battle between the bulls and the bears, within a longer-term war. The war never ends (as long as the stock continues trading) but there are endless battles (consolidation areas—a.k.a. bases/trading ranges) that develop over time. Consolidations are healthy and they come in all different shapes and sizes.

BREAKOUTS AND BREAKDOWNS

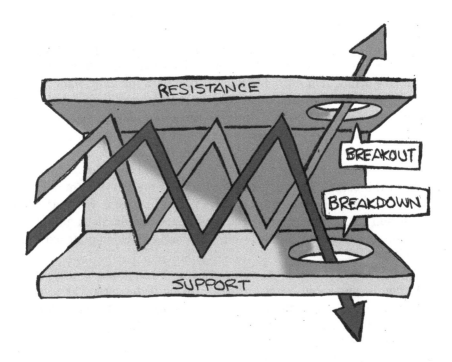

Stocks, however, don't generally stay in a fixed cycle for very long. Eventually, an external force may come along and cause a stock's price to break out above resistance or cause it to break down below support. If it breaks out, then the bulls won that battle, and if it breaks down, then the bears won that battle.

Generally, we expect a stock to break out when it displays bullish characteristics, and to break down when it displays bearish conditions. Traditionally, the crowd has been taught to buy a stock (a.k.a enter a long position) when a stock breaks out and to go short (a.k.a. enter a short position) when a stock breaks down.

To make things simple, we'll talk mostly about breakouts (please note that the guidelines for shorting breakdowns are the exact opposite). The idea is to buy when a stock breaks out above a line of resistance and then ride the momentum and sell for a profit sometime later, after the stock peaks and begins acting wonky (by which I mean the trend is over; the stock stopped going up or it topped out, broke a new higher level of support, and starts going down).

The crowd is usually taught to place a protective sell stop-loss order at a price a little lower than where they bought it (usually somewhere between 5% and 10% below their entry price in a stock, with the understanding that resistance now becomes support)—this way an automatic sell order will be triggered to cut traders' losses if things go the wrong way.

My main contention with this logic is that most breakouts (and breakdowns) fail, meaning that after the breakout, the stock rolls over and falls below the breakout level (and usually stops you out for a loss), effectively negating the breakout. Most breakdowns fail the same way (they move down, trigger a sell signal, then rally back above support and stop you out). Many times, to add insult to injury, after you are stopped out, the stock moves back in your desired direction and takes off. This feels like being punched in the gut—twice.

Often in the real world, smart money does the opposite of what "they" taught you in just about every textbook. Up until the early 2000s, buying breakouts worked marvelously, but now, in an age where every trader has a computer in their pocket and can make near-real-time trades, the classic breakout buy strategy is well known, and when buy orders start to come in, the market responds accordingly.

Smart money traders these days have to anticipate breakouts *before* they happen and take a position in a stock that is already in an uptrend and on the move. By no means am I suggesting you guess which stock is going to pop. My entry process is based on listening to the market and looking for clues that the stock is being accumulated (a.k.a. the big institutions are buying) and will likely run higher.

To be clear, there's nothing wrong with buying breakouts. If that works for you, by all means, do it. If not, this approach is different and, when executed properly, it can become very lucrative. To further clarify this point, it doesn't always work (nothing always works on Wall Street), but my approach gives you a very nice edge, a great low-risk entry point, and works marvelously over time.

ADVANCED ENTRY POINTS

In the previous chapter, on technical analysis, I told you about some interesting chart patterns with funny names: double bottoms, double tops, head and shoulders, cup with handle, rounded top and bottom, U-shaped base, and the Darvas box (a.k.a. rectangle and/or flat base), just to name a few. I look for these patterns when I study the charts of leading stocks.

Seeing one of these is a sign that the stock may be ready to break out of its current pattern. I call these "candy/setups." In a bull market, if a stock is going to move, it will most likely move higher. In a bear market, it will most likely move lower. I consider other factors as well—trendlines, fundamentals, the news. Most importantly, I want to stay in harmony with how the market is trending at that moment. I don't fight the tape.

At some point, I expect to see the stock price dip and then bounce off some line of support—maybe it's the 50-day moving average (which equals a 10-week moving average line on a weekly chart), or maybe it's a trendline I've drawn connecting recent lows, a prior chart high, or any other important inflection point you can identify as support (preferably on a weekly or monthly chart).

The most obvious reason for getting in before the breakout is that if the stock goes your way, you just created a very nice repeatable edge and you will risk less and make more money in the long run.

HOW TO BUY THE DIP—AFTER THE BOUNCE

Another way you can use my early entry points is to "buy the dip." Most people say "buy the dip," but that doesn't work because you have no way of knowing how deep the dip will be (percent decline) or how long it will last (a few days, weeks, months, or years). I have a different take: I like to buy the bounce after the dip. The easiest way to do that is to buy the stock as it is bouncing off of support and to place a protective sell stop just below support. This way I am able to cut my losses if the stock turns and goes the wrong way. Now let's see what these early entry points look like and how you can use them.

Here is an example of how it works:

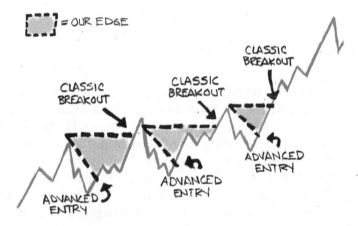

As you can see, over time, my early entry points will give you a very clear edge. Las Vegas was built with the house having a slight edge on every hand that is played in a casino. Having a clear definable "edge" is very powerful in any arena.

Take a look at the dotted horizontal line, which represents the classic breakout level. Most people are taught to buy breakouts. The problem I have with that approach is that if you only buy after the breakout, assuming you placed your stop below support, you're going to lose a lot more money if the breakout fails; and if you set your stop higher to limit your loss, the stock might fall, stop you out before it hits support, and then possibly bounce again and take off without you. It hurts to lose money, but it hurts more when you get stopped out of a monster stock and it takes off without you.

RISK AND REWARD

Here's a warning: this approach fails most of the time. Here's another warning: just about every credible trading system on Wall Street fails most of the time! However, even though it usually fails, it can still be tremendously profitable. According to my strategy, when we decide to enter a position, we automatically place a stop order just below support. Assuming that there is not too much slippage, my stop order will be filled close to where I placed it. Before I ever enter my buy order, I already know approximately how much money I am risking.

Aside from "what" and "when" to buy, the only other real question is "how much?" Here's my rule: no matter how excited I am about an idea—no matter how sure I am that it's going to work—I don't risk more than 1% of my portfolio. First, I calculate what 1% of my portfolio is worth.

Let's use the hypothetical $1 million that I used when I set up my paper trading experiment. One percent is $10,000. If I buy a stock at $10 a share and set my stop at $9, I could buy 10,000 shares. Here's how the math works: I will use $100,000 ($10/share times 10,000 shares = $100,000), and with my stop at $9, I will risk only $10,000 or 1% of my $1 million portfolio. I've established a floor for my risk: 1% is the maximum I want to risk on any one idea, and often I will risk less than 1%.

There is no ceiling, however, for my potential reward. After the market crashed in March 2020 during the COVID-19 pandemic, I added shares of Tesla to the FindLeadingStocks.com model portfolio. Over the next year, I rode a huge series of breakouts and at one point Tesla was up +499% from the entry point. To be clear, a gain of over 400% is an outlier and just an example of what is possible. The service had other outstanding stocks around the same time that saw double- and triple-digit gains, like Zoom, Microsoft, Adobe, and Apple, just to name a few.

Because I have tight stops on my losses, and because there are no limits on the potential gains—save for what the market will allow, it means I can lose on nine trades out of 10 and still pull a sizable profit if that tenth trade does very well. It doesn't matter how many times you win, it matters how much you win when you are right versus how much you lose when you are wrong. That's why I often say, "Keep your losses small and never fight the tape."

In reality, it would be unusual to be stopped out on nine trades and win only one. Usually, there will be a mix of winners and losers, but we work hard to structure the trades so that the value of the winners far outweighs the losers. In Wall Street parlance, that is known as asymmetric returns (example: risk 1 if you are wrong and make 10 if you are right).

To further mitigate my risk (a.k.a. limit my losses), after a stock moves higher, I'll raise my stop to breakeven. It means that once I have a profit on a trade of 5–10%, I move my protective sell stop to breakeven so I know I won't lose money on the trade. As a stock rises, I'll keep moving the stop up, locking in my profit. I make sure not to move the stop too high because I don't want to get stopped out if there is a temporary market fluctuation downward.

When I own a big winner, have a large cushion, and my conviction is high, I will use a "wide" stop, and leave the sell stop price down far enough below the current price so I am not stopped out on random noise. The idea is that I don't want to get stopped out on what my friend, business partner, and legendary hedge fund manager Jim Roppel calls normal wiggles and jiggles.

I'll look for a place below support, and put my stop there. (I've been stopped out before after a nice 30–50% rally, only to miss a +500% surge later.) The risk of keeping a wide stop is that you might give back a lot of profit if the stock does not go back up. That's also happened to me many times before. At the end of the day, you have to find a level you are comfortable with, then get out of the way and give the stock every chance in the world to succeed!

The idea with placing your stop is to understand risk and reward and really find a level you are comfortable with. Whatever approach you use, make sure you are mitigating your losses and sitting with your winners. Over time, that is the holy grail to trading that will let you fly a little faster than the American Tailwind. There's an old Wall Street adage that says, "You want to be patient with your winners and impatient with your losers." That's sage advice.

To recap, when I exit a profitable position, it is usually because the stock hit a stop that I put below support. I tend to place wide stops with plenty of room to accommodate normal short-term ups and downs. That means that when I exit, it's usually below the top (the exact high).

In a perfect world, we'd buy a stock at the bottom (its lowest point) and sell it at its top (the highest point of the rally), but it is impossible to know where those points are until they're in the past. My goal is to capture the bulk of a stock's move. I know I'll never pick the exact top or the exact bottom, and that's perfectly okay in my book.

"Buy and hold" investors may note that a stock, even though it has ended a rally, is likely to reach new highs over the long term. It's true, but the stock might also continue to fall and plunge below the place where I bought it. My strategy is to find trends, ride them, and get out when they run out of gas. Plain and simple.

So, are you ready to put your money to work and start building wealth? Good, because I want to empower you and help you develop your own winning strategy.

DEVELOPING YOUR OWN STRATEGY

If you're going to be a successful trader, you should develop your own strategy. That's what the best traders in history have done. Even if you model yours after what someone else does, I strongly recommend you make it your own. This way, when the bullets are flying, you can stick to it and you know it works for you.

Throughout this chapter, I've begun to lay the foundation for my A.M.P.D. trading strategy (discussed later in this chapter), but keep in mind that I developed this strategy to suit my own style. Remember, I told you that I've discovered I do best on a weekly time frame. I'm a big picture guy, and I do not do well with details (on an intraday basis). That's why my strategy works for me.

That said, lots of people use my strategy and adapt it to their own trading style, and many have been very successful with it. I want to show you how I make the stock market work for me (not against me) and give you the tools to develop your own strategy for beating the market.

PEOPLE LOVE STRUCTURE: DEVELOP RULES AND GUIDELINES

Back when I started my paper trading experiment, I had no unified strategy for investing. I was reading about other people's strategies, and since it didn't cost me any real money, I'd try them out. I lost lots of imaginary money. I didn't start having success until I started recognizing opportunities on my own and working on a set of rules that I developed—rules born out of the collective wisdom of the investors I had researched and modified based on my own market experience.

The best traders in the world have developed rules (or at the very least a hearty set of guidelines), and they use them consistently. It is much better to develop your own rules than to blindly follow someone else's rules. Why? Because what works for me might not work well for you and vice versa. Plus, after you take the time to create your own strategy, you're more likely to have the discipline to stick to it when the going gets tough (and believe me, it will get tough). If you blindly follow someone else's system, you will likely get subpar results and lose faith in the strategy and not be able to use it properly over multiple market cycles.

RULES VERSUS GUIDELINES

Some traders develop a set of rules so clear that they can literally program them into a computer algorithm that produces buy and sell signals based on a preset strategy. Other traders—most traders—operate with a set of guidelines that allow them to make discretionary decisions based upon factors that would otherwise fall outside an algorithm's ruleset. These are discretionary traders. I'm a discretionary trader, and unless you're a computer programmer, I suspect you'll be a discretionary trader as well.

In my early years (the 1990s and early 2000s), before I understood how markets worked (and before I understood myself), I was consumed with religiously following other people's rules. During my teens and early 20s, I studied the greatest traders and investors in the business and learned everything I could about how they played the game.

After several unsuccessful years following other people's rules, I came to a few realizations: I learned that two traders can follow the same rules and have different results. I also learned that two traders can deploy vastly different strategies and both win. I learned to look at successful traders' strategies more as guidelines than hard-and-fast rules. And most importantly, I learned to find my edge in order to capitalize on other traders' weaknesses. Put simply, I found an approach that worked for me.

FIND YOUR EDGE AND EXPLOIT IT

Most people do not want to hear what I am about to share with you, but it is the truth: most people are intellectually lazy and want the easy way out.

These people (hopefully, not you) want to be told what to do, and they want to blindly follow some "magical" system because it is "easier" than digging deep and doing the hard work needed to get ahead (which I call intellectual sit-ups). They jump from one "magical" "can't lose" crazy idea or new system to the next. They lose year after year. Rinse, wash, repeat. They run on a hamster wheel for their entire adult life and end up either broke or paying out of pocket for a lot of "market tuition." Or, in some rarer cases, they are intellectually committed to a concept (or person) and they blindly follow the magical system, even though they consistently lose money. And they justify this behavior by saying, "I've already invested so much money and so many years, I can't give up now." They are, in fact, doing the exact opposite thing that successful people do.

If you find yourself blindly following someone else's approach and it's not working, cut your losses and move on. Would you recommend someone stay in a losing trade for 5, 10, 20, or 50 years? Of course not. Successful people double down on what's working and drop what's not. Don't throw good time (and money) after bad. The faster you realize something is not working, the better. Change and move on. Find something that works for you and stay in your lane.

Remember, just because your friend made money doing XYZ doesn't mean it will work for you. The same is true for market tips; just about everyone has an opinion about the market (or a stock). In most cases, by the time you hear about that super-hot tip or magical strategy, it is too late, and you end up losing money. Successful people learn how to take action, stick with their winners, cut their losses, and walk away from bad ideas.

To be successful in the market you need to develop your own edge, and often that involves exploiting the difference between what the dumb money would do and what the smart money would do.

ARBITRAGE

I call the difference between what the dumb money does and what the smart money does "arbitrage." Traditionally, the term "arbitrage" describes how traders can take advantage of price fluctuations in different markets to make a profit. With markets wired up and moving at the speed of light, arbitrage doesn't work the same as it used to, but it helps explain why big trading houses invest millions upon millions for technical infrastructure that allows them to send and receive trading data microseconds faster than competitors. There's a type of arbitrage available based on the speed at which information moves.

Here's a more classic example of arbitrage: I once met a man who flew transport aircraft during the Korean War. For a period of his service, every day he flew a route between South Korea, Japan, and the Philippines. Each country had its own currency, and when this airman wanted to buy anything, he'd have to exchange whatever money he had in his pocket for the local currency. Before long, he discovered that the exchange rates in each country weren't always aligned; as a pilot, he was traveling faster than the news of currency fluctuations. He learned that he could take advantage of these misaligned currency markets and make a profit simply by exploiting the difference in exchange rates in the different countries. That is arbitrage in its purest form.

I take the concept a little deeper. I believe that arbitrage comes in many different forms, and it happens whenever there is a disparity in the value assigned to a single resource. Smart money knows how to create an edge by exploiting these differences.

Besides classic price arbitrage, which I explained earlier, the other types of arbitrage I've identified include intellectual arbitrage, time arbitrage, task arbitrage, and social arbitrage.

Intellectual Arbitrage

In many ways, intellectual arbitrage is the soul of this book. Intellectual arbitrage is the act of exploiting profit from the difference between smart money and dumb money. We've established that we all start in the dumb money circle and that most people, bless their hearts, remain there. That means that most traders in the market are making dumb money decisions.

Think about where you are today and where you were when you were 14 years old. Who is smarter? Who has more experience? Who do you think will make better, smarter decisions with their money?

The difference between the two is an expression of intellectual arbitrage on a personal level. That comes from learning new things, getting more experience in life, and learning from your previous mistakes (so you don't repeat them). When you're about to make a trade, it's often worth asking yourself, "What would the old me do?" Intellectual arbitrage can keep you from falling back into old (or negative) patterns.

To take this a step further, we also know that there is a difference between the smart money decisions you make and all the dumb money decisions being made in the market. In the 1800s, the great American showman P.T. Barnum was credited for saying, "There is a sucker born every minute." I like to say, "A new sucker enters the market every minute." That's not me being cruel; it's just the way the world works.

The sad truth is that most active traders can't beat the market and many lose money. I don't make the rules; I'm just playing by them. When the dumb money zigs, the smart money zags, and vice versa.

If you learn from your own mistakes and from other people's mistakes, you'll master the art of intellectual arbitrage, and you'll be able to turn other people's missed opportunities into your own.

Time Arbitrage

You'll hear this more than once in this book: profits are a function of time. If you were somehow able to magically buy 100 shares of a stock and simultaneously sell them at the exact same instant, there would be no change in price and the transaction would be useless. In order to make a profit, you must wait for even just a second or two for the price to move upward to sell it for a profit.

If you never sell a stock, you'll never realize the potential profit. If you sell too soon, you might miss out on a big winner. It works the other way as well: if you hold on to a sinking stock for too long, you'll risk losing big money. If you sell a stock that ticked downward too soon, you could miss a big upswing. Moreover, you can waste time in a stock that moves sideways for too long. If a position is not making you money, then it is losing you money because—even at breakeven—that money could be invested elsewhere making a profit (that's also known as the opportunity cost of a trade).

Much of this chapter is devoted to knowing when to enter and exit trades. This is often referred to as timing the market. Doing it takes patience. It means not buying into an exciting opportunity when you know the technicals aren't properly aligned. It means not chickening out and selling after the slightest gain to lock in your profit. It also means not watching the stock market tick every second. Mastering time arbitrage means finding the time frame that you are comfortable using to watch the market, make your trading decisions, and most importantly make money in that time frame.

The very week I'm writing this sentence, the market took a savage beating on Monday, and by Friday, it recovered everything it lost on Monday and posted a big gain for the week. Because I make my decisions on a weekly basis, this weekend, when I did my homework, Monday's dip was insignificant and became a blip on the radar. While traders everywhere were panicking and making emotional decisions, I was enjoying time with my family because I knew that I had my stops strategically placed and I was working a plan that I know makes me money over time. I was using time arbitrage to my advantage.

Task Arbitrage

While time arbitrage recognizes that the value of a single asset changes with time, task arbitrage acknowledges that the value of a single moment changes depending on how you use it. You can either invest your time, or you can spend it. Those who invest their time realize a long-term benefit; those who simply spend their time lose it to the past.

At any given moment, the smart money is doing what provides them the highest return on investment (R.O.I.). To be clear: that doesn't mean that smart money has to be working all the time—in fact, I hope that the highest and best use of your time is enjoying experiences with your family or doing the things that you love in life that bring you personal and spiritual fulfillment. That means that any time you spend not realizing your goals should be spent in the efficient pursuit of those goals.

Smart money knows how to manage their time. They focus on the tasks that move them toward their goals, and they outsource or blatantly dismiss all other "busy" and low-level activities. In the course of my consulting practice, people come to me all the time and complain that they are "too busy," but when we drill down on how they use their time, it turns out they are spending (most of) it on low-level activities and not investing it on high-level activities. There is a dumb-money myth that there is some award for working 60–70 hours a week. What do a billionaire and a drifter have in common? They both have 24 hours in a day. The billionaire invests their time and the drifter blacks out and spends it frivolously.

Years ago, Charlie Rose interviewed Warren Buffett and Bill Gates. One of the first things Bill said he learned from Warren was to focus on high-level activities and to keep a free schedule. Before Bill met Warren, he would micromanage just about every minute of his day, but Warren had only four things on his calendar for the entire month.

Every night, before you go to sleep, list things that you are grateful for (your wins for the day), identify the most important tasks you want to do the next day, and when the next day comes, get them done first. If one is a really big task, you'll need to break it up into smaller tasks—just don't let yourself be sidetracked by less important things. The world is full of distractions. Stay focused and win.

On another note, make sure you avoid activities that suck the life out of you, meaning they keep you "busy" but you are busy doing low-level activities that do not give you a good R.O.I. In fact, they might be giving you a negative R.O.I.

I refer to these activities as "time vultures" because these activities (or people) eat you alive and suck the life out of you. Dan K., a brilliant man I know, refers to them as time vampires. Whatever name you want to use, identify them and avoid them like the plague.

Social Arbitrage

Let's face it: some people are more valuable to you than others. I'm not talking about just money; I'm talking about the joy that comes with having a fulfilling relationship with someone. Maintaining strong relationships is key to maintaining a positive mental state, and in the next chapter, we'll discuss how important that is to being successful in your life and, ultimately, in the markets.

In life, there are people who give and people who take. In a healthy relationship, there is an equal exchange of give and take. Make sure you are engaged in healthy relationships and not toxic ones. If the relationship is toxic, figure out a way to fix it or end it and move on. Make sure your relationships are giving you a good R.O.I. The same system for ranking tasks can be used for ranking relationships. Create a life full of happy relationships and you will live a happy life.

There's an old axiom that says, "It's not what you know; it's who you know." The saying implies that you can gain more from other people (take) than you can give. I like to think of it in a different way. Become valuable to the people you respect and admire. That way the "right" people are drawn to you, and you don't have to chase the influential people who can benefit your life and open opportunities for you. Winners win. Surround yourself with winners and see what happens in your life.

CREATE A PLAN, THEN TRADE YOUR PLAN

My friend Joe used to say, "Create a plan, then trade your plan." What he means is once you've worked out your strategy, give it time to perform for you. Keep your emotions out of it. In the previous chapter, when I was listing off the pioneers of technical analysis, I mentioned Jesse Livermore. Livermore was a legendary trader and one of the most successful speculators in the 1900s. He famously shorted the market before the Great Depression and walked away from the Crash of 1929 with an extraordinary fortune. A prodigy with a knack for numbers, he left home at 16 and was drawn to Wall Street. In a very short time, he started to recognize patterns in stock charts and developed a system that helped him build several great fortunes. Unfortunately for Livermore, he didn't always stick to his plan; he made emotional decisions, and when he didn't follow his own rules, he lost great fortunes as well. Livermore experienced style drift, and instead of retiring wealthy and passing on his wealth, he committed suicide, buried under a mountain of debt.

Just as you are well-advised to stick to your system and avoid style drift, you also need to be realistic about whether your approach is producing profits for you. Your account statement(s) will always tell you whether what you are doing is working. If you are profitable, you're doing alright. If you're beating the market, good for you! If you are treading water or moving backward, it is safe to say you need to change your strategy.

Now, an important caveat to keep in mind: during certain brief periods, every strategy loses money. You will experience drawdowns—they are unavoidable—but the key is to make sure you win in the long run (your strategy has a positive expectancy). When analyzing whether or not to use a particular approach, be sure that the period you use to determine whether the strategy works is long enough to make it through at least three different market states.

KEEP IT SIMPLE

By now, things may feel like they're starting to get complicated. When that happens, take a step back and go to the beginning. In its simplest form, making a trade is making one of three choices: buy, sell, or hold. The strategy you build will help you decide what to buy, sell, or hold, and when to buy, sell, and hold.

Leadership guru John C. Maxwell said, "It's said that a wise person learns from his mistakes. A wiser one learns from others' mistakes. But the wisest person of all learns from others' successes." I have made—and learned from—just about every single possible trading mistake out there. But I've also been able to enjoy considerable success and that is why I wrote this book; I want to share my success with you. So here is a set of guidelines I created that will help you build your own strategy.

THE A.M.P.D. INVESTMENT SYSTEM

I used to call this the D.A.M.P. investment system, but I was told over and over again that "damp" has negative connotations, whereas perhaps the word "amped" might inspire more excitement. They were right, so this is now the A.M.P.D. trading system, but you'll forgive me if I walk you through it using the original order of the acronym, which stands for defense first, advanced entry, market conditions, and psychological analysis.

Defense First: Always Respect Risk

In this business, defense is the best offense. Anyone can be a cowboy and go all-in on a stock. Cowboys do not last very long on Wall Street—but successful risk managers do. Before I enter a single position, I know exactly where I am going to exit if I'm wrong and how much of my portfolio I'm going to risk. This way my stops are placed and my risk is clearly defined. Everything is planned before the trading week even starts, and I am able to make rational, not emotional, decisions irrespective of what news, event, or action occurs or doesn't occur at any given time. My risk is the distance between my entry price and my exit price. This way, the only important thing that matters during the week is whether or not the stocks hit any of my buy or sell stops; everything else is secondary.

The fastest way to go bankrupt on Wall Street is to ignore risk. It's how I lost all my money during my first trading misadventures. I got drunk on my early success; I felt invincible, and the market cut me to shreds. Playing strong defense (mastering risk) is the one concept every successful trader must learn in order to get ahead in this business. Just about every trading legend has reiterated this point in some fashion or another—undertrade, undertrade, undertrade. Or, as I prefer to say, always respect risk.

Advanced Entry and Exit Points

After you do your homework and find an idea (stock, exchange-traded fund, mutual fund, currency, commodity, or anything else you want to trade), it is of the utmost importance that you know when to enter and when to exit. In the simplest form, market technicians like to buy breakouts because that means the stock has cleared resistance. In a perfect world, breakouts work, but my experience has taught me otherwise. Instead of buying breakouts, I use advanced entry points and buy in the right side of a base or near support (if possible) with a close protective stop below support (or below a logical inflection point on a daily, weekly, or monthly chart). This assumes the stock is in an uptrend. In downtrends, I do the opposite: short near resistance or when an upward trendline is broken with a close protective exit above resistance.

We discussed the nature of quality before, how it's impossible to describe the color red to someone who's not seen it—or the taste of chocolate to someone who has never tasted it. To be a successful trader you should learn to read charts, watch for the evidence of the technical patterns that emerge, and test yourself to see if you can identify the high-quality setups and watch for breakouts. Feel free to keep a journal or become a paper trader as you develop these skills. Wait until you have a good feel for identifying sound bases and advanced entry points before you start putting real money on the line.

Market Conditions—Align Yourself with the Trend

Every bull and bear market in history had a definitive beginning, middle, and end. Bull and bear markets come in all different shapes and sizes, but remember: trends change, they evolve, and they do not last forever. Moreover, you can have a small downtrend within a broader bull market or a brief uptrend in a bear market. You'll never know if it is a short countertrend move or the actual end of a move and the subsequent beginning of a new trend. That's just a fact you have to get used to and learn to live with.

The future is unknown, and your job is to learn how to make the best possible decisions with the information you have at any given time. As you work with charts and start to recognize trendlines and anticipate price fluctuations based on moving averages, you'll begin to develop an intuitive feel for the state of the market. When the information changes, then you can change as well. In fact, when the market changes states, you should adapt your strategy or risk running counter to the trend. Remember, always keep your losses small, stay in harmony with the market, and never fight the tape!

Psychological Analysis

Previously I mentioned Warren Buffett's mentor, the celebrated investor Benjamin Graham, who said, "The investors' chief problem, and even his worst enemy, is likely to be himself." I think Graham is spot-on. It was true for me, probably true for him, and true for countless others.

When I finally got out of debt and decided to put real money behind my paper trading strategies, I chickened out. I was unemotional about the paper trades, but when I had real money on the line, I froze and sometimes lost my nerve.

I started making dumb money mistakes again. I wasn't in control of my own emotions as they related to money, and it negatively impacted my performance. I had to stop, look inside, and learn more about myself before I could become a successful trader. Essentially, I had to go back to the drawing board and consciously recreate my relationship with money—this time a healthy one.

Later in this book, I'm going to give you more nuts-and-bolts tools and tactics to help you define your personal trading strategy, but none of that will be useful unless you stop, take a look inside yourself, and really try to understand your relationship with money, how you feel about making big money, and what emotions drive your decision-making process—especially when it comes to building wealth. Spoiler alert: part of the process is based on greed and part of it on fear, and a lot of it stems from your formative years and how your subconscious mind internalizes money.

Once you start to see how your emotions, if left unchecked, can dominate your life and your trading decisions, you'll start to see the telltale signs of human nature in the stock charts you analyze, and you'll begin to understand the importance of psychological analysis and rewiring your brain to win. The good news is that anyone can rewire their brain to win.

Now, let's dive in deeper and discuss Psychological Analysis in more detail in the next chapter.

Create a healthy mindset.

CHAPTER 7

Psychological Analysis

What It Is and How to Use It

FIX YOUR MIND, FIX YOUR LIFE: CREATE A HEALTHY MINDSET AND OVERCOME A TOXIC ONE

After a few years of licking my psychological wounds and rebuilding my capital, I decided to change the story that I told myself about investing: "Taking money out of the market is easy." After that, when I placed well-researched, strategic, risk-adjusted trades, I did so with confidence, and with a positive expectation that I would win in the long term. I became the hero in my own story.

From that point onward, I've had plenty of ups and downs (no matter how good you are, there are always downs), but I've enjoyed steady success over time. Could I have been successful in the long term without believing in my heart that I truly had the ability to do so? No, I don't think I could. Externally, nothing changed—the market will always be there—but internally, I changed, and how I interacted with the market (and life) changed as well.

One important lesson I learned, and the lesson I want to impart to you is this: You are in full control of your beliefs, your decisions, and your actions. If you don't believe you can do it, the odds are you won't be able to. Or, if you do it, it will not be done as well as if you fully believed that you can do it. More than that, when you fail, you'll start creating (false) reasons why you cannot do it, almost to the point of self-sabotage. To make matters worse, all this destructive thinking usually happens on a subconscious level. Then, you'll start believing in those false negative reasons, or your negative story, you'll play the victim card, and unwittingly become the villain in your own story.

It is much easier to win from a position of strength, not weakness. Since you control your beliefs, you, and you alone, control your mindset. Remember, we can't control what happens to us in life (or in the market) but we can always control how we react to it.

To make money in the market, get yourself into a smart money mindset—one that is full of optimism, not pessimism. An easy way to do that is by controlling your attention. The cup can be half full or half empty—or it is half full now, but since I can always get more water, and I want to focus on what I have, not what I don't have, the cup is half full and I have more than enough water than I will ever need (because I can always get more cups of water).

Another helpful way to internalize this is to look at your return on investment (R.O.I.) for your attention and ask yourself whether this gives you a positive or negative R.O.I. Looking at the cup and internalizing it as being half empty is fear-based thinking, narrow-minded, in-the-box type thinking, and it gives you a negative R.O.I. You have unlimited water, why waste your time worrying and focusing on the fact that your cup is half empty? How does that help you? Instead, be grateful that you have water in the cup, know that you have unlimited more cups of water available to you anytime you want, and move on to something that is more important! Fill your mind with positive, not negative, thoughts, feelings, stories, and events.

Doing this will allow you to control your attention, thoughts, focus, and actions in life. Take it a step further and make it a daily practice. Make it part of your routine. Consciously make it a habit. Doing this will allow you to control your mental state and it will allow you to turn into a walking, talking, winning, money machine.

The next step you can take to drop a negative mindset is to adopt an attitude of gratitude. Train yourself to literally become thankful for *everything* (big and small) in your life. Think about the happy natural state of a two- or three-year-old. That is your goal. Pure love, optimism, happiness, and bliss—all day every day, especially when you are trading. Remember, there is nothing inherently wrong with taking money out of the market. In fact, I believe that there is something inherently wrong with you not taking money out of the market. Develop your alpha state (the best version of yourself) and go out there and win!

MENTAL CAPITAL

Capital comes in two forms: physical capital (your money) and mental capital (your mental health). Taking care of your mental capital is one of the best ways to get more physical capital.

Have you ever been mentally exhausted? We've all been physically exhausted after a long, strenuous day. People understand that we all have only so much energy in one day, and when we've spent it, we're tired until we get a good meal and some rest.

We can also become emotionally exhausted; anyone who has ever lost someone they love or goes through a difficult period knows that emotions can sometimes become so overwhelming that you need to recharge before you can face life again. I believe we can also become mentally exhausted—that the challenges of balancing work, and family, and finances, and health can build up, take a toll, and leave us with an empty gas tank, physically and mentally exhausted.

Elite athletes understand this. Not only do athletes need to maintain their physical capacities, but they must focus on their mental game as well. Sports psychology is very powerful. Many universities offer graduate programs on the subject. If elite athletes can benefit from psychological coaching, doesn't it stand to reason that anyone performing a task at an elite level could similarly be helped by some psychological analysis?

I mention this because being a trader who can consistently beat the market requires elite performance. Traders must always be at the top of their game, and their performance will suffer if they are physically or mentally exhausted.

As traders, we have to keep our "tanks full," and if we extend the gas tank metaphor, it suggests that our mental energy is something that is measurable—a valuable and limited resource. It is called mental capital.

I believe that your mental capital is more important than your physical capital—that is, your money. Before you can learn to control your physical capital, you must learn to control your mental capital. Most people are not aware of this concept and they do the opposite.

Prayer, meditation, exercise, rest, and unplugging from the noise around you are great, free, and easy ways to recharge your mental energy.

I coined the term "psychological analysis" for investing and trading to describe the process of understanding yourself and understanding how to get out of your own way. This way you can learn new skills that will allow you to join the smart money circle and destroy the mental walls that are keeping you from getting ahead.

The real skill necessary for beating the market is psychological analysis and, at the most basic level, that is self-mastery. To succeed as a trader, I have learned that mastering your inner game is 99% percent of the equation, and understanding market mechanics is only 1%. Don't believe me? Listen to my SmartMoneyCircle.com podcast and you will see countless huge multibillion-dollar money managers, all very successful and all with their own unique approach to making money on Wall Street. If you want more proof, you can go back and read about successful Wall Street traders; you will see that they each play the game by their own set of rules.

It is important to note that what I am about to share with you is not taught in business school and does not come from shiny academic textbooks. It comes from my experiences building wealth, accumulating knowledge, overcoming massive setbacks, studying the brightest minds in the world (the top 1%), interviewing some of the largest money managers on Wall Street, and figuring out what works and what doesn't—in the real world.

I am sharing with you what works for me and countless other people; this may not be popular but it is true and practical advice anyone can use.

HUMAN NATURE IS CONSTANT

Human nature never changes. If you walk into a crowded theater at any time in history, in any civilization, and yell "Fire!" in the local language, you will get a relatively predictable response. The reaction will be the same irrespective of the people's age, education, race, religion, creed, socioeconomic status, job, weight, political affiliation, height, or any other data point you can think of. Most will panic. Some will push over others to reach safety. Perhaps a few heroes will rise. The market may change, from the tulip mania to the dot-com bubble—and everything else before and after—but the one constant is that human nature never changes. The bubbles change, the busts change, the centuries change, but human nature never does.

I have studied every major economic and market cycle since the third century and it doesn't take a genius to learn that human nature never changes. The same patterns repeat time and time again throughout history. The patterns can be seen in the repeated rise and fall of empires. If you look for it, you can learn to recognize human nature at play in the markets. You cannot change human nature, and you cannot change the market, *but you can learn how to change yourself. Once you learn that, you can take control of your mental state—your focus and your behavior—then you can grow up, control your destiny, never play the "victim" card again, and live the life of your dreams.*

It is important to note that human nature, unchecked, will almost always lead to financial failure, not success. The same is true for other areas of your life, not just your finances. Most people are programmed to take the easy route and not push themselves— mentally or physically. In reality, pushing yourself is exactly what is needed to get ahead and succeed in just about any endeavor.

Without even knowing you, I can guess that, barring some physical or mental impairment, the primary reason you have not accomplished more in life is that you did not push yourself hard enough. Take a minute and think about any goal that you have accomplished. Did you do it by being lazy or by pushing yourself? The mind gives up before the body does. The ability to control your mind, behavior, decisions, actions, and state is what separates successful people from everyone else. Success is about controlling—and constantly growing—your mental capital. Be smart, push yourself, and if you use the principles in this book you will amass a fortune.

PAIN AND PLEASURE

There are some timeless and universal truths that pertain to your mental capital. One of them is your innate relationship with pain and pleasure. At the most basic level, your decisions are primarily motivated by your association with pain and pleasure. That's human nature 101. At the subconscious level (a.k.a. untrained mind), people tend to seek pleasure and avoid pain. When we make decisions, whether we realize it or not, we are influenced in large part by our pleasure-seeking and pain-avoiding tendencies.

We've talked about diet and exercise previously. Most Americans are overweight because their decisions about diet and exercise are governed— whether they want to admit it or not—by their innate tendency to avoid pain and seek pleasure. People often choose to eat cheeseburgers rather than salads because, in the short term, cheeseburgers provide more pleasure than salads. In the same vein, people do not exercise as much as they should because, in the short term, working out is uncomfortable—which, in their subconscious mind, creates pain.

Many people who are devoted to health and fitness might say, "No pain, no gain." The expression acknowledges the wisdom that, sometimes in life, decisions that lead to short-term pain can result in long-term pleasure—a long, healthy life. They also know that some choices that provide short-term pleasure have disastrous long-term painful consequences—such as diabetes, heart disease, and any other discomfort you can think of that comes from being out of shape.

Just as your fitness is defined by a series of decisions about diet and exercise, your financial fitness is defined by a series of decisions about buying and selling. Now that we understand that pain and pleasure impulses affect our fitness decisions, it makes sense that our trading decisions are likewise affected—and all our decisions about money for that matter (our spending decisions, saving decisions, investing decisions, etc.).

As a trader, with each trade you make, ask yourself whether you feel pain or pleasure. If you're cutting your losses on a sinking stock, you're probably feeling pain. If you are cashing out of a profitable rally, you're probably feeling pleasure. Take a minute and consider whether the emotion associated with the trade is affecting your decision-making process. Since there are always two parties involved in a trade, take a moment to consider what the person on the other side of the trade might be feeling. Are their emotions affecting their trade? Human nature says they probably are. If you're making a strategic, well-researched trade, following the broader trend, and the other side is making an emotional trade, chances are that you're on the better side of the trade.

An easy way to see this in action is to use my early entry points because that allows you to patiently wait on the sidelines while everyone else panics and sells during an otherwise normal and healthy dip. After the dip is over and the stock bounces, we get in—and most of the weaker/emotional traders are knocked out.

EMOTIONS ASSOCIATED WITH PAIN AND PLEASURE

The spectrum of human emotions is, of course, more complicated than simply pain and pleasure. Virtually every human emotion, however, can be seen as positive or negative. Each emotion, from love and hate to greed and disgust, can be sorted into negative/pain and/or "positive/ pleasure categories. If it's true that our emotions affect our trading decisions, then recognizing and categorizing our emotions is a critical part of assessing our mental capital.

Pain Emotions

Emotions that put us in a negative state can cause us to make irrational decisions regarding our money *(and just about all other aspects of our life for that matter)*. The following are a few to watch out for.

Fear

Fear occurs when you have a belief that something can threaten you or cause you harm. Fear is the anticipation of pain. On March 4, 1933, President Franklin D. Roosevelt famously said that there is nothing to fear but fear itself. Here is the full quote: "So, first of all, let me assert my firm belief that the only thing we have to fear is . . . fear itself—nameless, unreasoning, unjustified terror which paralyzes needed efforts to convert retreat into advance." Fear is such a powerful feeling that in today's world, most people get so worked up being fearful that being in a fearful (or worrisome) state becomes a habit and a "comfort" zone, even when 9 out of 10 times the thing they are worrying about or scared about never happens. Doesn't matter, they move on to the next thing to worry about.

The most obvious fear on Wall Street is losing money; however, losses are inevitable, and a trader who is too afraid of losing might not have the courage to stay the course with a winning trade. They can get spooked easily and bail out of a good position—even though the stock was acting fine and there was no real reason for the stock to be sold, except for a made-up fear that the stock would plunge and they would lose money.

On the other hand, many people in the market are afraid of being wrong, and to put off admitting failure, they stay in losing positions way too long, flushing good money down the toilet. Sadly, most people make fear-based decisions, and that causes them to do the exact wrong thing 9 times out of 10.

Anger and Sadness

Anger and sadness are two emotions we feel in reaction to pain. Sometimes when we suffer a loss, we feel both emotions at the same time. In the early days, before I learned to respect risk, I lost all my money trading a few different times, and I felt a ton of anger and sadness. Today, when I lose, I lose small because I've already calculated my acceptable risk before I enter a trade. Knowing it takes four to seven bad trades to get one winner, now when I have a loss, I just chalk it up to a necessary step on my way to the next big win. On Wall Street, the dumb money feels angry or sad when they lose money, but the smart money knows that losses are inevitable, they plan for how to handle their losses, and they always keep their losses small. The smart money never allows any single trade to impact their emotional state.

Disgust

We experience disgust when we feel something is wrong or dirty. It also occurs when we disapprove of something or find it unpleasant or offensive. Traders can feel disgusted with themselves for taking the bait on a hot stock tip that went sour. You may experience disgust if a high-profile CEO sends out an offensive social media post that sends a stock down. This may sound counterintuitive, but I've known people who felt a little dirty for making an "obscene" profit on a trade. Here's the truth: the market doesn't care whether you win or lose. Don't let disgust infiltrate your mind. Avoid these negative internal conversations, because nothing good comes out of them.

Remorse

We've all had buyer's remorse. Every trader has felt it after buying a stock that goes south. How many times in life have you kicked yourself after doing something stupid? Or worse yet, how many times have you regretted not having the courage to do something you were afraid of? Sometimes I feel a twinge of remorse when I identify a good setup and watch the stock breakout—after I've decided not to buy it. Remorse is a more complicated emotion than anger or sadness. We don't always recognize when we're feeling remorseful, and sometimes regret changes into simpler feelings that then negatively impact our decisions. In most cases, remorse is a backward-looking emotion. The market is a forward-looking apparatus. Any time spent looking backward is wasted. It takes away from you being in a positive state while hunting for your next big win, and in most cases, it just gives you a negative R.O.I.

Surprise

The fact that we ever use the term "what a nice surprise" implies that most surprises are assumed to not be nice. While traders are sometimes treated to nice surprises, on Wall Street, surprises are often associated with downside volatility—and downside volatility is almost never good. The dumb money is frequently surprised when one of their positions moves in a way they didn't expect. Conversely, the smart money has already acknowledged the risk associated with a trade and has therefore anticipated that the position could potentially change quickly and prepared (in advance) for the worst possible scenario. Everyone gets caught off-guard every now and then, but a good trader adapts quickly to the new conditions and resists the urge to panic.

Pleasure Emotions

Emotions associated with pleasure—especially those associated with short-term pleasure—can be just as destructive as the negative/painful emotions I just discussed. All emotions have the ability to provoke irrational decisions, so a good trader is just as wary of good feelings as they are of bad.

Happiness and Joy

When you make a trade that results in big gains, trust me, you're going to feel happy. That's great. Enjoy it. Just don't let it affect your future trading decisions. That is difficult at first. Sometimes that feeling will endear a particular stock to us, and we might be slow to dump it when our strategy says we should.

Some people get hooked on the burst of happiness they get from a big gain in the market. If you're looking to the stock market to make you happy, stop right now, because the stock market does not care about you and in the end, it destroys traders who make emotional decisions. Your ego, sense of self-worth, and any other feeling should be derived from within, or other sources, but definitely not the stock market.

The dumb money feels happy when they win or have a profitable trade. The smart money looks at their process and knows it is not about a handful of trades, it's about working the strategy over a series of thousands of trades over decades. It sounds funny, but a good trader has to shake off their wins just like they shake off their losses. A note of caution: avoid the calculator at all costs. When you find yourself on a winning streak and you pull out the calculator to figure out if X only goes up Y more dollars I can buy XYZ, you are very close to the end of your winning streak. Stay grounded, stay humble, and avoid the calculator at all costs. Deal with what is actually happening in the real world.

Greed

In the classic film *Wall Street*, the notorious Gordon Gekko says, "Greed, for lack of a better word, is good." As traders, we're all motivated by profit, but greed takes over when you become selfish and arrogant, when you ignore risk, forget your roots, and/or you want to be right more than you want to make money.

Good traders have a realistic expectation for what they can consistently take out of the market. Greedy traders have an insatiable appetite for money, and it can cause them to look for shortcuts and to take unreasonable risks. Greed, for lack of a better word, is not good, and like all other emotions, when it affects your decisions, you are destined for failure. To be clear, I'm not saying to forget about the money or anything like that. What I am saying is that if you focus on the money you will likely miss the ball. Instead, focus on your process, and if you have a good process, the money will come. The desire to win is good, the desire to constantly improve yourself is good, but greed itself serves no purpose and brings out unflattering parts of your personality.

Trust

Civilization cannot exist without trust. To survive in the world, humans have learned to trust their instincts, they've learned to trust their beliefs, and they've learned to trust other people. The market, however, is agnostic. It doesn't know you, and it doesn't care about you. The market is counterintuitive in nature, and the same qualities that serve you well in life can cause you to fail in the stock market.

The smart money learns how to overcome these pitfalls by checking their instincts/beliefs at the door, focusing instead on the data and working market-proven trading strategies to achieve superior risk-adjusted returns.

At the end of the Cold War, Ronald Reagan, trying to warm relations between the United States and the Soviet Union, adopted a policy of "trust but verify." In 2013, while negotiating with Russia over Syria, Secretary of State John Kerry took a position of "verify and verify." Trust that the market will be higher in a few decades, but for everything under 20 years, the market is a "verify, verify, *and* verify" arena.

Hope

Hope is a light in the darkness when there is no other light. Hope is the manifestation of our greatest expectations for the future. A trader's expectation for the future is powered by data and tempered by reality. A trader assumes that out of a certain number of trades, some will win and some will lose. If the trader is savvy, they know how to manage risk, mitigate losers, and maximize winners. A trader doesn't hope to make money in the market; a trader knows that over time with a data-driven strategy they are more likely than not to profit. *Hope is an excuse for not making rational decisions.* The dumb money hopes their trades work out because they have no other practical reasons to believe they will. The smart money learns to anticipate what may happen, then prepares for it.

Love

Many traditional marriage vows include the phrase "for richer and for poorer." That's very noble when it comes to your commitment to your husband or wife, but it's a terrible stock market investment strategy. Back in the 1990s, when I took all the money I had made selling candy and fireworks and invested it in SprintPCS stock—well, I fell in love with that stock, and unfortunately, I stuck with it "for richer and for poorer." I rode it all the way up and all the way down, and I missed every opportunity to make a profit on the investment. Dumb money falls in love with their stocks. Smart money, on the other hand, has learned to avoid developing an emotional attachment to their investments. This is much easier said than done (especially with very profitable and long-term positions), but it is necessary to become successful in this business. *It's better to date your positions; don't marry them.*

BREAKING OUT

It doesn't matter how old you are, where you live, what you do for a living, or how many degrees you have on the wall—in the end, you're a person, just like everyone else, and every person is subject to the forces of human nature. When I was younger and naive, I used to think that people were different from one another because, for example, some lived in a big city and some lived in the country; some went to college and some didn't. All wrong. Life has taught me that people are people—meaning we are all human and all have similar psychological motives, drivers, strengths, and weaknesses: human nature.

We've established here that human nature, unchecked, is not suited for success in the stock market. The emotions that come preprogrammed into our psyche prove detrimental to the sound, rational decision-making required to beat the market. But that's not to say we cannot rise above ourselves. It's human nature to panic when someone yells "fire" in a crowded theater, and while we know that most will flee wildly, and some will push others out of their way to save themselves, we've acknowledged that a few will stand out as heroes and help others. Those heroes know how to break free from human nature.

The key to becoming a successful trader is to become the hero of your own story and break free from the low-level shackles of human nature. I've claimed that we cannot change human nature, and we cannot change the market, but we can, I believe, change ourselves. We can change how we behave and react to situations. We have to start by wanting to change. Then we learn to resist our natural urge to pursue short-term pleasures and avoid immediate pain. Instead, we have to learn to recognize our emotions as we're experiencing them, in some cases anticipate them, and we have to be intellectually honest about how our emotions impact our decisions.

It means that you'll be learning to deny your emotions in order to make rational decisions. It might feel very uncomfortable.

At first, it might be painful. Remember, in most cases, success is on the other side of pain, and in that light, it will help you to change your outlook on pain. Instead of looking at pain with dread, think of it as something positive—a rite of passage, an obstacle that must be overcome to enjoy prosperity on the other side. Surviving pain is a necessary component to improving your life.

Once you embrace pain, the pain will not last long, and change (for the better) will come quickly. Remember, at first it may seem hard but over time it will become easy. That applies to just about anything in life, from learning how to read to learning how to ride a bicycle to a baby learning how to walk. It's painful to fall on your face, but the toddler, thankfully, at that age doesn't view it as painful and keeps going, and over time, walking becomes "easy." The same is true for bringing out the smart money superhero inside of you—or the A+/alpha version of yourself.

Once you do that, you'll have the tools you need to master your mental state and become the real hero of your own story.

The significance of the coat hanger.

CHAPTER 8

Master Your Mental State and Your Life Will Change

You can't control what happens in life; however, you can control how you think, behave, and react to it.

—Adam Sarhan

One of the major lessons you can learn from psychological analysis is how to control your mental state, so you can make smart, objective, and unemotional trading decisions over and over again—especially when you are under pressure.

People are best able to make objective, unemotional decisions—in the market and in life—when they are in an optimistic, strong, and/or positive state of mind. In order to create a positive mental state, you must first learn to recognize your current mental state at any given point in the day.

You must learn to take control of your mental state by focusing your attention on things that will positively affect your mindset. You must learn to filter out everything in life that is unimportant or that brings you down. You must align your wants and desires with your long-term goals. You have to be honest with yourself about your strengths and weaknesses, and then build an internal narrative where a person with those strengths and weaknesses is the hero. Essentially, you want to learn how to bring out the smart money superhero—every day! The smart money superhero can also be internalized as the A+ version of yourself or the alpha [*Enter your name*]. Since alpha means above-average returns, you want the above-average version of yourself to show up every day.

But before you can do any of that, you have to be honest with yourself about your relationship with yourself and with money. Then you must consciously create a new, empowering relationship with yourself, with money, and with the external world (everyone and everything around you).

YOUR RELATIONSHIP WITH MONEY

Most of us have an emotional attachment to our money. When I was young, I had a very poor (scarcity) relationship with money. I guarded the money I had earned selling candy and fireworks; that money was a symbol of my early entrepreneurial spirit, and it helped define who I was as a person. When I was a little older, the money I earned selling cell phones represented the sacrifices I made working nights and weekends while my college friends partied. Unbeknownst to me at the time, the money came to represent the pride I had in my work ethic.

Throughout my first forays in the market, I wasn't trading with dollars; I was trading with my entrepreneurial spirit. I was trading with my work ethic. The things I valued in myself, my own self-image, were wrapped up in the money I used to trade, and it caused me to make emotional—not objective—decisions, which caused me to lose the money, inflicting devastating emotional consequences. It became a big negative money-losing cycle—all created by my subconscious mind.

Ask yourself this question: How often do you make objective decisions about things you are emotionally attached to? Probably not often. Now, ask yourself if you are emotionally attached to your money. At first, it's hard for most people to admit, but dig deeper and you'll almost certainly find the honest answer is that you are very emotionally attached to your money. If you think you are "different," ask yourself how you would *feel* if you lost half of your net worth. What hopes and dreams have you attached to that money? What sense of security does that money provide?

Now ask yourself how you would *feel* if you lost half of the hangers in your closet. I'm guessing it would have very little to no impact on your emotional well-being.

The smart money trader views money for what it is: an object—just like a hanger in your closet. In time, you will learn to view money with the same emotional detachment you have for the hangers in your closet, and it will allow you to make more objective decisions about your trades. I always keep a hanger in my office. If you ever come visit, you will know what it means.

Here's another big negative belief we have with respect to our relationship with money: Have you ever heard the term "filthy rich"? It (mistakenly) implies that money is dirty and that someone who acquires a lot of it becomes dirty by association. The truth is, most people unconsciously view money as bad. That's one of the main reasons why 90% of people prevent themselves from ever getting to the top 10%. Think about the way you were raised. How did your parents talk about people who are rich? What do you think about rich people? I mean, people who swim in money. What did other influential people tell you about money during your childhood? Remember, most communication is nonverbal. For this exercise to work properly, think not only about what was told to you about money, think also about what other nonverbal messages were sent to you about being rich. I'll bet they weren't kind.

Most people feel uncomfortable saying (or believing) that they deserve to be rich (I use the word "rich" on purpose because even saying that you are rich has a slightly negative connotation to it for most people. Most people prefer to use the word "wealthy," but that difference just illustrates my point).

People subconsciously view money as bad or evil. Most people mistakenly think people with a lot of money are inherently bad or they do bad things. The reality is that money is neutral and has no bearing on whether someone is good or bad on the inside.

Pause for a moment and yell, "money is good!" then yell "I am rich!" How does that make you feel? Is it a little weird? If you feel at all uneasy, then you probably have a negative association with money and, most likely, you are subconsciously doing things to stop yourself from accumulating wealth.

The good news is that you can change your association just by telling yourself that money is good. In order to consistently make money, it is important to believe it is okay for you to make money and, more importantly, *have* money.

Give yourself permission to become rich; once you do you'll stop secretly self-sabotaging yourself, and you'll be able to start doing the work to master your mental state so you can make objective, nonemotional trading decisions. At the end of the day, once you learn how to trade well, the money will come. It is just a byproduct of being a good and very disciplined trader. If you chase the money, most likely you will keep chasing it forever.

The smart money is comfortable being rich. In fact, the smart money is only comfortable being rich; they cannot envision a world in which they do not have a lot of money. Learning how to become comfortable with money is a process. In some cases, it may happen instantly (if you are ready for it); in most cases it will take a lot of time and conscious effort to rewire your brain. Remember, you must unlearn everything you were taught about money and adopt a new healthy relationship with money.

Ignore this concept at your own risk because until you drop your unhealthy relationship with money and adopt a new, healthy relationship with money, you will continue to commit financial self-sabotage. People who are very comfortable with money know how to attract it, earn it, and keep it, and they can easily join the smart money circle.

UNDERSTANDING YOUR MENTAL STATE

Whenever I have the opportunity, I love to sit by the water—especially the beach or a big lake. Depending on the season, the weather, and the time of day, a lake always seems to have a different mood. Sometimes it's crystal clear, other times it is gray and choppy. Sometimes it's still and painted orange by the sunset. Sometimes it's blue and covered with ripples, and sometimes it sparkles like diamonds in the sunshine. Sometimes, a lake can exhibit all those states throughout the same day.

People, like lakes, have moods that can be influenced by outside factors. Unlike lakes, however, people have the power to control their moods, control what they focus on, how they react to external forces, to adjust their attitudes, and to control their mental state. Before you can adjust your mental state, you must have enough presence of mind to recognize what kind of mental state you are in. Most people are not aware of what state they are in and just go through life on autopilot or constantly reacting, in an almost helpless fashion (they love to play the victim), to what happens to them. Others are more "awake" and begin to understand the various states they are in throughout the day. Others are even more awake, and they can actually mindfully control their mental state.

At first, it may sound strange, but in order to be one of the awake people, you have to stop throughout the day and ask yourself what kind of state you are in. To keep it simple, you can be in either a positive state or a negative state. Clearly, there are many types of positive states (happy, excited, hopeful, elated, joyful, content, just to name a few) and there are many types of negative states (sad, blasé, depressed, angry, fearful, among others).

Simply knowing your mental state, however, isn't much help unless you decide to change it if you're suffering a negative mindset. Unfortunately, most people spend most of their life in a negative state and few can switch to—and then stay in—a positive state. Some people have brief glimpses of a positive state but then quickly (subconsciously) revert back to their default setting of a negative state. The truth is that you, and you alone, can manage your state (and your focus and behavior, for that matter) by just changing your wants and the questions you ask yourself (that is, how you rewire your brain—both your conscious and subconscious minds).

States become habits; some are good and some are not. Just like you can change just about any habit you have, the same is true about the habit you are in with respect to your state. And, just like most anything worthwhile in life, at first, changing it might be hard, but with consistent practice, it will become easy. And well worth it!

Don't take my word for it; just look at billionaires. Almost all of them, even uber-successful people, operate from a positive and very optimistic/usually very happy state. Google Richard Branson images and you will find him smiling in just about every picture. And I don't mean a fake smile, I'm talking about a true genuine ear-to-ear smile. Jim Rohn and Tony Robbins have a great line: "Success leaves clues." Trust me, when you truly adopt an attitude of gratitude, your entire world will change, and just about every relationship you have (with money, with yourself, with your family, with God/the universe, nature, your friends, and coworkers) will improve. Happiness is a choice. Choose happy. Be happy. It beats being unhappy every single time.

CONTROLLING YOUR INPUTS

Besides self-awareness, people have one great advantage over lakes when it comes to managing their states: to a large degree, people can control the external forces that may impact their mood. Remember, attention is the currency of your brain; how you use it really matters. Of course, most things in life are outside of our control; however, we can control how we react to them. Moreover, most of the time we can choose what things we devote our attention to, and we can choose how we look at the things that earn our attention.

The first thing I tell people to do is to cover the basics: get enough sleep, take care of your body, exercise, and eat right. That is the easy stuff you can do to dramatically improve your physical state quickly, and your physical state has a profound impact on your mental state.

Most traders sit at their desks all day for eight to 10 hours a day "working," but when you drill down, most of that time is not used effectively. Moreover, most people have lousy posture, so they are slumped over their desks. Their blood is not flowing. They are probably eating and drinking a lot of garbage (hopefully nothing worse) and then they wonder why they have low energy or are in a negative state.

What we feed our body really matters and the same is true for what we feed our mind and soul. What books are you reading? Are you learning something new every day, week, or month? Do you meditate? What spiritual practices help you stay centered? At the end of the day, people love progress. What progress are you making in your life in the short-term, intermediate-term, and long-term?

The next step is to filter out the noise. We live in a noisy world and most of that noise is created by people who want your attention and who have an agenda, and most of the time that agenda is designed to help someone else, not you. What you watch, what you read, who you talk to—all these things contribute to the noise you absorb every day. If it's not important to you, or if it doesn't contribute to a positive mental state, ignore it. Get it out of your mind. A helpful hint is to look at it as a binary outcome: you either have a positive return on investment (R.O.I.) or a negative one. If that item does not give you a positive R.O.I., is it worth your time to consume it? R.O.I. is not just about money; it can apply to many other things.

Focus on things that bring you joy. Find the opportunity to laugh often. As a quick exercise, I want to you stop reading; spend a few seconds and laugh as hard as you can right now. Try to think of something funny you did when you were a kid, something funny your kid did, or some YouTube video a friend sent you that was just hilarious. Just laugh for the sake of laughing. I mean let go and *laugh* really hard! Then, while you are in the middle of laughing, I want you to try to be in a negative state. It's physically impossible to laugh (a real laugh, not a fake superficial laugh) and be in a negative state. As comedian Steve Martin once said, "You can't play a sad song on a banjo."

Whenever you feel down or notice that you are in a negative state (which could be for any reason but it usually happens by default—especially after a losing trade), just take a minute and shift yourself into a positive state. Stop what you are doing, close your eyes, take five deep breaths, then start to laugh, and laugh very hard. Your state will instantly change. Whenever I notice I'm in a negative state I give myself 10–60 seconds to snap out of it. Otherwise, what's the point?

CONTROL YOUR FOCUS

Learn to focus. Attention is your brain's currency and we all have a limited amount of it. When I first began trading stocks as a teenager, I thought I could multitask, or focus on several things at once. As I began to learn more and more about how the brain works (not Adam's brain but every human brain), I learned that people can only consciously focus on one high-level thing at a time. Sure, anyone can text and drive, but we all know how smart that is. When you actually understand what is happening, you realize that those people are really consciously focusing on one thing: either texting or driving, not both.

I spent a very long time trying to figure out how people can do more than one thing at a time. What happens is our subconscious brain takes over for a lot of the mundane activities we have learned to do, and we have a false illusion that we can multitask when in fact our conscious brain is actually only focusing on one thing at a time. Have you ever driven somewhere and don't remember how you got there? You just spaced out during a big portion of the drive. If you keep your eyes on the road, visual cues may pull you back into reality, often with a pounding heart. When you are texting, however, you are focusing on your text and not the road; that's why there are so many distracted-driving fatalities.

When it comes to high-level things, you should think carefully about what you chose to focus on. Would you want your surgeon texting while in the middle of surgery? The same is true for trading. After all, you are trading your money. Beating the market is hard enough; it's even harder when you are acting dumb (dumb money is distracted, and smart money is focused). Wake up, focus, and pay attention.

Here's a fun exercise that I learned from Tony Robbins that perfectly illustrates this point. Tony asks people to look around the room for objects that are BLACK, and then he asks them to close their eyes and list some of those objects. Most people do pretty well at this. Then he asks them to keep their eyes closed and list some objects in the room that are BLUE. Here's where people stumble. They weren't looking for blue objects, so they have trouble remembering any blue objects. That's not what they were focused on, and people can only truly focus on one thing at a time. Take a minute and try it and try it on other people; the results are amazing.

Whenever you are in a bad mood—a negative mental state—ask yourself what are you focusing on (and you can change that instantly).

Think of this classic question: Is the cup half empty or half full? 10 out of 10 times, when you are in a negative state, you are asking negative questions and focusing on the proverbial cup being half empty. On the other hand, when you are happy, optimistic, and in a positive state, you are asking positive questions and focusing on the good in the situation.

All you have to do is learn how to identify your mental state, and then choose to focus on the positive. Instead of saying, "I can't afford this," change it to "How can I afford this?" "How can I acquire the skills necessary to excel and accomplish this goal?" When you learn to master this skill, your entire life will change.

KEEP IT SIMPLE

I've learned to simplify whenever possible. In most cases, I think of every-thing as being binary: either good or bad, either win (W) or lose (L), either risk or reward, either up or down. Sure, there are different gradients in between the extremes, but that is all noise and usually only serves to distract you from the important things you need to focus on. Most people have a hard time accepting that life is simple, and they complicate things unnecessarily. This causes them to get lost in the weeds, prevents them from seeing things clearly, and keeps them from achieving their goals. This timeless "truth" has existed since the beginning of time. Centuries ago, Confucius said, "Life is really simple, but we insist on making it complicated."

Centuries after Confucius (remember, human nature never changes), Albert Einstein said, "if you can't explain it to a six-year-old, you don't under-stand it yourself." The power of keeping things simple is another core belief we drive home in the smart money circle. The faster you accept this impor-tant fact, the faster you will understand the laws of money, nature, and life. The best traders can explain their strategy in extremely simple terms—so simple, in fact, that people often can't believe it.

Now, let me caution you, please do not mistake simple for stupid. There is a big difference. There is a certain elegance in being able to keep things simple, but it is human nature for people to want to complicate things, espe-cially things they do not understand. This happens all the time with inves-tors. Please avoid unnecessarily complicating things at all costs. The most successful investors, traders, and speculators on the planet have a simple plan, and all they do is execute their plan. You should too.

CONTROL YOUR DESIRES OR YOUR DESIRES WILL CONTROL YOU

It is important to note that you are free to want anything in the world (free will), and you are free to focus on anything (positive or negative) in any situation. Most people want multiple things that usually contradict each other. For example, Tim might want to lose weight, but he also wants to eat cake. Life is set up so we all have free will. You can want multiple things, but ultimately you must align your wants with your goals.

The first step is to take inventory of all your wants, then drop all the wants that detract from your goal—all the wants that are negative and/or destructive—and then you must adopt new healthy/positive wants that reinforce your goals. Focus on things that are positive in your life, not negative.

Now, think about what I just shared with you for a minute. Let's meet two traders: Trader A and Trader B. Trader A is happy, bubbly, optimistic, proud, and a pleasure to be around (in a positive state) and Trader B is always miserable, depressed, angry, upset, highly irritated, and paranoid (in a negative state). Trader A looks for opportunities in the market, and Trader B looks at problems and thinks everyone is out to get her. Who do you think will perform better?

Now, let's see how you can apply what you just learned. Ask yourself what state you are in when you trade. Are you able to notice when you slip into a negative state? If you are, what do you do about it? Do you just stay in a negative state? Or can you snap out of it quickly? The faster you learn how to control your state the better all aspects of your life will be.

KNOW—AND MASTER—THYSELF

When I first begin working with a new client, I ask them what animal best represents their spirit. Almost always, people tell me they are a lion or some other strong alpha-type animal. Virtually none of my clients see themselves as a sheep or a lamb. But then, I look at their results in the market (and in life) and then tell them a story about a stranger that they do not know who makes similar decisions, takes similar actions, and has similar (or even slightly better) results, and I ask them what animal they think best represents that stranger. Without fail, they almost always say a lamb or sheep. Then, I bring it back to them. I show them their portfolio and gently connect the dots. Poof! That almost always forces the person to look at themselves objectively and mentally wake up.

Judge yourself by the same criteria you use to assess other people—flaws and weaknesses included. Only then will you be able to know what areas you are good at and where you are weak. Here's the beautiful thing about life: even a metaphorical sheep can evolve and become a relentless and very skilled trader.

Being a good trader involves developing a market-proven strategy, working with market trends, making objective, unemotional decisions, learning how to listen to the market (by respecting and being in harmony with the way it is trending), and only making the very best trades.

A sheep may be controlled by fear and have trouble committing to a trade. Not all lions are good traders; many might be overconfident and risk more than they should. Both the sheep and the lion could be more successful if they recognized their weaknesses and accepted the strengths of the other. Each is capable of overcoming their own weaknesses and evolving into a better version of their former self.

If you are very weak at details but great at big-picture thinking, then find someone who can help you trade—to help you pull the trigger on a well-vetted idea. This way you don't have to make careless (and costly) mistakes when trying to do something you are weak at. Or maybe you are a great trader but a lousy analyst. In that case, find someone you can trust to help you identify good opportunities. At the end of the day, this is an idea and execution business. We all need good ideas and we need to execute those ideas very well. You may be asking yourself at this point how to get good ideas. You can subscribe to a good membership site, get ideas from an advisor, look at 13F filings—to see what the big investors are buying/selling in prior quarters—and scan the market and train your eye for winning setups.

Whatever the case may be, the key is to understand yourself, to identify your weaknesses, overcome them, and master yourself.

As a trader, you are playing in a very competitive arena. If you want to win, then you need to master the one variable you can control: yourself.

Introspection (honest self-reflection) helps me to remain humble and allows me to accept the best idea at the right time. One of my rules in life is to consciously check my ego at the door and always run with the best idea. I don't care where it came from, in my world the smartest idea always wins. Arrogance (which stems from your ego) is one of the biggest obstacles stopping you from getting ahead in life and in the market. Additionally, knowing I don't know (Aristotle said, "The more you know, the more you know you don't know") keeps me in a state where I am always learning, and I'm open to the potential that I might be wrong. That's hugely important on Wall Street and in life. I love to learn, and I love to win. If what I'm doing is wrong, then I want to stop doing it as fast as possible and do something that is right (which helps me win). I don't want to stay wrong. That's not smart. Ask yourself: "Is this smart?" If it is, do it; if it isn't, don't.

Your behavior and the quality of your decisions are directly impacted by the way you see and think about yourself and the world. If you believe you can't beat the market, you won't be able to beat the market. If you believe you don't deserve to make big money, you most likely won't make big money. Remember, the way you see and describe yourself (especially on a subconscious level) has a huge impact on your actions. Make sure your perceptions match reality so your actions make sense, and your results match your reasonable, risk-managed expectations.

If you change your internal story and take responsibility for everything you say, think, and do, and if you truly believe in yourself—then, in time, you will see magnificent results. Moreover, if you believe you can beat the market, you probably can acquire the skills necessary to beat the market. If you believe you deserve financial freedom and abundance, you will likely get it. Remember, it's not enough to believe. For a belief to manifest, you need to be relentless and constantly take considerable action until you win. Nothing happens without acting.

MAKING *GREAT* DECISIONS

Ultimately, the goal of achieving a positive mental state is to create a foundation for making great objective and unemotional trading decisions. The secret to achieving any major goal in life (and beating the market, for that matter) is to learn how to make great decisions (especially when you are under pressure). In order to make great decisions, you must learn how to make rational, not emotional, decisions and clearly weigh the potential risks and the rewards.

Just like many things in life, it sounds simple in theory but is difficult (for most untrained people) to execute in real time. I can tell you with absolute certainty, once you master this skill, you will enjoy life on a completely different level.

Making good decisions.

CHAPTER 9

How to Make Smarter Decisions

People make either smart decisions or dumb decisions (this is especially true when it comes to their money). Just about everyone begins in the dumb money circle, and most people stay there. Very few people have the mental and intellectual fortitude to do the heavy lifting required to rewire their brains and become part of the smart money circle. The good news is that there are no barriers to entry except for the mental obstacles you create for yourself. Anyone can start from scratch, and if they decide to acquire the knowledge needed to join the smart money circle, then change their actions accordingly, they will eventually join it. Your financial life will change for the better, and you will see things with more clarity and from a completely different perspective.

We've established that there are essentially only three decisions to make on Wall Street: buy, sell, and hold. That's all there is to trading. The key is to know what to trade and when to trade it. I've told you about my A.M.P.D. strategy. I told you how I vet stocks, with a disruptive element, and how I want to see repeatable patterns that show a stock is ready to move. I showed you how I determine advanced entry points, how I mitigate risk, and how my strategic stops determine when I exit a position. If you work this strategy over time, your wins will be big and your losses will be small, and you'll be able to consistently beat the market.

Yet, somehow, it is still more difficult than that. I've told you about human nature: people are people—and people make emotional decisions. It takes significant self-awareness to identify the forces that shape your decision-making. It takes practice to recognize your mental state at any given moment. It requires discipline to learn to shut out negative influences and maintain a positive mindset—and a positive mindset is necessary for making good decisions. Then, after all that, it takes discipline to be able to pull the trigger when the bullets are flying (when the market is moving fast) in real time—over and over again.

Nonetheless, armed with a sound, market-tested trading strategy, and reinforced by a positive mental state, we can still fumble and make bad calls (also known as a drawdown).

I've told you about the legendary speculator Jesse Livermore, who made and lost several great fortunes during his storied career. By 1905, at the age of 28, Livermore was a multimillionaire, living large and taking expensive vacations (he had his own railcar, which was the poshest way to travel in those days). One of the early technical traders, he had developed a strategy that worked, and as long as he worked it, it seemed to make him money. In 1907, a cotton trader named Teddy Price caught Livermore's ear, and he convinced him that cotton was going up. According to Livermore's technical analysis of the market, he should have sold, but for some reason—a reason Livermore was never able to explain—he kept buying. Then Teddy Price double-crossed him, and along with most other cotton speculators, he sold, bankrupting Livermore. Whether it was out of greed or trust, or some other emotion, Livermore allowed himself to be distracted and influenced by an outside source, and it cost him dearly. He would rebuild his fortune and repeat his folly a few more times throughout his trading career.

The movie *Moneyball* is a dramatic interpretation of Michael Lewis's book of the same name. It's the story of Billy Beane who, as general manager of the Oakland Athletics baseball team, adopted a statistics-based approach to building a winning team. It was an approach that flew in the face of conventional wisdom at the time. During a critical scene in the film, Billy Beane, as portrayed by Brad Pitt, sets up a deal to trade his All-Star player for lesser-known players—with less obvious talent—who were better fitted to his statistical approach. The technical analyst, portrayed by Jonah Hill, cautions Beane against the trade, saying, "This is the kind of decision that gets you fired." Risking his job and facing ridicule from the entire baseball establishment, Beane sticks to his guns. "Do we believe in this thing or not?"

In real life, that strategy was made famous by legendary systems trader John W. Henry, who basically applied a similar statistical/systematic approach for trading stock, currency, and commodity futures decades earlier. In fact, he made so much money trading that he eventually bought the Boston Red Sox and applied that approach to selecting players. That approach eventually helped him snap the Curse of the Bambino and the Boston Red Sox won their first World Series in 86 years.

Livermore got distracted and faced ruin when he deviated from his path. Beane, on the other hand, stood his ground, and (spoiler alert) proved his method and forever changed the game of baseball.

The quality of your decisions is the single most important factor that determines whether you wind up in the smart money circle or the dumb money circle. Making smart money decisions consistently over time (even when times are tough) requires more than just following a market strategy; it requires clear thinking that can stand up to fear, greed, doubt, love, just about every possible "distraction" under the sun, and against the so-called "wisdom of the crowd."

In order to stand up to those external forces, you have to learn how to rewire your brain to think like smart money. A smart money mindset is one that is focused on success; it is extremely self-motivated and intellectually honest at all times.

Smart money pushes themself intellectually as hard as they can. Smart money does the "right" thing at all times; it is positive/optimistic, learns from the past, lives in the present, plans for the future. Smart money is grateful and focuses relentlessly on self-improvement (doing the "hard" things that they and others do not want to do). Smart money helps others and is always focused on how to thrive. When life gives them lemons, they build a lemonade empire. Nothing will stop them. No excuses. They are dedicated and determined to rise above the crowd (and their former self) and win. Smart money is generous, enjoys helping others, and likes to give generously.

GOOD VERSUS EVIL: SMART MONEY VERSUS DUMB MONEY

I've told you before that I think in binary terms (it helps me have more clarity so I can make better decisions). Something is either good or it is evil. There may be a gradient in between, but all that is noise, cluttering your mind and complicating your decision-making. All classic stories are about a battle between good and evil. One of the things I have learned on my journey studying successful traders and counseling thousands of people since the early 2000s is that, at some level, we all have an internal struggle between good and evil (some more than others).

When we're building our internal narrative about how we approach trading—the one where you are the hero—I like to frame smart money as good, and dumb money as evil. The hero, we hope, will always choose good over evil, and the drama is often not between the hero and the external forces of evil, but instead, it's about the hero's internal struggle in choosing good and dismissing evil within.

The battle between good and evil exists in all of us and impacts us differently. We all have strengths and weaknesses, and most of us are all trying to improve ourselves in some capacity—and perhaps working to overcome a vice or two (or more). Maybe the improvement is as simple as reading more, exercising more, or spending more time with family. Perhaps the battle is more severe and is against some form of destructive behavior—financial, emotional, or physical self-sabotage. The good news is that we can decide to change our wants at any time. We can want to choose to do good at any time; we just have to want it more than the bad things that constantly distract and tempt us. Then, we must decide to do good and follow through with steady action that helps us do good—and keep wanting it and keep taking the good actions for as long as it takes.

Humans have an inexplicable capacity for self-sabotage, and all too often we choose to suffer in our daily lives because perhaps we lack the courage to make the tough decisions that can open us up to long-term success.

Over time, after choosing good long enough and developing "new good" habits, thoughts, and actions, doing the right thing becomes much easier. You will develop a habit of choosing good and that will become your new normal. Effectively, you will raise your standards and perform at a higher level.

Remember what I shared with you earlier: at first, it's hard; then it's easy. The same is true for choosing good and adopting new good smart money habits (in any area of your life). Remember, people are creatures of habit; if you fill your day with good habits, your life will be filled with good things. Conversely, if you fill your day with bad habits, bad things will happen. Life is simple. Don't make it more complicated.

Now, to be clear, just because you do "good" things doesn't mean bad things will not happen from time to time. They will, and that's normal because they will be few and far between, and when they do happen, you will know how to deal with them much better because you will be much stronger. The same is true if you make bad decisions—good things will happen but they will be few and far between. Again, focus on what you can control, the quality of your decisions, and how you react to what happens to you. The rest will take care of itself.

THE DANGER OF EMOTIONAL LOGIC

I met an accountant once who made lots of great smart money decisions. He drove an old Buick sedan that he bought from an estate sale. The car wasn't fancy, and it wasn't pretty, but it was well-maintained, had low miles, and it suited the needs of his family—and he bought it for a fantastic bargain price. Likewise, he bought his home at a foreclosure auction because the previous occupant had been convicted of serious federal crimes. He ended up with a palatial home on a three acre-lot for the price of a three-bedroom, two-bathroom ranch-style house in a suburban neighborhood. These were both highly practical, unemotional purchases. They were smart money purchases.

For most people, their home and their car are the most expensive things they'll ever own. Who among us has been able to make such unemotional decisions about our home or car? When we shop for a house, we often "fall in love" with a property where we can imagine raising our family or living out our golden years. Real estate agents rely on this. When we buy our automobiles, if we're honest, we're often more concerned about what the car says about us, whether it's suited to the level of success we feel we've achieved. A luxury car is something we may feel we "deserve." Listen: it's okay to have a home we love; it's okay to drive a car that makes us feel good about ourselves—as long as they don't detract from our goals.

The point is that we need to know when our emotions are influencing our buying decisions because when we trade in the market, we don't need to love our stocks, and we don't need our trades to make us feel good about ourselves. We trade in the market to make money, and, as I hope you have learned by now, the smart money makes objective/rational decisions with their money, not emotional ones.

I once knew a trader who convinced himself he deserved a brand-new Mercedes S-Class—the big one. He had just had a good year, he told himself he "deserved" it, and he decided it would create the proper "air of success" with potential clients. The truth is he just wanted the biggest fanciest car he could possibly afford because it would make him feel good. He never drove around with his clients; he was using what I call emotional logic to reverse-justify his decision to buy a top-of-the-line status symbol luxury car.

Most people buy things based on their emotions and justify those decisions with "logic." In most cases, they are using inferior logic that, by definition, is skewed because they have already made the decision and they manufacture some logic that is designed to support that decision. Dumb money uses this emotional logic to justify everything they buy—and especially their trades in the market.

In this business, money is your inventory. You use some (or all) of it whenever you want to buy or sell anything. So, it is of the utmost importance to understand how to make sound, objective, rational, superior decisions and not subjective, emotional, inferior decisions. Since most people make emotional decisions and use emotional logic to justify their decisions, then it should come as no surprise that the default setting for most people in the market is to make lousy emotional decisions and fall into the dumb money circle. This presents a major opportunity for whoever understands this timeless law of human nature and is strong enough and self-aware enough to do something about it. The same is true in business or just about any other competitive professional arena.

Now, armed with that knowledge, think about all of your buying decisions and ask yourself what will you do differently going forward to begin making rational, and not emotional, decisions.

Here are some ideas, but there are many other ways to accomplish this goal: they all are versions of "preparation." The key is to prepare very well before the market opens and then step back and focus on trading your plan.

First, write down your thoughts about the market every night or every weekend and share them with someone else. This way you "get out of your head" and have accountability for your ideas. Also, when your ideas are written down there is a clear archive of them that you can look back on forever. This way you can go back and study your thoughts and compare them to how the market actually performed. Over time, you will learn how to change your perception to become more aligned with what is actually happening on Wall Street.

Another powerful way to make rational, not emotional, decisions is to keep score on a whiteboard near your desk. Write down the trades you want to take before the market opens and then see how many trades you managed to execute when the market was open. When you "see" something but don't pull the trigger, ask yourself why. Why did you miss it? Most likely it will be because you got distracted. Then over time, you will figure out ways to get and stay focused. There will always be some stocks that you miss or get away from you and that's okay—as long as you followed your plan. No one can catch every single big monster stock in the market. That's not realistic, and you only need one or two really good moves each year and you will be loving life! The key is to learn how to plan ahead and then execute/trade your plan.

STUDY THE CROWD

Imagine how much easier investing would be if there wasn't a crowd—other people in the market against whom we compare our own success. It was the behavior of the crowd, the circle of cotton speculators, that convinced Jesse Livermore to bet against his own logic. It was the crowd, the baseball establishment, that put pressure on Billy Beane to abandon his statistical approach to baseball. The crowd is one of the biggest things that can put you off your game and prevent you from making smart money decisions.

RETAIL VERSUS INSTITUTIONAL INVESTORS

So, who is "the crowd" and how do you outsmart them? The trading world is divided into two primary groups: retail investors (a.k.a. individual investors) and institutional investors (a.k.a. professional investors). Within each group, there are two subgroups: the smart money (some who win) and the dumb money (some who lose).

On average, people on Wall Street like to say that retail traders lose and institutional traders win. Well, as is the case with most generalizations and stereotypes, that is not always true. In practice, the normal bell curve applies to both retail and institutional traders. In both cases, some are lousy, most are mediocre, and very few are great. Additionally, if you dive a little deeper, you will know there are so many different schools of thought that the normal bell curve will apply to each—meaning some fundamental traders are good, most are mediocre, and very few are great. The same applies to momentum traders, quant traders, technicians, and just about any other style you can think of.

Why? Because at the end of the day, when you peel back the onion, we are all people, and as we have learned, people are people. Human nature never changes, and it governs nearly all of our decisions. Remember that whenever you (or anyone you know) think that "this time is different" or that the "rules" do not apply to them, that thinking is most likely wrong. That is just human nature taking over and causing them to make biased, and not rational decisions.

"THEY" WHO?

You probably think you are different, but most people follow the crowd either on a conscious or subconscious level. Why? Because it makes them feel safe, and feeling safe is a very powerful emotion.

To keep it simple, I define "they" as everyone else who participates in the market. The normal bell curve applies here as well: some people in the crowd are smart, most are average, and some are not. That is just the way the world works. A note of caution: it is okay to follow the crowd if you are making money, but always stress-test your ideas to make sure the smartest idea wins. If you do follow the crowd, make sure it is on purpose and based on rational, not emotional, logic.

If you spend any time with anyone who works on Wall Street, or if you consume just about anything in the financial media, you will hear people say "they" are buying or "they" are selling. This is not a new concept; it has existed since the beginning of time and exists in every aspect of life. If you drive by a new real estate development, you might think, "Wow! I can't believe what 'they' did with that space." Or, if you see something in bad shape you might suggest that "they" really should do something about it. So, naturally, people (a.k.a. "they") say the same thing about capital markets.

Back in 1912, G.C. Selden wrote a timeless book titled *Psychology of the Stock Market* and dedicated an entire chapter to this subject. In fact, Chapter 3 in his book is entitled "They" and Selden presciently pointed out that everyone believes in "they" and each person will tell you "they" is someone else. Selden writes:

> If you were to go around Wall Street and ask various classes of traders who They are, you would get nearly as many different answers as the number of people interviewed. One would say, "The house of Morgan"; another, "Standard Oil and associated interests"—which is pretty broad, when you stop to think of it; another, "The big banking interests"; still another, "Professional traders on the floor"; a fifth, "Pools in the favorite stocks, which act more or less in concert"; a sixth might say, "Shrewd and successful speculators, whoever and

wherever they are"; while to the seventh, They may typify merely active traders as a whole, whom he conceives to make prices by falling over each other to buy or to sell.

Another legendary book titled *Extraordinary Popular Delusions and the Madness of Crowds*, written by Charles MacKay in 1841, does a great job explaining how crowds behave (spoiler alert, mostly irrationally) and the madness of crowds. Remember, every market in the world is made up of various crowds and most of them are grouped together. Why? Because human nature never changes, and most people just blindly follow the "crowd." The crowd is another version of "they."

These powerful observations support my thesis and underscore the importance of psychological analysis: human nature is timeless and that is what drives asset prices (both up and down). My research supports Seldon's and MacKay's findings, and they are both right that there is no magic "they." People are social animals and most people prefer the psychological safety of adopting someone else's opinion, instead of taking the time and putting in the work to truly think for themselves.

Thrive on other people's stupidity. You can't undo dumb money mistakes, so you might as well profit off them. The crowd suffers from a common psychological bias known as groupthink (which you'll hear more about in the next chapter). Carl Icahn articulates this phenomenon best in his Twitter biography which, as of this writing, reads: ". . . Some people get rich studying artificial intelligence. Me, I make money studying natural stupidity." If you prefer, you can call this approach "intellectual arbitrage."

ANALYZE THREE SIDES

So, does the smart money ignore the crowd? No. The smart money knows that the crowd affects the market, so they consider the crowd in an objective way. At the most basic level, there are three parts of the crowd to consider: people who agree with you, what the crowd thinks (a.k.a. consensus), and the people who disagree with you.

Keep in mind, the crowd is not *always* wrong, but they are usually wrong or at the very least late to the party. For some reason, by the time the crowd figures "it" out, usually the big move is already over—or very close to being over. Jumping on the bandwagon in the market simply means you're helping drive the price up for the people who were already in. There are times where that could (briefly) work, but in the long term, it is not a winning strategy.

Here is how I avoid groupthink and keep myself from falling into this very common psychological trap: I grab a pen and a blank piece of paper and write down three columns titled Me, Crowd, Against. Then, I write down at least three reasons why I want to do something (buy, sell, or hold) in the Me column. Then, in the Crowd column, I write down what I suspect "they" think, and then I imagine what traders who are against my position might think, and I write three things down in the Against column.

I do this for all my trading decisions because it forces me to get out of my head and see things from other people's points of view. It also forces me to admit when the crowd is affecting my decision-making and stress-test my ideas (maybe I'm missing something important). It also helps me see what the "against" circle would think and then at the end of the day, just like Ray Dalio, I go with the smartest idea. At face value, this exercise might seem tedious, but over time it is incredibly rewarding (just like walking for an hour a day to exercise might seem tedious but, in the end, is worth it).

If you want to take it a step further, find the smartest people you know and ask them to do the same exercise, and ask them to send you their findings. In my world, the smartest idea wins. Put your ego aside and embrace whatever idea will give you the best return on your investment.

THEY (DON'T) WANT YOU TO LOSE

A note of caution about the crowd. I've heard traders say, "'They' want me to lose." That is not true. I fundamentally refuse to accept any disempowering logic that implies that I am a victim and/or that someone else can control my destiny. The truth is the exact opposite. You are in full control at all times. You control your decisions. You control your results. You create your life. Anyone who buys into disempowering logic is misguided and exhibiting childish behavior at best. Disempowering logic is something that the smart money circle does not tolerate or believe in.

Some people believe that there is a magical group of people who are conspiring against you, but my experience tells me otherwise. As you know by now, I am a very direct and very practical person. I do not believe in outlandish conspiracies or wild ideas that cannot be supported by facts. I do believe in concrete facts, sound logic, and what works in the real world. I do not think there is a secret group of people that no one has ever heard of who is out there to take your money and has existed on Wall Street since the beginning of time.

What I do know is that this is an extremely competitive arena where the best-performing people win. It is that simple. Instead of blaming other people for your shortcomings (which is what the dumb money does), I urge you to do what I do: take the opposite approach—take full responsibility for your actions, and work hard on improving your performance—always and everywhere. Even if they want you to lose, so what? A lot of people want a lot of things to happen. In the end, results matter; everything else is noise.

I also know that most people on Wall Street have a long bias (meaning they profit when stocks go up) so they are constantly buying stocks, even when stocks decline. Sometimes during bearish phases in the market, they buy stocks because they feel a stock is undervalued or is "cheap." Most conspiracy-oriented people would call this "the plunge protection team." I would be naïve not to know that, at times, "they" (investors who buy when stocks fall) act in tandem. Once you know this, you can profit off it by expecting buyers to show up when stocks fall and being ready to buy after a big decline. Eventually, the market will turn higher after pessimism abates. The same is true when the stock (or the market) rips higher; it keeps going because the fear of missing out (a.k.a. FOMO) kicks in and buyers jump on top of each other. The same is also true when a stock breaks down and falls; it keeps falling because people panic and sell (because they are scared it will keep falling). These are normal human tendencies that recur over and over again.

The bottom line is that the market is full of people who want to win, and you are free to buy, sell, or hold at any time you want. The best-performing people win. It's that simple. Focus on winning and improving your process, and the money will follow. The money is the by-product of your trading. Over time, when you trade well, you will win, and by definition make money. If you trade poorly, or if you focus on the money, you will not be focused on trading well and will most likely lose. Focus on trading well, and the money will come.

THINK CLEARLY (A.K.A. ACCURATELY)

"Accurate thinking" is one of the timeless lessons Napoleon Hill wrote about in his classic book *Think and Grow Rich*. Out of everything he mentioned, for me, accurate thinking is one of the most powerful lessons that usually gets the least amount of credit: in order to excel in life, you must think accurately. It's that simple. My version of this is to think clearly. I always seek clarity, and the clearer I see things, the better and faster things get done, and the more I win. I see the members of my Find Leading Stocks service do this, and I have hundreds of stories to share from traders of all different walks of life.

Here's a story that illustrates the importance of thinking clearly that will show you the power behind accurate thinking:

Jack (I changed his name to respect his privacy), one of my private advisory clients and long-time members, has been with me since the summer of 2008 (before Lehman crashed). When we first met, in June 2008, he had a liquid net worth of around $800,000 and was worth a lot more on paper. He was always busy, leveraged to the hilt (stocks and real estate), and literally couldn't sleep at night. He was in a panic-like state almost all day every day. He did not have a clear view of his financial future, felt lost, and felt like he did not have control. He was always "putting out fires" (do you ever feel like that?). Deep down he knew something had to change, but he didn't know what to do.

His stock portfolio was a mess, he owned 200 stocks and a handful of exchange-traded funds (ETFs) and mutual funds that were pretty much all correlated to the S&P 500 (which means that if the S&P 500 went up, he did well, and if it went down, he lost money). He owned real estate on both coasts (this was before the 2008 crash) and, unbeknownst to him at the time, his crown jewel was his business (to which he afforded the least amount of his attention).

Essentially, he was a jack of all trades and master of none. Within the first five minutes of meeting him, as he began telling me what was going on,

I had to literally stop him and put him on the right track (I don't usually do that within five minutes, but this guy was all over the map and needed my help).

Now, it doesn't take a genius to realize that what he was doing was not sustainable and he was spread way too thin. I am a very straightforward kind of guy, and I told him what he needed to hear—not what he wanted to hear (I'm told that's one of my greatest strengths and why people stay with me). My advice was simple: sell everything and go to 100% cash. I told him to sell his stocks, ETFs, mutual funds, and all his speculative real estate (except his primary residence). I explained why, showed him my logic behind my view (over that summer I also moved to cash because markets across the board were wildly inflated). At first, my advice blew his mind, but after three hours, he understood my logic and agreed.

By the end of the summer, he was in cash, and, luckily for him, he had sold his real estate as well. That action allowed him to completely avoid the brutal 2008 crash, saving him millions of dollars in the process—and that's just the physical capital and does not include the priceless mental capital he saved. Then, after he cleared his plate, we dove deeper, and we started to focus on his business.

In the next 24 months, during the Great Recession (the worst recession the world has seen since the Great Depression), we grew his business by over 500%. His business grew from $500,000 in EBITDA (earnings before interest, tax, depreciation, and amortization) to over $3,000,000 in EBITDA. Instead of "investing" his money in low-level and outright distracting activities (at the time, stocks and real estate were too volatile to consider), he reinvested his time, energy, focus, and capital into buying more practices and growing his business. Keep in mind, we thrived while his competition collapsed due to the Great Recession. I say "we" because I became a partner in that business, and I'm proud to have been a part of Jack's growth every step of the way.

I've told you this story because it is the epitome of smart money thinking. Virtually all of Jack's noncash assets—the stocks and the real estate—were not strategic investments; they were part of a hobbled-together portfolio that didn't follow a unifying strategy that someone else (his financial advisor) put together for him.

Because we perceived that both markets (stocks and real estate) were overvalued, it made rational sense to liquidate the entire portfolio and rebuild it with a new goal in mind and by making a series of objective, non-emotional decisions. There was a lot of noise back then, and it was hard to ignore what the crowd was doing and saying. In the end, it was smarter to focus exclusively on what was important for Jack and his family and where he had a clear edge.

While I knew the markets were overvalued, we couldn't have known then how deep the coming Great Recession would be. In some respects, Jack benefited from great timing, but there's a lesson in there: always do the right thing, the smart thing—regardless of what the rest of the world is doing. If you make objective, unemotional decisions, if you respect risk, if you don't fight the tape, and if you don't let yourself be swayed by the crowd, then you'll very often find that, even though you couldn't have predicted a big market disruption, you were, nevertheless, prepared for it.

(*In case you are wondering, Jack was able to invest in both stocks and real estate again, but he now does it in a much more manageable fashion, and he has learned how to think clearly and respect risk. He later told me that because he was so leveraged, if he hadn't sold, he would have been wiped out, lost everything—including his business. Take a minute and let that powerful lesson sink in. One decision literally changed his life forever.*)

Surmounting mental walls.

CHAPTER 10

What's Holding You Back?

Mental Walls and Cognitive Biases

The great aim of education is not knowledge, but action.

—*Herbert Spencer*

WHAT ARE MENTAL WALLS?

Have you ever hit a wall learning something new or doing just about anything? Don't worry, you're not alone—we all have at one point or another. It's a normal part of the learning curve. At the beginning when you learn something there is a big spurt of growth, then eventually you plateau and hit a wall. Most people back off at that point and jump to the next shiny object. But a few push hard, break the wall down, and then enjoy another big growth spurt until they hit another wall at a higher level. This process goes on and on until they master the skill. "Mental walls" is a term I use to describe those mental obstacles that prevent us from getting ahead.

When Indiana Jones leaps across a chasm, either in pursuit of treasure or to escape some hazard, we, the movie's audience, expect that he'll make it—but just barely. We know he'll end up dangling from the edge, and that he'll somehow climb his way out of peril. This is written into the script to create drama, of course, but it reflects a reality of human nature: people often put in just as much work as is necessary not to fail. If that pit was five feet wider, Indiana Jones would still make it—but just barely.

If you're looking for a real-life example, watch the summer Olympics. When the athletes competing in the high jump clear the bar, they tend to just barely clear it, no matter how high the bar is set. It would be almost comical to see an athlete fly several feet above the bar. It suggests that the physical barrier isn't the real obstacle; the real obstacle is the mental barrier. Often it's our own minds that prevent us from jumping further or reaching higher. I call these self-imposed obstacles "mental walls." A mental wall is any barrier built in your mind that stops you from achieving your goals.

When I first established my paper trading project, I decided to imagine that I had $1 million under management. Why $1 million? Real Wall Street fund managers are responsible for hundreds of millions or billions of dollars. I've worked with people who manage multibillion-dollar funds. Even when I was operating a simulated investment account using fake money, my imagination, at the time, only allowed me to conceive of working with $1 million. That limit of my imagination was just one of the many mental walls holding me back in those early days.

Each of us has mental walls, and our mental walls put stricter limits on our potential success in the market than any physical constraint. Mental walls impact all aspects of your life and come in all different shapes and sizes. Some walls are small (they only last for a brief amount of time) and some are big (they last a lifetime). Like most concepts in this book, I will simplify it in binary terms: you either control your mental walls or they control you.

Most mental walls are created in our subconscious mind (where the dumb money beast tends to reside) and we are not aware of them. If unchecked, you can unknowingly pass them down to future generations. Just think, did your upbringing imprint upon you any constraining or limiting beliefs? I bet it did.

One of the most common limiting beliefs that seems to perpetually float around in many middle and working-class families is that, somehow, having a lot of money is bad. We've already discussed the idea of negative thinking around the term "filthy rich" and I trust that, at this point, you get that point.

The good news is that you can also pass down positive/healthy thoughts and beliefs, but the onus is on you to cultivate those beliefs and develop that healthy mindset. Your future and your family's future depend on you recognizing your mental walls and finding a way to break them down. I have yet to encounter a mental wall that can't be destroyed with the right tools, the right habits, and the right mental outlook. It is amazing how much progress you will make when you begin to systematically identify and destroy your mental walls! As each wall is destroyed you enjoy a deeper sense of freedom and you begin to accomplish things you could not even dream of in almost all areas of your life!

A NEW WAY TO LOOK AT WEALTH

Before we get deeper into identifying mental walls, let me help you destroy the "filthy rich" negative mindset. Money is neutral. It is neither good nor bad. It exists as a necessary component of a complex civilization. It is a tool, like fire. Fire can be used to cook a hearty meal, or it can be used to burn down a house. Likewise, money can be used to create comfort, security, and opportunity, or it can be used to exploit people, stifle competition, and feed unhealthy/greedy desires.

When you hear the term "filthy rich," perhaps you think of some industrial revolution-era curmudgeon like Ebenezer Scrooge wringing his hands while his workers toil. On the other hand, you might think of someone like Warren Buffett, who has dedicated his life to spending the bulk of his fortune on philanthropic endeavors (and encouraged other billionaires to do the same).

Money is good or bad based only on what we do with it. Only you get to decide whether your money is good or bad. The smart money knows that money is good. The more money you have the more good you can do, the more jobs you can create, the more people you can help, the more charity you can give, and the more taxes you pay. All of these help the greater good and money just amplifies the amount of good you can do. A note of warning: money can also amplify the amount of bad you can do, so make sure you are in control and use it to do good—a lot of good!

There also seems to be an ongoing misconception that wealth is a zero-sum game, that in order for one person to win, another has to lose—as if the whole world is one big pie, and if you take two slices, it means someone else doesn't get any. That's a huge myth. If it was true, all the wealth in the world would stay the same, just like the pieces on a chessboard. Since the global economy continues to grow just about every year, by definition the "pie" continues to get bigger and bigger. Trust me, there is more than enough pie to go around several hundred million times. In fact, there are new pies being made all the time. Why? Because people love pies, and bakers know that if they make pies people will buy them. The savvy investor knows that if they give more money to the baker to help them buy more ingredients to make more pies, the baker will earn a bigger profit, the investor will see a nice return on the investment, and in the end, there are more pies. The baker then finds there are economies of scale when making lots of pies, and they invent ways to make more pies for less money, open new locations, and so on and so forth. Then, other investors fund other bakers to get in on the action, and as more pies flood the market the price of pies goes down, and people who once could not afford a pie can now enjoy pie and everyone wins. In a zero-sum game, one person wins, and the other person loses. That's a negative, invalid, scarcity mindset that has absolutely no place in the real world.

Pies aside, the point is that capital markets create new wealth all the time. When you invest money in a good company, the company will use that capital to create value in society, which will stimulate—and grow—the economy, and create more wealth for everyone involved. The company can use that money to create a product or service that people want and or need and are willing to pay for—and they will make a profit, return the capital to the investor with a healthy return on investment, and, once again, everyone wins.

As a trader, your speculative dollars create liquidity and feed the market that companies use to access capital. Look at the world around you. There's never been so much wealth. We can get virtually any product we want, delivered to our front door within a day (if not a few hours), we stream movies on any device, from anywhere in the world that has the internet, 24/7. Some cars can drive themselves, tourists can buy a ticket on a rocket to space. Anyone who grew up before the 2000s would have a very hard time imagining the kind of wealth that exists now and the amazing world we live in. It is really a huge blessing.

As a profit-motivated trader, you are a fundamental driver of the economy and a producer of wealth. Hopefully, as you build your wealth, you'll choose to use it for good.

MENTAL WALLS

Over the years, I've worked with thousands of clients and every one of them, no matter how wealthy they were, had mental walls standing between them and the full success they were capable of. As I helped my clients identify and destroy their own mental walls, I discovered new mental walls of my own that I never realized were there. To help expedite your learning curve and help you succeed, I made a list of some of the mental walls I've encountered during my career. As you read through them, perhaps you'll recognize some of these mental walls in yourself; it's the first step in tearing them down.

Knowledge Wall

How many times have you failed to accomplish a goal simply because you didn't know how to do it? I've had home improvement projects that I've put off because I had no idea how to get started, but once I finally looked up the how-to on the internet, I was bombarded with countless tutorials, guides, and videos. Most of the projects have turned out to be easier than I thought. I had to get over the knowledge wall before I could solve the problem.

(On a side note, I'm lucky if I can tie my shoes in the morning; physical tasks are not my forte. Again, this goes back to knowing yourself and really knowing your strengths and your weaknesses. But I digress, now back to the knowledge wall . . .)

We're lucky that we live in an age where we have so much information (the sum of all human knowledge thus far) at our fingertips. I grew up in a world where the closest thing to a search engine was the periodic guide to literature at the local library. Our challenge now is to figure out how to sort through that information, decide what's important, dismiss what's not, and translate the information into action. Most people get overwhelmed by all the information out there and shut down or just look away and hope the problem will go away. That is the exact opposite of what successful people do. Learning how to research a problem and to identify a solution is the best way to eliminate the knowledge wall for any goal you set.

In the markets, there is a lot of information, and it takes discipline to navigate it all. I spend hours each week doing research on the market, which is a labor of love, poring through thousands of stock charts, trying to interpret the price action to find great set-ups that might translate to actionable ideas.

FindLeadingStocks.com is a business that is built on me sharing my trading ideas and market thoughts with our members, and many of them have had success trading off the ideas I've presented. Time is your most valuable asset and knowledge is your most valuable commodity. Breaking down the knowledge wall is a key step to getting ahead. Become resourceful. Become solution-oriented. The knowledge is out there; go out and get it. If you don't have time to learn it yourself, sometimes you can hire someone who can help you. The goal is to get the right knowledge so you can destroy the (lack of) knowledge wall and win!

Certainty (Belief) Wall

The certainty (belief) wall is very powerful and impacts millions of people. Have you ever met someone who has a lot of potential but low self-esteem, someone who never (or barely) uses their talent and wastes decades of their life in a negative state? That is what I call the certainty (belief) wall. They simply do not believe they can do it and, as a result, they don't do it. Then, that reinforces their negative belief and they do less and less. This is a vicious negative cycle that impacts millions of people across the world. The solution is to strengthen your belief and take massive action until you accomplish your goal. Then, your belief will strengthen and you will accomplish more/ bigger goals. That is a smart money belief cycle. Do not take my word for it—Tony Robbins talks about a different version of this, which he calls the success cycle. He's spot-on.

I've met so many people who were hesitant to start their own businesses because they were nervous about not having a steady paycheck. They decided to stay with the relative certainty of the company they worked for. Some of those people were later unceremoniously laid off. Certainty is an illusion. The future is unknown, and each one of us is either navigating into the unknown or following someone else into the unknown—but nobody knows for sure where we're headed. To be clear, there is nothing wrong with working at a big company; that's not my point. The point is that these people wanted to leave, they wanted to do something else, start a business, and do something they were passionate about, but couldn't bring themselves to pull the trigger.

People have an innate need for certainty, but life itself is uncertain. For most people, that creates a tremendous amount of cognitive dissonance (internal conflict) and they try to resolve it (unconsciously) by avoiding it and doing nothing. If you want to achieve your goals, you must learn how to become comfortable navigating the unknown—otherwise, you'll spend your entire life helping someone else achieve their goals.

The market is definitely uncertain. That uncertainty stops a lot of people from trading and investing. They sit on the sidelines, make excuses such as "the market is not for me," or in some cases, they invest but stay in "cash" almost all the time, they miss big moves up, and/or they are out of the market and spend all their money and don't save anything. This is dumb money thinking. Inflation erodes the value of cash every year, so by doing nothing, you're going backward. If you can't stomach uncertainty, you can at least ride the American Tailwind. But if you are willing to destroy the certainty wall, you may have what it takes to accomplish your dreams in life and beat the market. You alone control your beliefs and you have the power to believe you can do it (or believe you can't).

Execution Wall

Perhaps one reason people get stuck and can't break down the knowledge wall is because, once they know how to do something, they know they'll have another task added to their to-do list (human nature is lazy), and they will have to go and do it! Do you have a to-do list? Most people do, at least in their heads. If not, I'll bet your boss has one for you—or your spouse does. Once you know how to get something done, doing becomes a matter of motivation. I saw an internet meme that read, "It just took me five minutes to do something I've been putting off for five months." Can you relate?

I don't like to-do lists. I prefer to make "results lists." From a practical sense, it's the same thing, but since we're talking about knocking down psychological barriers, perhaps a little psychology is in order. Instead of "clean the pool," consider writing "enjoy the pool this weekend." If I have the goal of enjoying the pool in mind, I'll be more motivated to clean it (and do whatever else is necessary to accomplish my goal—which means I will do a lot more than just one mundane task). The key is to rewire your brain to focus on the goal, not the task. Also, while "enjoy the pool" may imply "clean the pool," it doesn't eliminate the possibility of "hire a pool guy (or gal)." It doesn't matter how it gets done; just get it done.

Warren Buffett said in one of his annual letters, "You are awarded no points in business endeavors for 'degree of difficulty.'" Then he went on to quote Ronald Reagan, who cautioned: "It's said that hard work never killed anyone, but I say why take the chance?" This means to work smart, not hard.

Financial Wall

When I started my business in my dorm room in grad school, I didn't have any money. I was undercapitalized and I hit a financial wall. What do you do in that situation? Give up? Just because the bank won't give you a loan, is that the end of the conversation? Absolutely not. I found a way and you can find a way, too. The world is awash with capital and the reality is that there is a scarcity of good, investable ideas out there. If you can't find funding, it means that your idea isn't good or that you're not selling it correctly. Either way, there's a solution: find someone to help you sell the idea, or find a new idea. Or both. Again, become resourceful and find a solution!

The same holds true for personal goals. Do you have a dream vacation you'd like to take but you can't go because it's too expensive? Is that the end of the story for you? Or are you going to figure out how to make it happen? You can ask your boss for a raise. You can find a new job. You can get a second job. You can start a business. The possibilities are endless, and none of them are crazy if you have a goal and you make a plan to reach that goal.

In my early days as a financial advisor, I'd show some couples that they didn't have enough money in their budget to reach their retirement goals. They could either reduce their spending, earn more money, or lower their expectations for retirement. It amazed me how many people choose to lower their retirement goals rather than get resourceful and figure out how to increase their investment budgets. Be creative. Set a goal, research ways to reach that goal, and then make a plan and put it into action.

Emotional Wall

As you know by now, a central point of this entire book is that emotions drive most of our decisions. We've discussed how most people zigzag through life, caught in a tug-of-war between conflicting emotions. The result, to the untrained mind, is either inaction or worse: self-destructive actions. None of us is immune to our emotions, but a goal of psychological analysis is to identify when our emotions are affecting our decisions and to consciously make objective/rational decisions instead.

My favorite way to do this is to get into a calm mental state and build a plan based on the objective facts as we know them. Then, when the facts change we can pivot and change as well. When we go into the world, we may be swayed by the forces of our emotions, but if we prepare to win (by creating a sound time-tested plan we trust), and we execute it well (we stick to our plan), then we'll get through okay.

I'm just like everyone else, and I can get caught up in my emotions if I look at the market all day every day. That's why I don't do that, and instead, I make all my trading decisions on the weekend when the markets are closed. My decisions are not influenced by the daily turbulence of the markets or by the latest headline du jour. Every week, I create a game plan that helps me keep my emotions separated from my trading decisions. Then during the week, I get out of the way and just trade my plan. Now, that is what works for me; other people might do this exercise daily, monthly, quarterly, or annually. It is up to you to discover what works for you.

COGNITIVE BIASES

I've just introduced you to five big mental walls that I've encountered over the years working with my clients and how to destroy them. Soon, I'm going to introduce you to several more, but first, we have to talk about cognitive biases. A cognitive bias is a fundamental mental flaw (a.k.a. blind spot) in how you interpret the world around you. If your perception is skewed by wrong (and or negative) beliefs of the market (or the world for that matter), it's going to negatively affect your decisions and your results in life and in the market. Remember, price is a function of perception (not your perception, but the market's perception). Your primary job is to be aligned with that perception and take smart risk-adjusted positions to test your ideas in the market—when appropriate—to see if they work in real time. When you are wrong, be wrong small, and when you are right, be right big (more than you lose). Over time, that will create life-changing wealth for you and your family.

The most insidious aspect of a cognitive bias is that, in most cases, you can't see it—or perhaps more precisely, it's all you see, so you're denied the broader perspective that would allow you to recognize that it is not an accurate perception of the world. It's a warped lens that gives you a funhouse-type comforting view of reality. It's comforting to you because it reinforces your ego and your innate desire to be right. Most people on Wall Street would prefer to be right than to make money. That's why most people lose. Again, this makes no sense but it happens all day every day. (Why? Because your emotions, not your logic, drive most of your decisions.)

I've been stressing that the key to success in the markets is developing the ability to make objective, unemotional trading decisions. Let's add "unbiased" to the list. Before we can make unbiased decisions, we have to make an effort to correct our perception and get as clear and unbiased a view of the world—and, in particular, the market—as possible. In practice, that means that if the market goes up this week and you thought it would go down, you are wrong. It's that simple. The good news about the market is that you get a report card (your statement) every day and you can always see how you are doing. The smart money works hard to align themselves with what is happening— and most importantly—what is going to happen next. That is where the big money is made.

Now, the next step on our journey is to identify our cognitive biases and destroy them. To begin with, it is important for you to know that we all have cognitive biases. In its simplest form, a cognitive bias is a systematic pattern of making subjective—and sometimes prejudiced—decisions. Often, these are wrong decisions because they are not aligned with what is actually happening in the real world. For example, you might be bearish (think the market will decline) but the market keeps going up. You have a choice: you can stay bearish and keep losing money or you can respect what is actually happening and turn bullish (and make money by pushing your ego aside and aligning yourself with what is actually happening). We've discussed the power and importance of thinking clearly, and that power is corrupted when you have countless biases that get in the way and prevent you from making rational decisions. That is exactly what happens to the untrained mind.

BIASED THINKING: (DON'T BE) FOOLED BY RANDOMNESS OR THE EFFICIENT MARKET HYPOTHESIS THEORY

Understanding that there are many types of cognitive biases, it makes sense then that there would be competing views on the reality of the market. Two of these pervasive views are "fooled by randomness" and the "efficient market hypothesis." Fooled by randomness would have us believe that humans invent reasons for the way that the market behaves, when in fact, many of the fluctuations are just random. The efficient market hypothesis (EMH) suggests that share prices reflect all the available information about the market, which implies that consistent alpha generation—a fancy term for beating the market—is impossible. I would strongly recommend that you do not buy into this defeatist mentality. Feel free to look these perspectives up online and make your own judgment, but I fundamentally disagree with these flawed perspectives.

Primarily, these market theories imply that you can't consistently beat the market even though countless other people have—and continue to do so year after year. If consistently generating alpha is impossible, how do we explain the awe-inspiring returns of market legends such as Warren Buffett, George Soros, Stanley Druckenmiller, Carl Icahn, Jim Roppel, T. Boone Pickens, Paul Tudor Jones, Martin Zweig, William O'Neil, Marty Schwartz, Gary Kaltbaum, Peter Lynch, or David Tepper—just to name a few? That's not to mention legendary firms like Fidelity, Invesco, and countless other brilliant fund managers and millions of individual investors who consistently outperform their peers and the market. How about all the other Market Wizards that Jack Schwager interviewed in his great *Market Wizard* books? How can all these different people consistently beat the market if it is impossible to beat the market?

I've met a few of these legends. I have also been fortunate enough to have worked with a few of them or interviewed them on my Smart Money Circle show, and I can tell you with absolute certainty that, in my humble opinion, beating the market is skill, not luck.

Is each of these luminaries simply the beneficiary of extraordinary good luck? Have they all just flipped a coin a hundred times and it almost always landed on heads? I'm terrible at games of chance, yet I consistently beat the market and have enjoyed numerous years with stunning gains of double- and triple-digit annual returns. If the market is random and truly efficient, how would that be possible? Now, if that only happened once or twice, sure, anyone can say it is a random fluke, but the fact that so many people do it year after year and decade after decade clearly tells me otherwise.

Another key gripe I have with all the negative thinking packaged into these market theories—especially the efficient market hypothesis—is that individual market participants receive information at different times, and, more importantly, they interpret the information differently and, therefore, react to the information differently. I can tell you first-hand that I have seen one piece of information interpreted so differently by so many experts that it would make your head spin. If multiple parties cannot agree on the significance of a single piece of information, how could a stock ever represent a complete and accurate measure of all the information in the market, especially because the price is always moving?

These theories fly in the face of the real-life results I just showed you. Perhaps I'm biased. Maybe I'm operating with a warped perspective of reality. Here's the thing: if I do have a warped perspective of the market, it works for me. In my worldview, it's possible to beat the market consistently, and I do. Why would I adopt a worldview where I don't win just because that is what other people believe? In my world, that makes no sense.

I feel those flawed, limiting, negative market theories are an oversimplification of the fact that human nature is at play in the market, that human nature causes people to make unobjective, emotional, and biased decisions, and because of that, most people fail. Let me be clear, acquiring the skills necessary to beat the market is hard, but that doesn't mean it's impossible. Just like getting six-pack abs is hard, but that doesn't mean it's impossible. If you push yourself and do the sit-ups, you will get the results. If not, you won't. Most people aren't willing to put in the work necessary to do the mental sit-ups that are required to consistently beat the market. That's why I say they are better off to ride the Great American Tailwind.

STOP (OR LIMIT) YOUR BIASED THINKING

If someone believes the market is unbeatable, how do you think they will act and behave? Do you think they will have an edge or push themselves intellectually? If someone else *does* believe they can beat the market, ask yourself the same questions. Which person do you want to be?

While biased thinking can prevent people from being successful, it also has the compound effect of convincing people they are "killing it" in the market when they're seeing mediocre returns at best. It's like seeing an adult who plays tennis against a bunch of children and then convince themselves they're ready for Wimbledon. I always laugh when I meet these people (once you know what to look for it becomes incredibly obvious and you can see it a mile away).

Sadly, most of the world walks around in this borderline delusional state. This is also known as the delusion of grandeur—or thinking you are bigger or better than you actually are. There are other people who are aware of their biases but they make no real effort to change their worldview. Hanging on to a belief that you cannot do something makes it easier not to try, I suppose. That leaves a tiny percentage of people (and I mean tiny) who can recognize their biases and actually do something about dealing with them. Therein lies your opportunity and your chance at changing your life.

Please understand, there's no judgment here—I am just stating facts. If you have a mind, you have biases. It's part of being human, and no matter how much you try, at some level, you'll still have biases. The trick is to identify the biases that are keeping you from reaching your goals (or better yet, the biases that are keeping you from setting big enough goals in the first place).

Successful people excel because they think and do the opposite of what the dumb money thinks and does. They know they have biases, mental walls, and weaknesses, but they reject the notion that those shortcomings will prevent them from reaching their goals.

Successful people take action, break down their mental walls, find solutions, and get to the next level. Unsuccessful people ignore their shortcomings or create a dumb story where they are victims of an unfair world, a series of unfortunate events—or any other excuse you can think of. The dumb money loves excuses and "wins" by losing. The smart money loves to win and learns how to control their mind to push themselves intellectually and in some cases physically to show up every day (even when things are tough) and win!

In the next chapters, if you're interested in recognizing your cognitive biases and identifying the mental walls that might be holding you back from your full potential, I'm going to list a bunch of cognitive biases that I've encountered in myself and my clients and several corresponding mental walls that I've seen successful people destroy.

What affects your view of the world.

CHAPTER 11

Create a Smarter You with an Unbiased Mind

Cognitive biases affect our ability to see the world accurately. Mental walls are psychological barriers that prevent us from taking action to achieve our goals. Cognitive biases are like the bricks in our mental walls, and together they can prevent us from reaching our full potential. There are too many cognitive biases to name them all, but over the years, I've encountered several common ones that traders and investors struggle with. I hope that sharing these with you helps you recognize which biases influence your thinking so you can adjust your perspective and see the world more clearly. Remember, taking the time to identify and break down your mental walls will help you become more successful and make better decisions in all areas of your life.

ANCHORING

Anchoring occurs when someone relies too heavily on a single piece of information—the anchor—that impacts future decisions. In the market, traders may become fixated on an old price, their entry price, their exit price, or a recent inflection point (a recent high or low), and that data becomes an anchor and has an outsized impact on their subsequent judgment. As new information becomes available, that information is compared to the anchor. As time passes, the initial anchor tends to lose its influence, like gravity. In the market, the initial price you paid to buy a stock often becomes an anchor, and it impacts your future decisions to buy, sell, or hold.

In reality, the price you paid is an arbitrary data point that has no relevance on whether it is a good idea to buy or sell the stock at any point in the future. One solution to overcome this bias is to do your best to ignore your prior actions with the stock and view it as if it was the first time you are looking at it. Then, write down the pros and cons for each trade and make a decision based on the data in front of you.

Remember, the market is a forward-looking apparatus; it doesn't know you, and it doesn't care about where you bought or sold something. If you care about it, you'll end up driving yourself crazy and battling yourself and the market. That is foolish, and it produces a negative return on investment. The market is going to do whatever it wants to do and your job is to get out of your own way and align yourself with what is happening—and what is going to happen—at all times.

CONFIRMATION BIAS

Confirmation bias occurs when you look for information that supports your chosen beliefs. Imagine an investor who believes that they cannot beat the market; they will tend to seek information that supports their opinion. They might even become evangelists of the efficient market hypothesis—or just about anything else that supports their preconceived notions. Even if their opinion is wrong, they don't care, because they have a psychological motive for finding information to support and bolster their delusion. Perhaps they feel it absolves them of a bad decision or helps them claim they are a victim of the system or some other larger force. In some form or another, it gives them comfort and it makes them "feel" good to find information that confirms their existing beliefs. Even if those beliefs are false, they don't care, because they get pleasure out of that confirmation and that's what they care about.

Whatever the reason, their destructive actions are likely subconscious, and they're not even aware they are doing them. A good trader will focus like a hawk on finding the truth and identifying data that helps produce the results they want in the future—not something arbitrary that happened in the past that is used mainly to support their frail ego.

IRRATIONAL ESCALATION BIAS

You can also call this the "sunk costs effect." In business, a sunk cost is a loss that cannot be recovered. In the market, there is an errant opinion running rampant that suggests that if you take a loss on paper, you don't realize the loss until you sell. Inexperienced traders get in trouble with this because they are losing money on paper (meaning, the position goes against them after they buy it) and they don't know what to do. The smart money already planned a risk-managed stop on their trade and sells quickly when things go wrong. Dumb money holds on and hopes the stock will get back to even. Sometimes they'll even buy more, hoping to balance out their loss if the stock rallies—but that's an irrational escalation. Don't throw good money after bad. A trader is going to lose more trades than they win. The trick is to focus on winning trades, keep your losses small, and let your winners run.

CONSERVATISM BIAS

Conservatism bias describes how people tend to fight to protect their beliefs and dismiss new information. Most people do not want to change their beliefs—even when presented with new factual evidence. Most people tend to overvalue old data when it supports their beliefs and dismiss new data when it runs contrary to their beliefs. The market doesn't care about you, and it doesn't care about your beliefs. I'm astounded at how often I see traders ignore the reality of the data right before their eyes because it doesn't support their opinion about how the market should behave. The market is going to behave the way it wants to behave. Listen to the market. Strive to align yourself with what is happening in the market. Never fight the tape.

HYPERBOLIC DISCOUNTING

Hyperbolic discounting is a common bias that refers to your willingness to settle for smaller, more immediate, results rather than wait for larger results that will come in the future.

For example, if I offered you $100 right now, or $200 if you were willing to wait a month, which one would you choose? As a trader, I hope you'd choose $200 in a month. That's a great return. Most people, however, tend to take what they can get now at the expense of benefiting more in the future.

Hyperbolic discounting impacts your decision-making, especially in the short term. It works in reverse as well: people tend to focus on the short-term consequences of their decisions and dismiss the long-term consequences.

Here is an example of how that works in the real world. It feels good to eat a cookie right now, but long-term, it is bad for you. In the market, profits are a function of time. A trader has to wait. Don't take the easy way out. A fast $1 gain today could become a $10–100 gain in a few months. Most of the time, in life and in the market, the short-term results are the opposite of the long-term results. The smart money knows that every decision has short-term and long-term consequences.

Earlier in this book, I suggested that investors function in the long term and traders function in the short term. That is a practical definition. When we talk about the long term in relation to psychological analysis, we're talking about any period of time that demands patience. It is deferred gratification that requires a rational mind to see beyond the immediate desires of the emotional heart.

Let me be very clear: the smart money focuses on long-term results. They do not get tempted by the short-term gratification of something if its long-term consequences are bad. Remember, just about every decision you make can be boiled down to the same elements that impact a trade: risk and reward. What is the risk and the reward of doing X? Does the reward outweigh the risk? If yes, I'll place the trade; if not, I don't. It's that simple.

ILLUSION OF CONTROL

We all suffer from this bias on multiple levels. The illusion of control bias is the tendency for people to overestimate their ability to control events, people, and other things around them. This happens everywhere in life. Right now you think you are in control of your life, but anything can happen to you at any time. Some people think they can control other people, which is a complete illusion. This book is designed to help you take control of your life by seeing clearly and making objective, unemotional, unbiased decisions. You can control how you see the world and, with some mental discipline, you can learn to control your decisions—but just about everything else is out of your hands. In markets, people think they can control the outcomes, but they cannot. Focus only on the information that is important to you, manage your risk, and always try to do the right thing by making objective decisions. If you do that, you'll win some and you'll lose some, but I bet you'll come out way ahead in the end.

INFORMATION BIAS

We live in the age of information and most of that information is completely useless. Much of it doesn't make sense and is conflicting. Becoming a savvy consumer of information is essential to being a good trader—and to becoming successful in just about any aspect of life. Information bias (also called observation bias or measurement bias) occurs when information is either calculated, used, or interpreted erroneously. According to Johns Hopkins, information bias strikes when: ". . . information is collected differently between two groups, leading to an error in the conclusion of the association." In markets, this happens all the time because there is so much information out there and most people have a very difficult time knowing what to do with it. As technical traders, we have an advantage here: price is primary and everything else is secondary. Understand what data is important to you for executing your strategy and then filter out the noise and focus on the facts that impact your bottom line. Fundamental investors look at cash flow, earnings, the margin of safety, valuations, and other metrics to determine whether they should make an investment and that works great as well. However you make your investment decisions, it is of the utmost importance that you are able to focus on the important information that will help you get the results you want and dismiss everything else.

NEGLECT OF PROBABILITY

Neglect of probability happens when you get so caught up in the prize that you ignore the probability that you will actually win and enjoy the prize. This happens all the time, on and off Wall Street. A great way to illustrate this common bias is to look at the lottery. We all know that the probability of winning the lottery is extremely low, but the size of the prize is big enough to make us ignore the odds and take a shot. People tend to focus on the outcome when they take a chance rather than on the probability that such an outcome will actually occur. Neglect of probability can cause some people to take on long odds if the potential outcome is big enough, and it can keep people from making a good bet when there is a long-shot chance of catastrophic loss. In the market, good traders know better than to gamble, and they don't make trades they're substantially certain to lose. When a trader has a reasonable expectation that a stock will move up, however, they can mitigate risk by placing a stop-loss order to sell when they buy a stock to protect the position and limit the potential loss. Once you understand this dynamic, neglect of probability will be greatly mitigated or not impact your decisions again. Remember, my number-one rule in trading is to always respect risk.

POST-PURCHASE RATIONALIZATION

Ever hear of buyer's remorse? That happens when you feel bad after you buy something. Whenever we spend or invest money, we want to feel good about it. Sometimes we'll create a story after the fact to justify our decision. This is called post-purchase rationalization. If our goal is to make objective, unemotional, unbiased trading decisions, post-purchase rationalization is a complete waste of time. Ideally, if we vetted the idea, mitigated our risk, and understand that we'll have some small losses before we score a big win, we shouldn't have any emotions associated with our trades. Looking for a reason to feel good after the fact simply invites emotion into a circumstance where there should be no emotions. Make all your rationalizations before you make a decision, and use objective criteria to reach your conclusions. Before I make a decision, I do my best to analyze all the angles, and I pay extra attention to the reasons why I should not make that decision. If there is a compelling case to move forward, I do; if not, I don't. Ray Dalio says the best idea wins; I say the smartest idea wins. It's essentially the same thing—remove your ego and go with the smartest idea.

STATUS QUO BIAS

Most people do their best to preserve their status quo. Essentially, they learn how to become comfortable in the uncomfortable. You might have heard the expression "Don't rock the boat!" Most people are uncomfortable with change, because they fear the unknown, and therefore they perceive change as a loss. They'd rather live with the devil they know than the devil they don't. It means that people display a strong tendency to preserve the current state of affairs (status quo). If you are happy with the status quo then you have no business trading in the market. Put your cash in some low-yield, low-risk bond that stays a step ahead of inflation and enjoy your perfect never-changing life. If you're in the market, you're looking for change; you want to make money and compound your returns. You can't make money in the market without change. Reject the status quo and embrace change.

WISHFUL THINKING BIAS

It's important to maintain an optimistic mindset, but not at the expense of ignoring hard facts and reality. Victims of wishful thinking bias craft a story in their mind of what they want their result to be, and they make decisions based on their fantasy rather than the evidence in front of them. It's like planning a camping trip with dreams of roasting marshmallows without considering the weather, there might be heavy wind, or rain, or other factors such as mosquitoes, or the fact that there might be no running water, that might impact your wishful thinking. Wishful thinking often occurs when people have a conflict between what they desire and what they know. As a trader, you'll encounter some ideas that you think are amazing, and you'll be tempted to ignore your normal risk tolerance. Get out of your head and focus on what is actually happening. Always remain objective and make decisions based on the facts in front of you at any given time. Feeling too excited about an idea is a red flag. Take a step away from it and reassess it later—or, better yet, ask an informed colleague you trust to help you understand whether you're being objective or not. If you want to read more about this bias, check out delusions of grandeur.

RISK AVERSION

Risk aversion is a very powerful bias that impacts all of us just about every time we think about the market or make a decision. The fear of losing money is a more powerful motivator than the prospect of making money. Psychological studies show that people generally would prefer to avoid losing $1 than to make $1. Some research shows that losses are twice as powerful, psychologically, as gains. That means that it takes two wins to psychologically neutralize a single loss.

My strategy allows me to keep my losses small and my wins big, and I've learned that the best intermediate-term active position traders are only right around 30% of the time. This means they are wrong 7 out of 10 trades. When I lose, I tell myself I'm that much closer to the next big win. If you do that enough times, it becomes second nature and a loss just becomes the cost of doing business.

As a trader you do not have to pay rent; you do not need to hire an army of employees or have any other major costs of doing business. So, for me, losing trades are the cost of doing business. They happen to the best of us and they are inevitable.

To further help remove your emotions from your trading and reduce this cognitive bias, I always identify the maximum risk I'm willing to take before I enter a position. This way I am okay with the worst-case scenario before I enter a position and then I tighten my stop and never widen it, so I keep on reducing risk as long as the stock is going up. Tightening your stop means you bring your stop loss closer to your entry price, and widening your stop is doing the opposite. The wider your stop the more you have at risk.

FRAMING BIAS

The framing bias works similarly to risk aversion. Just as most people would rather prevent a loss than realize a gain, the framing bias occurs when a person's response to a choice is influenced by how the options are presented—how they are framed. Would you rather put money in an investment that has a 50% chance of success or one that has a 50% chance of failure? It's the same investment, but one presentation frames the positive and the other frames the negative; human beings are drawn to the positive. Now, what if I were to show you a great opportunity to make $1,000,000 that has a 20% chance of success? That sounds pretty good until you realize that means there's an 80% chance of failure. People tend to minimize risk when choices are framed in a positive light and overemphasize risk when framed in a negative light.

In the market, framing bias is never quite so clear, but the effect is that when we're excited about the upside of a prospect, we tend to underestimate the risk. My friend, business partner, and legendary trader Jim Roppel taught me the importance of creating guardrails for yourself. Figure out how to stress-test your own ideas. Learn to find the flaws in your logic, and figure out a better way to make decisions. Essentially, you want to protect yourself from yourself. You can reach out and find a trading guide or coach. Write down your thoughts, then step back and revisit them in a few hours or in a few days to make sure they are valid and your ideas are still good. Share them with a (smart) friend who can help you find your blind spots. I do this every weekend and share my ideas with some of the smartest people I know on FindLeadingStocks.com. The feedback from my members is priceless.

DISPOSITION EFFECT

The disposition effect describes an investor's tendency to sell assets that are increasing in value and hold on to assets that are declining in value. Warren Buffett said that most investors are fearful when they should be greedy and greedy when they should be fearful. There's this recurring phenomenon in the stock market where unseasoned traders tend to cash out of a position as soon as they make a little money—often way before the stock shows signs of trouble. They're afraid the stock will reverse and they will lose all of their hard-fought gains. They are emotionally attached to their money. They are operating from a position of fear, not strength. They do not trust their strategy, the market, or their ability to make money. On the other hand, people also have a strange tendency to hold on to their losers because they are afraid to admit to being wrong, or they hope (or pray) a stock will get back to even so they can sell. Sometimes they even buy more, hoping to recover some of their loss should the stock rebound.

That's why smart money limits their losses and lets their winners run. To lock in my gains, I use trailing stops, by picking levels every week below the market where I will exit if the stock falls (assuming I'm long). No matter what, be grateful for the gains you make and avoid the temptation to beat yourself up for missing big gains. Just look forward and start hunting for the next big win. Remember, nobody can consistently pick the exact top or the exact bottom, and the good news is you do not have to! My goal is to capture the bulk of the move, and I can't do that by entering and exiting every time a stock moves up or down a few points.

Remember what Jesse Livermore said: "After spending many years in Wall Street and after making and losing millions of dollars I want to tell you this: it never was my thinking that made the big money for me. It was always my sitting. Got that? My sitting tight!" Another great Wall Street adage is to be patient with your winners and impatient with your losers.

DENIAL

The denial bias happens when people reject a fact that is too uncomfortable for them to accept. Sigmund Freud was the first person that I know of who identified this bias (although it had a different name at the time). Denial is so powerful because it requires an individual to concoct a web of lies to circumvent the truth they are trying to avoid, and as a result, it makes a negative impact on a broad spectrum of associated decisions. This is a common psychological defense mechanism that helps people defend against trauma, but it's absolutely catastrophic for a trader who must see things honestly and clearly to be successful in the market. It may be hard, but you must face your failures. Get out of your head. Focus on the facts and align yourself with what is happening in the real world.

OUTCOME BIAS

It is important to judge your decisions based on the information you had when the decision was made, and not the outcome. Is drunk driving a good idea? Of course not! Well, what if someone drove home drunk but didn't crash? The outcome was that they got home safely and nothing "bad" happened. But clearly, anyone with an ounce of common sense would know that was a very bad decision—even though it was not a bad outcome in that one example.

Now, when we talk about trading, there are a lot of unknowns in the market, and when you work a proven, actively managed trading strategy, it is virtually guaranteed to produce losing trades—most of the time, in fact. Just because you get a bad outcome doesn't mean you made a bad decision; it's outcome bias if you think otherwise.

A trading decision needs to be judged based on the facts and information at the time the decision was made and not on any single outcome. If you buy a stock whenever it meets your criteria and after 100 trades the overall result is profitable (your strategy has a positive expectancy), then you wouldn't judge any single losing trade based on that individual outcome. Many traders look at one or two losing trades, panic because they "lost" money, and then give up and look for a new shiny object (a.k.a. a new strategy or super-secret formula). If they keep doing that over time, they'll lose a lot of money.

It's much better to judge the quality of your decisions by the facts that were available to you at the time. Avoid the temptation to judge a decision based on a single outcome. Look at hundreds or thousands of outcomes to see if your process is good. If those facts were available at the time you made the decision and you missed them, then address that so it does not happen again and adjust accordingly. If they weren't there, accept the loss and move on and find the next win.

Separately, it is important to avoid the trap of letting your ego be hurt when you have a losing trade. If you follow your rules, losses are just a cost of doing business, and you move on to the next trade. Losses are normal; they are not fun, but beating yourself up over a loss is a losing trade every single time.

RECENCY BIAS

Recency bias happens when people place a higher value on recent information and discount historical information. Imagine a trader who convinces himself that any particular rally will last indefinitely, spurred by the fact that an anticipated market correction is overdue. Perhaps they begin to think it won't happen. They focus on the recent data, and they dismiss the patterns seen in the past several decades of the market's ups and downs. Eventually, every rally ends. Facts are facts.

Focus on all data equally. Develop a weekly (or daily) written system where you write your thoughts on the market when the market is closed. When everything is out of your head and written "on paper," you can look back at your wins and losses and see what you were thinking at the time before the decision was made. This exercise is tremendously valuable and will help you on multiple levels. It will give you much-needed structure, it will help you get out of your head, it will help you overcome some of your biases, it will help you be accountable, it will help you detect strong and weak patterns that you might not have realized exist within yourself, it will help you identify your blind spots, and it will give you a written track record of your thinking. Doing this, or some version of this, you can learn from your mistakes, focus on your strengths, and constantly improve your performance.

HASTY GENERALIZATION

A hasty generalization occurs when people quickly jump to a conclusion without carefully weighing all the data. Typically, the conclusion is not logically justified by sufficient or unbiased evidence, and the decision is not optimal because it is made without processing all the pertinent information. A decision based on too many assumptions and broad, generally accepted market wisdom is likely to fail. Do your own homework. Develop your own process for evaluating an opportunity and apply your process consistently across the board. Create a system where you plan your trades ahead of time. This way you can step back, remove yourself from the emotional trading rollercoaster, and trade your plan.

GROUPTHINK

Dumb money is intellectually lazy and tends to accept the logic of a group instead of formulating an independent opinion. In the market, the crowd is not always wrong, but they are often wrong—or at least late to the game. By the time the crowd is talking about it, it's usually too late to get into an idea for a profit. In most cases, when virtually "everyone" is talking about something, it is a good contrary indicator and a sign that the trend is about to change.

A few great examples of this can be found near important tops or bottoms in the market. In late 1999 and early 2000, just about everyone was bullish on dotcom stocks, and the Nasdaq 100 (QQQ) topped out in March 2000, and then the Nasdaq 100 plunged 84% and that turned out to be the exact top for that cycle.

By the end of 2008, nearly everyone was talking about how "bad" things were in the economy, and the stock market bottomed in March 2009. These are just two recent examples but the market is littered with countless other examples.

When you learn to analyze the data, make your own decisions, and form your own independent opinions, your life will change for the better. There will always be someone smarter, richer, or doing better than you, and that is okay. Find the smartest people you can, listen to what they are saying, and follow them closely. Then, after you take in their points of view, plus your own, you can stress test your thinking and see if you missed anything. Even Warren Buffett has Charlie Munger to lean on and vice versa. Investor Ray Dalio built a very smart team around him to "thoughtfully disagree" with him whenever necessary. Once your idea is thoroughly vetted and you are ready, pull the trigger—but remember to always take full responsibility for every decision you make (and every decision you don't make). It's your life. It's your money. Own it. Control it. Crush it!

HALO EFFECT

The halo effect occurs when people judge a book by its cover and not the content within. This happens all the time in all aspects of life. How many times have you seen a picture of someone who looks nice but turns out to have done some despicable thing? Many companies spend millions of dollars to build a positive corporate image and a brand that people can trust while their quarterly reports show evidence of a troubled corporation with heavy debt and misman-aged assets. Enron was a stock market darling until a single financial reporter, Bethany McClean, finally looked seriously at the energy company's financials and discovered it was a house of cards poised to fall. Her example shows us why it's important to do your own research and not judge a book by its cover.

Don't be blinded by a company's halo. Step back and do your due dili-gence. Study the company, learn their story, study the stock, see how it behaves, stress-test your idea with other (smarter) people. Don't just blindly jump in and out of stocks on whims. Another important and related point is to separate the stock from the company. You can have a good company and a lousy stock or a good-performing stock but the company loses a ton of money.

PERSONAL BLIND SPOT BIAS

I saved this bias for last because it impacts all of us in a very big way. The personal blind spot bias means that you can see flaws in others but not in yourself—or at least not as easily in yourself. If you don't think any of these biases apply to you, then you have a personal blind spot bias. Someone with a personal blind spot bias cannot see themselves objectively. It's easy to point out other people's weaknesses, but it can be hard to admit to our own.

An easy way to illustrate this point would be to ask 100 newlyweds after they walk down the aisle and say "I do," how many think they will get divorced? Almost no hands will go up, but statistically, we know that about 50% of them are wrong. I've been speaking to investors all over the globe since the 1990s, and every time I ask a group of traders, "How many of you think you will beat the market?" almost everyone raises their hand.

Meanwhile, we know that only a handful of them will generate alpha (beat the market). The easiest way to overcome this bias is to remove yourself from the equation and think about someone else. What advice would you give another trader you never met before? Another helpful tactic is to join a group of like-minded traders, create a fun fictitious cartoon character, give it a name, and/or do anything you can to remove yourself from the equation and to internalize all your decisions objectively.

Understand that you are human and you have strengths and weaknesses. Understand that, if you have a mind (which you do), then you have biases. You will win and you will lose. Stocks you own will gap up and they will gap down. It happens to everyone. You are not different. Really drill down, understand yourself better than you ever have before, and remove yourself from the decision-making process as much as you can.

Be intellectually honest with yourself. Be accountable. Go with the best idea, even if it is not your idea. Listen to the market. Ask yourself which bias impacted your decision, what you can do to mitigate that impact, and know that this time is not different. As a helpful tool, always ask yourself: Is this smart? Take it a step further and ask: Is this the smartest decision I can make right now? Notice, I'm not asking myself what I want to do or anything else. I am committed to making the best (smartest) decisions possible—even if that means I don't do what I want.

For example, I might want to do X but I know Y is the right thing to do. Nine out of 10 times (or 10 out of 10 times) I'll do Y. Just about every time I do what I know is not the smartest thing, it turns out bad in the end. That's a deeper look into my process, how I handle biases, and what I do to win. This process has served me very well over the years.

While this is not a comprehensive list of cognitive biases, it should be enough to illustrate how biases can negatively impact how you perceive the market, individual stocks, your decisions, and even yourself. If you cannot see clearly, you'll be unable to make great decisions or achieve your full potential in the market.

Breaking down mental walls.

CHAPTER 12

Ever Hit a Wall? Destroy It and Master the Learning Cycle

Over or through—never around.

—Theodore Roosevelt

A WALK THROUGH ROCK CREEK PARK

More than one unsuspecting acquaintance of Theodore Roosevelt was led upon a point-to-point walk through Washington, DC's Rock Creek Park. "Point-to-point" meant that the hikers would plot a course straight through the park, regardless of the obstacles in the way, and they would not deviate from it. It often required climbing boulders, and it inevitably necessitated fording the waters of the meandering Rock Creek itself—at least once. "Over or though," Roosevelt would say. "Never around."

As practical navigation advice, point-to-point might not be such a good idea, but as a metaphor for dealing with obstacles in life, it's fantastic. Obstacles, whether tangibly in Rock Creek Park or metaphorically in our lives, will either stop us in our tracks or force us in a direction that deviates from our goal. Often, if we spend our time navigating around all the obstacles, we'll find ourselves walking in circles, never arriving at our destination.

If you're like me, you don't face a lot of physical obstacles anymore (except maybe traffic). Our obstacles are mental and more figurative; there are things standing in the way of us achieving our goals in life. Some of these obstacles may be external: a workplace rival, a difficult relationship, an illness. Some are internal. In my experience, however, it's not the external obstacles that hold people back, it's our internal obstacles—your mental walls.

In the previous chapter, I gave you a list of cognitive biases that impact how humans misperceive and distort the reality of the world they are presented with. These cognitive biases serve as the building blocks for mental walls that stop us from taking the actions necessary to recognize and achieve our potential. For years, I've been working with my clients to help them identify their mental walls, and the solution, as Roosevelt said, is "over or through—never around." The reason I want to address these mental walls directly is because, just like most any other real problem, they do not just magically go away on their own. They do, however, go away, when you address them and deal with them directly.

I'd like to share a few mental walls I have encountered during my career helping traders accomplish their goals. My hope is that you may recognize a few that may be keeping you from realizing your dreams, and encourage you to destroy them and discover other mental walls that may be holding you, or your loved ones, back that you can destroy as well. Once you recognize and destroy these mental walls you will see things much better, you will have a much higher sense of clarity, and you will live life at a completely better level.

EGO

For many of us, we become set in our ways as we get older. We've achieved some level of success, perhaps we've developed a little bit of an ego (admit it), and we're less open to new ideas. We can become stuck in our own heads. We get stuck with the "identity" that we created for ourselves years ago—most of the time without really thinking about it or consciously choosing it. The truth is, the world is constantly changing all around us. Technology changes. The market changes. Be open to changing with it. Open your mind. Tell yourself a new (better) story. Just because you never did X for the past few decades doesn't mean you can't start doing X now—if that is the smartest thing for you to do.

Just because you found something that worked for you in the past (anchoring bias), doesn't mean there's not a better way now. I've seen people spend (a.k.a. waste) a significant amount of mental capital defending themselves and their ideas purely to bolster their ego. They don't want to hear new ideas that don't agree with their worldview (denial, illusion of control, just to name a couple), and they focus on people and things that tend to support their long-standing beliefs (confirmation bias, conservatism bias). Worst of all, they are often the sort of people who don't realize they're plagued with all these biases (personal blind spot).

Let's pretend that you discovered an opportunity that was likely to double your money in 30 days. Then let's pretend that I come along and show you an opportunity that was just as likely to quadruple your money in the same time period. Are you going to stick with your idea just because it's yours? Or are you going to put your money into my idea and double your profit? It's a hard-headed stubborn fool who passes up profits for the sake of pride—yet this happens all the time on Wall Street. One of Ray Dalio's timeless principles is "the best idea wins." One of my guiding principles is "the smartest idea wins," and it doesn't matter to me whose idea it was—even just a random person.

Winners win. Losers lose, and they love creating drama and coming up with every excuse under the sun of why it wasn't their fault. I'm very goal-driven and results-oriented. Anything (legal and ethical) that gives me the results I want and that gets me closer to my goal is okay by me. And because we all have some ego, let me say this: when you pick up the check at dinner, your friends will not ask you if the money came from your idea or someone else's. Some of my best ideas have come from other people, legends, who have walked the earth before me: William J. O'Neil, Paul Tudor Jones, and all the other Market Wizards, Jim Roppel, Gary Kaltbaum, Stan Weinstein, Nicolas Darvas, Jack D. Schwager, Robert D. Edwards, John Magee, Jesse Livermore, Tony Robbins, Jim Rohn, Ray Dalio, and the countless other unsung heroes who have shared (and continue to share) their knowledge with others. Get out of your head. Relax, adopt an open mind, and enjoy a much richer life. Align yourself with the truth, drop false ego-based beliefs, and focus on the next smartest decision you can make.

Ed Seykota, a famous trend-following trader, used to say, "Win or lose, everybody gets what they want out of the market. Some people seem to like to lose, so they win by losing money." Some people want the drama around telling a story about how they got stopped out or "battled" Wall Street. So they end up engaging in self-sabotage and get the drama. Others just want to win, so they dig deep and do what is necessary to figure out how to win. Either way, in the end you get what you want from the market and in life. It's important to note that most people do not know what they want most and as a result end up not getting what they say they want. Always ask yourself what you want most.

Often, people will go to great lengths to protect their ego, and those efforts often include self-destructive and outright dumb behavior.

Have you ever heard of a "drama queen"? There are "drama kings" too. They are people who manufacture drama and create chaos everywhere they go. The primary purpose for creating drama is that it makes the creator of the drama the center of attention for everyone caught up in their vortex. It's also used to disguise or justify failure. Remember, attention is binary: you either give it or take it. People with a big ego wall have an insatiable appetite to constantly take attention (to no avail). Our egos can be so delicate that when we make a bad decision, we want to find something else to blame it on, and if we can create a complicated narrative (a.k.a. drama) we can blame the drama and further support our frail ego. The drama keeps us at the center of attention, or some unjust conspiracy (denial, illusion of control, information bias), where we feel we preserve our ego so we can continue to float around in our self-centric universe. It's a spiral of self-destructive behavior that can lead to disaster on Wall Street. Just ask Bernie Madoff—or any other egomaniac. The smart money knows how to destroy the ego wall by giving attention to the market, focusing on what is happening, not what they think will happen, and doing what is "right" (being committed to making money and being—and staying—in harmony with the market) and not what they think is right (stubbornly defending their false beliefs). Let that sink in. There's a *huge* difference there. Be humble. The best traders are humble. The best people are humble. Focus on being humble anywhere and everywhere. Master humility and you will live a much better life.

FEAR

During the depths of the Great Depression, Franklin Delano Roosevelt said something profound about fear. You know the famous line "The only thing we have to fear is fear itself," but not so many people know the rest of the "fear itself" quote. Roosevelt called fear a "nameless, unreasoning, unjustified terror which paralyzes needed efforts to convert retreat into advance."

On Wall Street, the most obvious fear is the fear of losing money. It is what keeps most people out of the market. They're so emotionally attached to their money, they'd rather let the slow creep of inflation devalue their wealth than risk taking a hit on a trade (risk aversion bias, disposition effect). Beyond losing money, however, in my dealings with clients—particularly clients who have a reputation for managing a considerable sum of money—I've found that most people are more afraid of being wrong than of losing money. The ego is a powerful thing, and for some, a consequential failure is a direct assault on a person's measure of their self-worth.

Let me unburden your mind: in order to become a successful trader and beat the market, you are going to lose sometimes, and you're going to be wrong often. Embrace it. Own it. Get over it. I've told you before, it takes four to seven losers for me to find a winner. The same is true for Hollywood studios—most movies do not turn into a huge blockbuster—and that's okay. The most successful players in baseball only hit 33% of the time and strike out nearly 70% of the time. Babe Ruth was the home run king but he also held the record for the most strikeouts. The smart money knows that when navigating the unknown, the trick is to keep your losses small and let your winners run. It's a timeless truth, and it really is that simple.

A little bit of fear is okay; it gives us a healthy respect for risk, and my first rule of trading is to respect risk. But if fear is keeping you from making a decision, then it's the kind of "unreasoning, unjustified terror" that FDR described in his inauguration speech. The smart money uses fear (they don't allow fear to use them), and they understand that it is good to be wrong because the faster you identify your mistakes, the quicker you will realize your victories. The best way to get over a fear of failure is to fail and get comfortable failing. Know that failing is a necessary and good thing because it helps you get to your next winner. Know that everyone fails, not just you. Know that failing is a great opportunity to learn and excel. Once you rewire your brain to know that failing is "good" and not "bad" you will learn from your mistakes, not make them again (hopefully), and you will have the strength to get up and keep going and find your next (bigger) win. Failing is good because it teaches you what not to do. Embrace it. Fail gracefully. And use it to your advantage. Get out fast, fail small. Always stay focused on your next win.

One of the biggest fears that humans have harbored in their hearts since the dawn of time is the fear of the unknown. A child's fear of the dark is based on the fear of the unknown. An adult's fear of death is rooted in not knowing what lies beyond in the "undiscovered country," as Shakespeare put it. The future is unknown, too, and speculating in the market is about betting your fortune on the unknown future—and that can be terrifying. But one thing is for certain: the future is going to happen whether we are afraid of it or not. A good trader is not necessarily someone who feels no fear; a good trader is someone who respects fear, overcomes fear, and takes control of their future. It takes courage to become a great trader. The good news is that, with the right mental outlook, anyone can become a great trader.

Another great way to destroy the fear wall is to clearly define and understand your risk before you enter a trade. Once you learn how to become comfortable with your maximum risk (worst-case scenario), the "fear" pretty much disappears. Since you know in advance the worst-case scenario, and decide you are okay with it, you place the trade. If not, reduce your risk until you are comfortable with the worst-case scenario.

PAIN

The pain wall is very closely related to the fear wall. Before I go any further, it is important to note that pain comes in two forms: physical pain and mental/emotional pain. For the scope of this book, I will be referring to mental/emotional pain, not physical pain, even though they are closely related. (Remember, these are mental walls.)

Remember, people are innately programmed to avoid pain and seek pleasure. Pain is not inherently good or bad. When used properly, pain is just a derivative of some form of weakness manifesting itself and the pain can be overcome with the right mental outlook.

George Addair once said, "Everything you've ever wanted is sitting on the other side of fear." In most cases, the same is true for pain. Ray Dalio talks about the "pain jungle"; he knows that most pain is a false figment of your untrained subconscious mind and it usually prevents you from getting what you truly want. The easiest way to break the pain wall is to stay focused on the goal, not the pain, and your life will change for the better.

If you are a fan of the 1987 film *The Princess Bride* then you know how the Dread Pirate Roberts feels about pain. "Life is pain, Highness," he says. "Anyone who says differently is selling something." Pain is a fact of life. It is unavoidable. We experience pain as a loss, and risk aversion bias kicks in, as does hyperbolic discounting, as we're willing to trade future gains to preserve our comfortable status quo.

Losing money is painful. Failure is painful. Being told you're wrong is painful. Spending countless hours studying the market and not making big money is painful. So what? Success is on the other side of pain. That was the lesson to be taken from Teddy Roosevelt's point-to-point walks: any goal worth achieving is going to require enduring some pain. In this book, I've compared trading to fitness multiple times. At first, denying yourself treats and forcing yourself to exercise is painful, but it is necessary for staying fit, and that is nothing compared to the "real pain" that comes from being unhealthy in your future.

In the 1962 film *Lawrence of Arabia*, T. E. Lawrence, as portrayed by Peter O'Toole, performs a parlor trick where he extinguishes a lit match with his bare fingers. A colleague, William Potter, tries to reproduce the trick and burns himself. "Oh, it damn well hurts!" he exclaims. "Certainly it hurts," Lawrence replies. "Well, what's the trick, then?" Potter asks. "The trick, William Potter," Lawrence says, "is not minding that it hurts." In most cases, the event itself is not that painful but the mental relationship you associate with that event is what creates most of the pain. In most cases, you mind the pain a lot more than you need to. In most cases, you create the pain and make it a big deal by staying focused on it and living in the past or worrying about the future. Instead, let it all go, play the game to win, and live in (and fully enjoy) the present moment.

If you want to be a successful trader, you are going to have to endure losses that will, to the untrained mind, trigger pain. The smart money learns to embrace pain because they know it means they are growing and doing the work needed to reach their goal. The trick to beating the market is to keep growing, keep learning, and not mind that it hurts.

The framing bias teaches us that people are more inclined to select an option when it's presented to us in the most favorable light, and it causes us to ignore or downplay the risks. Sometimes choices are framed as easy or hard. Our hearts want to take the easy way, but by now, we've learned that the hard path, the painful path, is usually the better one. When you're making long-term decisions, all else being equal, it's best to grow, and if that means taking the painful route, do it—if you want to get to your destination.

SHORT-TERM THINKING

In our discussion of mental biases, we discussed hyperbolic discounting. It means that we're willing to settle for smaller, immediate gains rather than wait for larger gains in the future. We've also explored how things that are comfortable now (eating treats and not exercising) often lead to negative long-term consequences. You may also remember the disposition effect, which causes some investors to sell a rising stock before it realizes its potential and some to hold on to their losers. These are all examples of short-term thinking.

Oftentimes, we're victims of short-term thinking because we fear the uncertainty of the future or because we simply lack the discipline required to endure a little discomfort right now for deferred gratification later. Other times, we make short-term decisions out of necessity: we sell because we need to liquidate an asset or we fail to capitalize on an opportunity because we don't have cash on hand to invest.

In the market, the term "strong hands" is used to describe a trader who has the cash and the conviction to take a strong position when a favorable risk/reward scenario shows up. The smart money with strong hands has the wherewithal to outlast the "weak hands"—those who don't have the conviction and/or the capital to do what is necessary to win. The strong hands do what is best for the long term; the weak hands live (and often die) in the short term.

Here's a supermarket example: imagine that a grocery store is having a sale on chicken—buy two and get the third for free. Someone who doesn't have enough cash (or enough room in the freezer) for the extra chicken cannot take advantage of the deal. They have weak hands and they're forced to make a short-term decision. Someone with the cash to spare and plenty of room in the freezer can take advantage of the deal. They have strong hands, and they can afford to think (and prepare to win) in the long term. Over time, the savings add up, and the shopper with strong hands will get a lot more for a lot less. The same principle applies to many areas of life.

The market works the same way. The traders who are able to take action that will benefit them in the long term will most of the time do much better than those who act on their short-term impulses.

I have already told you that profits are a function of time. Jesse Livermore stressed that sitting on a position is the best way to make big money on a trade. That is why I say there are three basic decisions to make in the market: buy, sell, and hold. I've told you that I make all my trading decisions on a weekly basis. Usually, I make the decision to buy, sell, or hold, only once a week. Often, as a stock rallies a couple of times, I'll decide to move my stop order higher a few times, essentially making a handful of sell decisions over the life of the trade. The vast majority of the time, my decision is to hold. If I stay in a position for 36 weeks, I'll have decided to buy it once, and I'll have decided to sell (move my stop order) perhaps five times. That means I'll have decided to hold 30 times. If you look at every tick on the chart all day every day, it will be extremely difficult for you to be this disciplined.

I work on an intermediate- to long-term timeframe when I trade. When I hold a position, unless it quickly falls below my predetermined sell stop, I tend to stay in for months if not more than a year or longer. Some people trade in short-term intervals. We call them "day traders." I repeat often that there is no one right way to make money on Wall Street—as long as you're realizing profits over time. That said, I've yet to meet a day trader who consistently beats the market year after year.

Once you change your perspective, step back, and really understand that profits are a function of time, you will be able to break down the short-term thinking wall. Remember, the great American Tailwind happens over the long term, the stock market is a forward-looking apparatus, and it often punishes traders who operate with short-term thinking. Trade accordingly.

ADULTING WALL (OVERCOMING CHILDISH BEHAVIOR)

"Adulting" is a recently created word that newly minted grown-ups use to describe the behavior required to navigate the world as an independent human being. Sigmund Freud pointed out that we all have unmet childhood wants and needs, a latent desire for attention that we have to renounce in order to grow up. My friend Dr. Joan likes to say, "Kill the dumb fat kid inside of you, and you will achieve things you can't even imagine."

I learned a lot about adult behavior while studying how my children interacted with their friends when they were between the ages of two and seven. They are very pure and innocent at that age, they are not very self-aware, and they are driven by their wants and desires without a lot of rational thought or emotional baggage. It's raw human nature on display at its finest. As we become adults, most of us learn to regulate the little kid that still resides in our hearts, but the child still emerges sometimes and lurks in our untrained subconscious mind.

I'd like to point out all the cognitive biases that contribute to the adulting wall, but there are way too many. Children are often psychologically anchored to a single event in the past. Children prefer the status quo. They are unable to imagine themselves from another person's point of view (personal blind spot). They ignore what they don't like and have little concept of the consequences of their actions (information bias, denial, wishful thinking). They're subject to groupthink and they blame others when they fail.

Blaming others is one of the most common childhood traits that follow people into adulthood. I also call this playing the victim card. When people fail, they often like to imagine that someone else is responsible for their failures. Perhaps blaming others and playing the victim card is good for some short-term sympathy, but victims don't succeed in the stock market. Losers lose and winners win. If you've failed, it doesn't matter whose fault it was because the result is the same. Blaming others or playing the victim has no return on investment (R.O.I.). Learn from your mistakes and get back in the game—and *win!*

Children are governed by their emotions. Psychological analysis is all about removing emotions from our decision-making process and relying instead on objective logic and unbiased facts. Children are terrible at making objective, unemotional decisions. I've yet to see a four-year-old say, "I've got a pretty big day tomorrow, I should probably turn in early and get a good night's sleep." I have, however, seen plenty of little kids throw themselves to the ground and have a tantrum at the mention of bedtime (or just about anything else that they do not want to do—even if it is good for them).

Another important element to understand is that attention is binary and children love attention. In fact, they thrive on it. If you talk to a young child you can keep them engaged as long as you give attention (ask them what their favorite color is, their favorite movie, food, and so on, and you will have them engaged for as long as you want). The second you take attention and tell them about your day, or what happened at work, or in the market—they will almost immediately check out. Think about that as you go through your day. Are you giving attention or taking it? Children need attention. The smart money does not need attention. Instead, it gives attention to everything and everyone around them—including the market.

When we're making important decisions, perhaps it's not a bad idea to ask ourselves what decision a child might make, and then go with the smartest decision—the one that is good for you, not the one that you want to do. For example, I want to eat the cookie, but I know I should do sit-ups instead. Remember, your success is the direct result of your decisions, and in the market, the choice is always yours.

As silly as the word "adulting" may sound, perhaps it's worth admitting that being a successful grown-up requires you to renounce your childhood wants and add new success-based wants instead. If nothing else, perhaps making an effort to recognize the adulting wall will help us admit that we sometimes act like children—and we can change that behavior. All we have to do is realize that it is happening and then catch ourselves in the act when it does. Most importantly, we want to adopt better, more mature behavior that will give us the results we really want.

LACK OF VISION WALL

I believe the biggest reason people fail to reach their potential is that they don't ever even begin to imagine what they are capable of. And even of those who dare to imagine great things, all too often, they do not really believe it is possible. That leaves the very few who are able to imagine it and really believe it. Those people are the ones who are not only able to achieve it but also to achieve much more!

Just like there is a rampant myth that being rich is somehow filthy, there's also something pounded into children that says "don't get too big for your britches" and "don't get out of line." Many children are encouraged to follow "safe" and "practical" paths rather than being empowered to take a chance and strive for extraordinary goals.

Oprah Winfrey, over the course of her long run on the legendary daytime talk show, interviewed more than 37,000 people. From presidents to pop stars to everyday people, Oprah pried into the heads of every type of person you can imagine. There's one thing she found they all had in common: they had insecurities about how they performed. Winfrey says, "After every interview, you know what they would say? 'Was that okay? How was that? How did I do?' In one form or another, somebody always said that."

Oprah herself seems to never have suffered from any lack of self-esteem. In an essay entitled "Every Person Has a Purpose," Oprah recalls watching her grandmother doing housework:

> I vividly remember standing on my grandmother's small screened-in back porch, churning butter while she boiled clothes in a big black cast-iron pot in the yard. As she pulled the steaming clothes from the pot to hang on the line to dry, she called to me, "Oprah Gail, you better watch me now, 'cause one day you gon' have to know how to do this for yourself."

Oprah writes that a small voice inside her replied: "This will not be your life. Your life will be more than hanging clothes on a line."

But even Oprah, with all her confidence, needed a little help to recognize her full potential. In November of 2005, Oprah revealed on her show that advice from movie critic Roger Ebert led her to accept a syndication deal that allowed her to become a household name. As Ebert recalls it, in his essay "How I Gave Oprah Her Start," Oprah said, "I don't know what to do. The ABC stations want to syndicate my show. So does King World. The problem with syndication is that if your show isn't successful, you're off the air in three months. The ABC stations own themselves, so they can keep you on. Which way do you think I should go?"

Ebert had a show in syndication, and he knew how successful it could be. He did some back-of-the-envelope math on a napkin for Oprah to show her how much she could earn doing a full-hour show five days a week at the quality of her broadcast. When he showed her the napkin, Oprah said, "Rog, I'm going with King World." Obviously, Oprah went on to achieve wild success in her chosen profession.

Oprah is a great example that anyone can become successful and achieve more than we were raised to be—if we have a vision, a strong enough purpose, and believe in ourselves. She also shows us that, even with all the confidence in the world, we still need people in our lives who believe in us, who can mentor us, who understand our talents, and who can show us opportunities that we cannot see ourselves.

Question the self-image you have carried with you from your childhood, and look for the negative beliefs that could be holding you back. Then, find people in your life who see you in a different light, without the biases you carry from your youth—people who care about you, or who can help you. Ask for their advice, read their books, follow them, learn from them, attend their seminars (or webinars), call them, email them, and listen to what they have to say. Then apply what you learn! One final thought about the vision wall is to aim high, and then after you hit it, aim higher. People love progress, set realistic and ambitious goals, achieve them, and then set larger goals. Along the way, believe in yourself, get the skills needed to accomplish your goals, stay humble, stay thankful, live, and really enjoy the present moment, stay focused, and you can really live your dream life!

OTHER DUMB MONEY WALLS

There are so many more mental walls that can keep people from finding success—far too many to list there, but here are some parting thoughts on the topic:

Take control of your life. Control it by making better decisions. Control how you react to what happens to you. Think and plan ahead (I can't stress this enough). Plan to win. Identify your bad habits. Fix them. People are creatures of habit; we have good habits and bad habits. The key is to focus on eliminating the bad habits and developing more good habits. Aristotle said, "We are what we repeatedly do. Excellence then is not an act, but a habit." Success is the culmination of good habits. They say it takes 21 days to develop a new habit. Why not get started now?

Exercise self-control in all things. Either your mind controls you, or you control your mind. Far too many high-powered executive types have a work hard/play hard mentality, and all too often it means they work crazy hours and then abuse their body with terrible food and frequently drink until they black out. Be smart. Don't do this. This is not a recipe for long-term success. I tell my smart money members to take care of the basics: take care of your mind, body, and spirit. Sleep well, eat well, read a lot, and exercise. Having self-control is paramount to your success. Learn to balance your life.

Finally, I want you to focus on finding the truth and doing the right thing. Do the smart thing. Even if that means doing something that you do not want to do (do the sit-ups; don't eat the cookie).

When you encounter new information, be as objective as you can to determine whether it is true and has an important impact on your life. This is especially important when you encounter bad news. To be successful in the market, and in life, you have to operate with facts; otherwise, all your decisions will be compromised. Once you're confident about the information you have, use it to make the right decisions. If you seek the truth and strive to do good in all aspects of your life, you'll thrive. Just like if you do the sit-ups and don't eat the treats, you will get results and win.

IDENTIFY YOUR WALLS AND DESTROY THEM

Helping clients identify and tear down their mental walls has become one of the most popular components of my private client membership program. I have seen some miraculous transformations from both people (personal walls) and businesses (business walls) after we identify and destroy their walls. The good news is that you can always improve. In fact, you are always improving whether you are aware of it or not. The only question is how fast you want to improve. Think about how much you know today versus how much you knew 10 or 20 years ago. Which version of you is smarter? We are all growing—all day, every day. The smart money just pushes harder (grows faster) than the dumb money. When they hit a wall, they destroy it and keep learning; they keep growing. They win. Take control of the dumb money beast, bring out the smart money superhero, and you can win too!

I believe we all have an innate desire to serve a higher purpose. Use it to your advantage. Everything I do—all the businesses I invest in—are purpose-driven. Purpose helps increase retention (both consumers and employees), and it helps everyone stay focused on a higher purpose and not get trapped in their own heads. Find your purpose in life, and let the wealth you build in the market be driven by your purpose. Use it to do good.

There's an old saying that the mind gives up before the body. It is so true on so many levels. When you understand that you are not your mind and learn how to control it you will experience a whole new world. We all hit various types of walls as we make our way through life. It doesn't matter if you are fishing, playing tennis, learning how to cook, growing a business, or trading stocks. We all hit walls all day every day. The smart money (successful people) learn how to identify and quickly destroy their walls. That's what separates them from the crowd.

Just about every worthwhile endeavor requires intellectual tenacity. Do the intellectual sit-ups. It's the ability for the mind to push on when the beast wants to stop. Just fostering your intellectual tenacity alone will give you success beyond your wildest dreams. This is a big component for our members.

Here is a little glimpse for those of you who want to excel: the first step is to pick a lofty goal. Second, ask yourself what information you are missing to accomplish that goal. Third, become a student, seek that information, and begin the learning cycle. At first, you'll learn quickly, but you'll inevitably hit a wall soon, and your progress will plateau. Don't get stuck there. Push hard.

Anticipate the walls that will hold you back and create a plan to destroy them. Instead of being stuck in the normal negative cycle of learning something then stopping after you hit a wall, you can push through and get to the next level. I can't do the sit-ups (intellectual or physical) for you, you have to do them. Keep pushing and you will win. The stock market is one of the best ways to accumulate wealth in the history of the world. Use it to your advantage, profit from it, don't let it use you, and stay in control, and you will achieve more than you can ever dream of!

Risk versus reward.

CHAPTER 13

The Most Important Skill to Master on Wall Street

There are an infinite number of ways to make money in markets and in life. Your job is to find one that works for you.

—*Adam Sarhan*

ALWAYS RESPECT RISK

As a trader, your single most important job is to compound your returns over time, and the best way to do that is to successfully manage risk. The market is a place where people can exchange risk for a potential reward.

If you step back and study history, the single common denominator with just about everyone who failed in this business (big and small investors alike) is that they did not manage risk effectively. The most successful traders, investors, institutions—and just about any other entity you can think of—all know how to respect risk. In fact, when you do not respect risk, you are essentially engraving your own epitaph, and it is just a matter of time until you blow up and or lose most (or all) of your money.

There is an old adage on Wall Street that says, Everyone is a genius in a bull market. That means that just about anything you do on the long side will work in a bull market (when stocks are going up). But if you go back and study any bear market you will see it is a completely different story. I encourage you to study prior bull and bear markets. Read about all the tragic suicides that came after the Great Depression—or how the entire investment banking model collapsed in the 2008 financial crisis—or enter any crazy story you can think of that happened when someone or something failed. It all occurred because of lousy risk management. I can say without a shadow of a doubt that just about every single person who has ever gone bankrupt in this business has done so because they did not respect risk. That's why my first commandment for trading is to play defense first and always respect risk. In a nutshell, proper risk management is designed to reduce the potential for losses while increasing the potential for profits.

Many people look at the market as a big casino and they think trading is gambling. It's not. Is there an element of risk? Absolutely. But there is an element of risk to starting a business, driving a car, or crossing the road, for that matter. Are the millions of people driving their cars right now gamblers? No. Are the millions of people who own a business gambling? I sure hope not! The same is true for investing and trading. Risks exist in just about everything we do in life. Some risks are large and some are small. It all comes down to your intentions: if you intend to gamble with your money, at least go to Las Vegas, because there they will give you free drinks.

Successful traders are not gamblers. Traders take informed and highly calculated risks. They do the hard work that most unsuccessful people do not want to do. They do not risk their money unless they have a very attractive risk-versus-reward opportunity. They do not risk their money until they have taken the time to fully understand themselves and fully understand how markets work (the risk(s) and the potential reward(s)). They find a strategy that works for them, they test their strategy, and they don't start trading until after they develop a winning approach (with a positive expectation) that works in both bull and bear markets. It doesn't matter what strategy you choose; the most important thing is that you understand the risk(s) and the rewards of that strategy and make sure you are okay with them.

You should understand that public freely traded markets (anywhere in the world) are just a big place where risk is traded in exchange for a potential reward. It doesn't matter what strategy you use; the only way you can make money on Wall Street is by risking your money. It is that simple.

Successful traders respect risk and understand the relationship between risk and reward. They know how to stay solvent (that is, keep money in their account—even when the market is falling), consistently take money out of the market, and as a result, they do well over time.

If you can master this concept, you will thrive in this business. Interestingly, it does not matter whether you are trading stocks, gold, sugar, corn, coffee, cotton, bonds, the U.S. dollar, or bitcoin—at the end of the day, you want to exchange risk for reward. Put simply, you are buying (and selling) risk and reward with every decision you make.

Therefore, learning to manage risk properly will give you a clear definable edge that will put you light years ahead of the crowd. Most people only look at the reward side of the trade and they ignore the risk. They pull out the calculator and start calculating how much money they are going to make and ignore (or dismiss) the risk. That's why most people fail to make it big in this business. They are ignoring a critical part of the equation.

Why do we buy risk? Well, the answer is for an equal or, hopefully, greater reward. The market is constantly moving, and it is physically impossible for anyone to accurately and consistently predict the future, so why do we all do what we do? Because if we are right in our analysis (understand the relationship between risk and reward), then the reward will greatly outweigh the risk. Moreover, when you learn to think like a trader (risk vs. reward), you learn how to keep your losses small so you only have to be right a small amount of time and you can do very well.

Proper risk management begins with a healthy attitude regarding risk. It is not always simple to understand how risk is perceived by each investor or what motivates risk-taking, but surely, there is a mental process involved, which may make or break each investment decision at any point in time. Risk-taking involves an emotional state that results from making uncertain decisions and may contain subjective elements that vary for each person. To begin, you must be okay taking risks. Andy, a good friend of mine, likes to say, "You have to risk it for the biscuit."

However, if you are not comfortable with the level of risk you are taking then you will likely abandon your strategy and/or sell impulsively and eventually get erratic results. You will likely zig when you should zag and vice versa. If you risk too little you will never win big, and if you risk too much you will suffer devastating drawdowns and expose yourself to the risk of ruin.

The risk of ruin (a.k.a. the disaster theory) is a concept that is derived from gaming theory, and it explains the delicate relationship between risk and reward. The key is to know how much you should risk without risking so much that you end up in a complete disaster, losing all or a large portion of your capital. Remember, your primary goal should be capital preservation and then your next goal should be capital appreciation. You can't grow your capital if you don't have any capital to begin with. At the most basic level, you want to stay in the game and participate in the Great American Tailwind.

Markets will be here forever. They serve a critical function in our society. They make our society great. They create enormous wealth. The only question is, will you be around to participate and enjoy the glory? Once you determine the optimal amount you are willing to risk per trade, you want to always limit your losses when you're wrong and be very patient with your winners when you're right. The key is to find a healthy balance where you are comfortable with the risk you are taking and are risking enough to move the needle so that when you are right, you clean up.

BASIC RISK MITIGATION STRATEGY

Becoming a successful trader is all about balancing risk versus reward. We risk a dollar for the chance to make a dollar—or, hopefully, more. (Some strategies allow people to risk a dollar if they are wrong and make a nickel or a dime if they are right, but that usually revolves around selling options and is not for the faint of heart.) Most people are better off looking for asymmetric returns.

On the simplest level, a trader wants to realize the greatest reward for the lowest amount of risk. The beauty of the stock market is that you can control your risk in nearly every transaction. The way you do that is by deciding exactly where you are going to enter, exactly where you are going to exit, and how much you are going to risk if you are wrong.

Specifically, when you buy a stock, you can also place a stop order at a predetermined price below your buy that will automatically trigger a sale if the price moves against you. On rare occasions, a stock can gap down while the market is closed, and open below your stop, but for the vast majority of circumstances, your stop order will limit the amount of money you risk in any single trade. Big gaps—up and down—tend to occur during earnings season or when some other major catalyst occurs. Even then there are strategies you can use to offset that risk, such as buying puts to protect your long position and/or buying calls to protect your short position.

Let's say you have done your homework and found a few good stocks to buy. The technicals and fundamentals all line up, and you are good to go. Now what? How much of your portfolio should you put to work on any given idea?

The biggest and most successful funds in the world usually do not risk more than 1% of their portfolio per idea (and most risk less than that). Why? Because most trades fail. The best traders in the world usually average three wins and seven losses for every 10 trades. Even with that record they still put up amazing returns because, when they are wrong, they lose small and when they are right they win big. To further illustrate how this works in real life (and, while I'm at it, to show you how foolish it is to care about someone's win ratio), imagine you have 10 trades, and you lose one unit on nine of those trades. That means you are negative nine. On the tenth trade, you win 20. After all is said and done, you walk out up 11, even though you only won on one out of 10 trades! The secret is to keep your losses small. I'll talk about this more in the next section.

Some people risk more on a single trade, but the problem is, the more you risk, the greater the possibility of ruin. If you risk 100% of your portfolio on every trade, it will only take one bad trade to wipe you out. Clearly, that is too much risk. If you risk 50% on every trade, only two bad trades wipe you out. If you risk 25% on every trade, four bad trades wipe you out, and so on and so forth. So, be mindful of how much you risk on any one idea.

Some of the best traders I know only risk around 20–25 basis points (0.20–0.25%) of their portfolio on any one trade and still do extremely well. Legendary global macro trader Bruce Kovner said, "I would say that risk management is the most important thing to be well understood. Undertrade, undertrade, undertrade is my second piece of advice. Whatever you think your position ought to be, cut it at least in half." This comes directly from one of the smartest traders in history.

If you want to risk 1% of your portfolio on any one trade, then all you have to do is start by calculating what 1% of your portfolio is in dollar terms. It's really simple math. You would risk $1 for every $100 you have in your portfolio. For example, you would risk $10,000 if you have a $1,000,000 portfolio.

The second step is to figure out where you want to enter and where you want to exit the trade. Then, take the difference and divide that number by the dollar amount you want to risk. For example, if you buy a stock at $100 and sell it at $95, then you are risking $5 from entry to exit. If you have a $100,000 portfolio, 1% of your portfolio is $1,000. You would buy 200 shares (200 × 5 = $1,000). That means that if you buy the stock at $100 and it immediately goes against you and you are stopped out at $95 for a full loss, your portfolio will lose $1,000, or 1% of your portfolio.

Another easier method you can use to determine your risk-managed position size (note that this approach works for stocks, but it does not work well with other markets such as currencies and commodities) is to keep it simple and take a 10% position and exit if the stock drops 10% below your initial entry price, meaning that if you have a $500,000 portfolio you would buy $50,000 in each idea and exit if the stock drops 10% below your entry point. In this case, you will also risk 1% of your portfolio from entry to exit, per idea, and keep a wide enough stop that you are not stopped out on noise (a normal meaningless retracement). On another, and closely related, topic: there is no magic number with respect to where to place your stop loss, but for the most part anything between 4% and 10% is appropriate for most traders.

Risk, like value and beauty, is very subjective. What you are comfortable risking can be completely different than someone else, and in the end, you both can win. That's the magic of markets—and life, for that matter. Everyone is free to do whatever they feel works for them. Your mindset, which is based on your subjective reality, is key and will always influence any risk objectivity when the final decision is made on any decision. Since risk is subjective, try to stay consistent so you are risking equal or close to equal amounts for every trade. This way you are very aware of how much money you are risking and, more importantly, what will happen to your portfolio if the market moves against you.

WIN RATE (KNOW THE STATS)

As previously mentioned, the vast majority of trades are losing trades and that's okay—in fact, the faster you learn and accept that as par for the course, the faster you will be able to learn how to develop the skills necessary to win consistently on Wall Street. I strongly urge you to avoid the temptation to follow the "genius" who is running around telling you they have a high percentage win rate. That's impossible, because the absolute best traders in the world have a relatively low win-loss ratio. Anyone can get lucky and win over a few trades—that is meaningless in the long run.

If the percent of winning trades versus losing trades does not matter, what does? Easy: the size of your winners versus the size of your losers. Let's look at the 15 trades in the following chart. Only around one-third are winners and nearly two-thirds are losers. Is this normal? Absolutely; it is because the six winners each won more than all the losers combined. For example: If each loss was one unit and each win was three, at the end of the period you will have lost nine units and won 18—which means you walked out plus nine, even though you only won six out of 15 trades. The key is to look at the size of your winners versus the size of your losers.

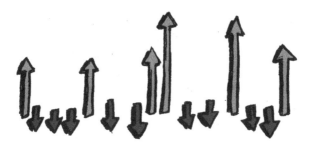

The smart money uses stop-loss orders to limit our losses, but we do not do anything to arbitrarily limit our gains. Why? Because there is virtually no limit to how high a stock can go. Sometimes an upward trend can last much longer than you think it will, and only one or two big upward trends can easily make your year—or career, for that matter! So prematurely exiting winners just for the sake of locking in gains is typically not advisable unless the stock gives you a very compelling reason to do so. As a stock price rallies, I will move my stops up to preserve my earnings, but I'm careful not to move them up too much because I don't want to get stopped out prematurely by natural price fluctuations.

The core of this risk mitigation strategy is to listen to the market, dump your losers early, and let your winners run.

WHY WE CUT AND RUN FROM LOSERS

There is a terrible myth that new traders and investors often regard as gospel. It says that when a stock you own falls, you don't actually lose money until you sell it and realize the loss. This is complete nonsense. A loss on paper (an unrealized loss) is still a loss. Some people do not sell, even though they know they should. They create excuses and try to justify it by saying it'll come back. They are in denial and they are directly violating my first commandment of trading: always respect risk. The key aspect of making this risk management plan work is to always sell once you've lost the maximum you were willing to risk—or less, if possible. If the stock is just not performing well after you buy it and you are in a strong market, there is a big opportunity cost of tying up your money in a broken stock. Sell weakness, and move on.

Here is why holding on to losers is so dangerous: if you buy a stock at $100 and it goes down 20% (to $80), you need a 25% gain ($20 is 25% of $80) to get back to even. If your position declines by 50%, you need a 100% gain to get back to even. Let me ask you this: If something loses half its value, what are the odds that it will double in price in the foreseeable future? They are very, very low. So, why would you ever let your stocks fall anywhere close to that much? Yet, people do this all day long—and that is one of the major reasons they lose. Take some time and review this basic table so you can properly understand how powerful this concept is and what you should always keep your losses small:

Loss	Get Back to Break Even
-5%	5.3%
-10%	11.1%
-15%	17.6%
-20%	25%
-30%	42.9%
-40%	66.7%
-50%	100%
-60%	150%
-70%	233.3%
-80%	400%
-90%	900%

ALWAYS REDUCE, NEVER INCREASE, RISK

Successful traders always look to reduce their risk after entry; they never increase it. The three questions you want to ask before entering a trade are:

1. Where to enter?
2. Where to exit?
3. How much to risk if wrong?

That means you have to pick a place to exit if the trade moves against you. That is your initial stop-loss point. Once you are in the trade, it is very tempting for beginners to widen the stop (a.k.a. cancel the stop or move it so you don't have to sell) and stay in the trade longer if the price moves against you.

Successful traders never do this; in fact, they do the exact opposite: they may exit completely if the stock is not acting well, or they may tighten their stop—but they never widen it.

Once I enter a trade, if the stock goes up by 5–10%, I do my best to move my stop to breakeven because that allows me to protect my capital and only risk the money I earn from the market. Tightening your stop too fast may cause you to get prematurely stopped out and the stock can take off without you. Unfortunately, there is no magical formula for when to tighten it to breakeven. It all depends on a slew of factors: your performance, your conviction, the state of the market, how the stock is performing—just to name a few.

The next step after raising your stop to breakeven is to raise it again and lock in a profit. I'm often asked if I ever let a winner turn into a loser. It depends on the size of the gain. If it's tiny (0–5%) I do, but above that, I'll exit for at least breakeven or preferably for a profit. Again, these are just guidelines and you are free to use your discretion and create a formula that works for you.

Everyone runs hot and cold; this happens in just about every performance business in the world (actors, athletes, musicians, comics, and traders, for just a few examples). If you perform well, you get paid well; if not, "good luck." That's just the nature of a competitive performance-based business. During your career, you will invariably experience several hot and cold streaks, and people will want to know if they should adjust risk when they are hot or cold. Again, there is no right or wrong answer, but I have found it best to reduce your risk when you are in a drawdown (cold) and keep it steady or increase it slightly when you are in a hot streak. It is very clear in hindsight, but very difficult to do in real time. So, to keep it simple, keep your risk steady when you are winning and steadily reduce it—or stop trading completely—when you are losing. Never increase your risk beyond what you were willing to take on when you originally placed the trade. Follow your rules; they are there for a reason.

OTHER TYPES OF RISK

As a general rule of thumb, the higher the risk, the higher the potential return (although that is not always the case). To profit from this relationship, you have to find what degree of risk you are comfortable taking and learn how to properly analyze the potential reward. Remember, every investment has a hidden opportunity cost that should also be factored into the equation. In addition, there are several other types of risk that may impact your bottom line. Next are a few more for your consideration.

Market (a.k.a. Systematic) Risk

Market risk (or systematic risk) refers to the daily volatility in the market. I take it a step further and focus on the risk of the entire market moving against me. If you are long, the risk of the market moving into a steep downtrend or an outright bear market is considered a market risk because that would obviously hurt your portfolio. Conversely, if you are short and the market rallies sharply and a new bull market is born, that could greatly impact your portfolio. Additionally, if you are in cash (or not properly invested), the market can take off without you. Basically, market risk, in my mind, occurs when you are not properly aligned with the market and the market is trending (up or down) and you are not riding that trend.

Specific (a.k.a. Unsystematic) Risk

Specific risk refers to a risk that may directly impact your position. For example, if you own shares in a company and all of a sudden there is a scandal or some other negative news that may impact the stock price, that is known as a specific risk. Or, if you are trading commodities and all of a sudden there is a news event, drought, or a flood—that is a specific risk that could greatly impact the price of that commodity.

Interest Rate Risk

Interest rates are constantly moving and are influenced heavily by global central banks. Therefore, interest rate risk refers to what may happen to your investment if interest rates move in an adverse fashion. This is mainly for bond investments and other interest-rate-sensitive areas of the market.

Credit Risk

Credit risk refers to the underlying risk that your investment will default on its debt. The 2008 financial crisis taught us that credit risk comes in all different shapes and sizes and is difficult to determine properly.

Liquidity Risk

Liquidity risk occurs if a company or financial institution is not able to meet its short-term liabilities. This can largely be avoided by properly managing cash flow, but in times of duress, liquidity often becomes a major concern. Additionally, liquidity risk refers to a stock (or market) not being liquid enough to exit when you want to exit. This isn't a risk for most people with smaller accounts but this is a big deal for people who manage large pools of money.

Currency and Political Risk

Currency risk refers to large swings in a currency that may impact your investments. Political risk (which can impact currency risk), occurs when the political climate is volatile.

Operational Risk

Operational risk occurs when people lose money due to their inability to operate properly. That could be the inability to execute effectively, employee errors, system failures, software issues, or some other operational problem.

Gapping

The one element that can defeat your stop-loss approach to mitigating risk in the market is "gapping." You can't always control your risk in the stock market because a stock could gap up or down (literally open much higher or much lower) overnight based on a major external event (a common example would be a big earnings report), but the odds of that happening outside of earnings season is relatively low.

LEVERAGE

Leverage occurs when you borrow money to increase your investable capital. You should always remember that leverage can work for you (when the market moves in your direction) and against you (when the market moves against you). Personally, I only use leverage when I have very strong convictions.

Every major blowup in financial history has come from people who misused leverage and or did not respect risk (some examples are Long-Term Capital Management, Amaranth, the 2007–2009 bear market, Lehman Brothers, Bear Stearns, AIG, Washington Mutual, and Wachovia).

Keep your name off this list. When you don't know what to do, simply don't risk your money. There is no rule that says you have to always be invested. In fact, there are many periods when I'm 100% in cash, and I view cash as a perfectly valid position. There's nothing wrong with being in cash when there is nothing to do or you need time off to clear your head.

PSYCHOLOGICAL ANALYSIS

We all know the 80/20 rule or the Pareto principle. As with other aspects of life, this rule also applies to markets as well. The Pareto principle, which is named after economist Vilfredo Pareto, describes an unequal relationship between inputs and outputs. The principle states that 20% of the input is responsible for 80% of the output (results). I would push it a little further and create the Sarhan 99/1 rule—99% of your success on Wall Street is based on your psychology and 1% on everything else. Why? Because your psychology controls your actions, and if your psychology is strong, your actions will be strong as well—it's not the other way around. Being successful in this business is about making smart decisions and taking proper action over and over again—even as you are getting punched in the face (such as when you are in a drawdown). When you dig a little deeper, the only way you can act well is by not freezing up and having the courage and discipline to pull the trigger when required (having the right mindset).

A very important part of being successful in life (and in markets) is to take responsibility for everything. It's a universal truth that anyone who takes responsibility for their life tends to live a better life than people who do not. Just because you take responsibility does not mean you will not encounter problems; it just means that you will be mentally stronger and have a much better chance of being fulfilled and happy. This is especially true in markets. The market is not out to get you; in fact, it does not even know you. Avoid the urge to take things personally or play the victim. Be humble and take responsibility for every aspect of your life. Take control, find solutions, and win!

Most people get stuck when making tough decisions, and that is exactly what causes most people to lose money on Wall Street. This business is about making sound decisions quickly, handling losses gracefully, focusing on your next winner, and adjusting when the facts change.

An easy way to make sound decisions and overcome anxiety is to think about the worst-case scenario if you make a particular decision. Before I make any decision, I always ask, what's my maximum risk (the worst thing that can happen if I make this decision)?

Once that is clearly defined, I then ask, what is my potential reward? If the reward is greater than the risk, I'll place the trade. If not, I won't.

That's really it when it comes down to how I make nearly all my decisions. Life is really simple when you elevate your thinking and learn how to keep things simple.

It is important to stay consistent and humble because the second you start pulling out the calculator and living in la-la land because of the pleasure from a hot streak, you are most likely to encounter a nasty drawdown. The opposite is also true. The second you are about to give up due to the pain of a losing streak, watch out—you are probably on the verge of a new hot streak. Unsuccessful traders get caught up in the emotional highs and lows and make careless decisions that end up causing their financial ruin.

The unsuccessful trader will increase risk after a winning streak, then get slammed when the inevitable drawdown occurs. Then after the losing streak, still smarting from their loss, they decrease risk, and it takes forever just to get back to even—not to mention get back to an old equity high (a new high in their portfolio). Then, they get impatient and increase risk after a few good trades only to get buried in the next drawdown. This destructive cycle continues until they are wiped out.

I'm not going to pretend to know why people have hot and cold streaks; I have my theories, but all that matters is that they happen consistently to everyone (remember, focus on what is happening, not why you think something is happening).

At this point, it is critical for you to understand that ***this time is not different*** and that is just the nature of how markets work. You are not special and, no, this is not the first time this has happened to someone. It might just be the first time you experienced it. So, please do your best to avoid the temptation to get arrogant and think you are special. You aren't. We all experience the highs and lows of trading. The only difference is that successful people can anticipate to the inevitable highs and lows (and their reaction to them), stay humble throughout the entire process, and maintain a healthy attitude—and always respect risk. My good friend Michael Lamothe likes to say, investing is a marathon, not a sprint.

Venturing into the unknown.

CHAPTER 14

What Happens Next

Navigating to the Right of the Chart

THE RIGHT SIDE OF THE CHART—THE ONLY PLACE TO MAKE MONEY

When you study a stock chart, it can tell you almost everything you'd want to know about the price of a stock in the past. You can follow its ups and downs on a weekly, daily, or monthly basis—practically any time frame you want—from the moment the stock started trading to its most recent tick. But a stock chart cannot show you the future. The last tick on the right side of the chart is the last recorded moment in the market. The same is true for analyzing important fundamental data such as earnings, economic data, sales, return on equity, pre-tax margins, or any other data point you want to use. We have no information about what happens next—or to the right of the most recent tick on the chart.

Another way to explain this concept is that the left side of the chart tells you about all the filled orders in the market, but the right side moves based on future unfilled orders.

To make sure it is crystal clear, I want to reiterate this important concept: most people focus on the price chart (the past), but the real key is to understand and master the right side (future unfilled orders). The best way to do that is to learn how the smart and dumb money think, then learn how to expect what they are going to do at any given time.

No doubt, as you've followed a stock chart backward through time, you've noticed the highs and lows, and thought, "If only I had bought there. If only I had sold here." You might see the imprint of the Great 2008 Recession and wonder what life would be like if you had the nerve to buy during the turbulent lows. You might see the remarkable "V-shaped" recovery from the COVID-19 bottom in March 2020 and kick yourself for not buying big at the bottom.

We cannot go back in time and take advantage of the knowledge we have now. The only place to make money in the market is in the future—to the right of the chart. The only place to place a trade or interact with the market is right now, in the present moment. Since we can see the left side and the right side is blank, most people spend all their time dwelling on the past. In practice, what happens is they end up getting stuck in the weeds and overanalyzing information that will not help them find new winners: analysis paralysis.

I always like to keep things simple, so I'll remind you: there are only three things that can happen on the right side of the chart: the price can either go up, down, or sideways. The smart money uses the left side to get a small edge on what may happen going forward, but they are always prepared for what may happen or what may go wrong on the right side. On March 23, 2020, I published "a special report" to FindLeadingStocks.com members and said it was time to buy. I didn't know that would be the exact low but I did know that the market was offering an extremely attractive risk/reward ratio and that I was backed by the Federal Reserve. We started buying over the next few weeks and walked out with a few hundred percent returns in several monster stocks such as Zoom, Tesla, Amazon, Apple, and Wayfair, just to name a few. In fact, 2020 turned out to be one of our best years—ever! All because I kept things simple and understood a very good risk-versus-reward opportunity when I saw one.

NAVIGATING THE UNKNOWN

To be successful in the market (and in life), you need to learn how to be comfortable navigating the unknown. This is a very difficult concept for most people to grasp because the future is uncertain, and people like certainty and structure. By definition, to thrive in the market you have to learn how to change your default settings and learn how to become comfortable with the unknown.

The good news is that the skills needed to navigate the future are simple when you know how to develop them. I navigate the unknown by simplifying everything to risk versus reward and making the best decision I can with the information I have at the time. I ask myself, "What is the worst possible thing that can happen (risk)?" and "What is the best possible thing (reward)?" If the reward outweighs the risk, then I'll move forward with confidence.

It is literally impossible for anyone to consistently predict the future. No one can know what the market will do all the time. It's an odd concept at first, but your job is to learn how to navigate the unknown—and that is not an easy feat.

It would be helpful for you to start thinking in terms of probabilities, not certainties. That is a foreign concept for most people because that is the exact opposite of how most of the world around us works and it does not feel natural. People have a deep-rooted desire for certainty and the market by definition is uncertain. Therein lies one of the most common reasons people fail to beat the market. Successful investors have to rewire their brains to embrace uncertainty and navigate the unknown gracefully.

I'll illustrate this concept with another real-world tangible example. Just about any qualified dentist can successfully fix a cavity, and any qualified Certified Public Accountant can file your taxes—that's what I call a predictable outcome.

On the other hand, a lawyer cannot guarantee a win in court, and a trader cannot guarantee outsize massive returns in the market. No one on Earth can tell you exactly what to do and (legally) guarantee that the stock will go up after you buy it. Welcome to the wonderful world of unpredictable outcomes. A good lawyer, however, will win more than they lose over time, and a good trader makes money in the aggregate over the long run. As a trader, you do not need to predict market action with 100% certainty to do very well in this business. In fact, if you learn to manage risk properly, you catch a handful of big winners each year and still do extremely well.

THE UNPREDICTABILITY OF MARKETS

Why are the markets so difficult to predict? To borrow a phrase from the physicists, the market demonstrates "unstable aperiodic behavior in deterministic nonlinear dynamism." This behavior is better known as "chaos theory." Scientists who study chaos theory define it as "the science of surprises, of the nonlinear and the unpredictable." At its core, chaos theory shows us how to interact with the unexpected. Linear science deals with predictable outcomes such as gravity, electricity, or chemical reactions. Most of the time in those disciplines, there is a clear, logical, mathematical explanation for how things behave.

Meanwhile, chaos theory deals with nonlinear situations that have unpredictable outcomes such as turbulence, weather, the stock market, and so on. By understanding that some experiences are chaotic by nature and have unpredictable outcomes, the trained mind can prepare for what may happen—which is a huge edge over other market participants.

A seasoned pilot can steer an airplane through turbulence much better than a novice, simply because the pilot has spent countless hours training for it and is prepared for just about any likely event that may happen in that scenario. The same is true for the seasoned trader who knows the market can only move up, down, or sideways, and has studied countless prior bull and bear markets. Once you learn how the market or stock you are analyzing behaves, you will instantly have a huge edge on your competition, take actions that will allow you to generate wealth, and avoid actions that adversely impact your long-term well-being. We've previously discussed the idea of "quality"—meaning you can't know what the color red looks like, or what chocolate tastes like until you experience it for yourself. An experienced pilot comes to know the quality of turbulence just as an experienced trader comes to know the quality of market fluctuations.

In the stock market, past results are not indicative of future returns. That said, understanding and learning from history is priceless. For example, if I told you that a big blue-chip stock like Apple or Microsoft moved 10% in one hour, could you tell me if that is normal for that stock? If you study history, you would know that it is extremely abnormal for a big blue-chip stock to swing so wildly in one hour. Stocks, like people, behave differently, and you will get a better feel of this with enough experience.

What does that mean in layman's terms? The market is called "aperiodic" because it never repeats itself precisely the same way. Weather is also aperiodic. It may be colder in the winter than in the summer, so there is a degree of cyclicality, but the day-to-day changes are never exactly the same year after year. A thunderstorm last Fourth of July doesn't mean there will be a thunderstorm on the Fourth this year. The same dynamic applies to the markets. There are similarities from one period to another, but it's never identical. In Mark Twain's words, "History doesn't repeat, but it often rhymes."

The markets also act with a surprising degree of instability. Small forces can create disproportionately large reactions. A surprising economic report, an off-the-cuff comment by a Central Bank official, a small change in earnings—or any other disruptive headline—could emerge, and any one of these data points can roil the market. That behavior does not occur in what the scientists call a "stable" system.

Capital markets and the physical universe are extremely complex, so we should not be that surprised to learn that chaos theory applies to financial markets. Considering how little we know about the totality of market conditions and all the variables of human nature—and how incredibly complex the system is—it should come as no surprise that most pundits' predictions are not accurate.

The responsibility to buy, sell, or hold lies on your shoulders, not someone else's. Now, that does not mean you should blindly dismiss other people's opinions or remarks—on the contrary, there are a lot of good newsletters, research reports, and credible people who want to share their expertise with you—but the key is to always remember that the buck starts and stops with you. Successful people take *full* responsibility for all their actions, including what information to consume and what information to dismiss. Find a smart, trusted, experienced person (or team of people), consume their ideas, and ignore everything else. Find winners and stick with them. Over time, you will do very well.

THE SMART MONEY LOOKS FORWARD

The smart money looks forward, and the dumb money looks backward. People are constantly looking backward while trying to predict the future, and this disconnect is one of the main reasons most people have trouble getting ahead. People struggle to beat the market, they struggle to get into the smart money circle, and they struggle to get out of their own way. If you drive a car only looking in the rearview mirror you will crash. Look forward, your future is bright. Plan for it and win!

At the end of the day, we are all looking at the same data; the big difference is how we use it. Put simply, the smart money makes money from the data while the dumb money consistently loses money and wastes time blaming others and arguing about nonsense. Trust me, I can speak from experience, having started out with nothing and spending many years struggling to figure it out. Smart money knows how to use the information we all have access to in order to make better decisions. It may sound very simple (because it is), but it is extremely powerful.

As a quick reminder, the data (economic and earnings) tells us what already happened, whereas the market moves on the perception of what will happen (future/unknown data). The market is a forward-looking mechanism, and the price of a stock today is influenced by what people think might happen in the future, not what's already happened.

When it comes down to it, just about everything that happened to you in the past is mostly irrelevant when it comes to making decisions in the present. That includes any arbitrary feelings about a recent loss. The market doesn't care what price you paid for a stock; it's going to behave independently. The market doesn't care about any of the baggage you bring along; that's why whenever something negative happens, or you are stopped out of a trade for a loss, the faster you get over that event the better.

At first, it may seem difficult, but over time you will learn how to consciously train your brain to look forward and move on. The easiest way to do that is to turn a loss into a learning experience. Don't dwell on it; analyze it objectively, and then look forward. Once you master this very powerful skill you will be light years ahead of the crowd.

The past is over and the future has not yet happened. All that matters is right now—and then the next moment. All you can do at this moment is look for your next best decision. Eternity is made up of a series of never-ending present moments. Learn to live in and love the present moment. Trade in the now, live in the now, love the now. You will thrive when you learn how to rewire your brain to focus on the now because time is the most valuable asset you have; use it wisely, don't spend it. (As an aside, a couple of great books to read on this subject are *The Power of Now* by Eckhart Tolle and *The Miracle of Mindfulness* by Thich Nhat Hanh.)

FORGIVE AND MOVE FORWARD

The market is made up of a series of never-ending ticks. Each tick represents a precious moment in time. The last tick, and every tick to the left, is in the past and does not make you money. To be clear, I am not saying to ignore the past, or to not study chart patterns; that's foolish. What I'm saying is to not get caught up in the past or carry the psychological baggage from past losses into the now and your future. Focus on the present and the future, not the past. There will always be another tick (opportunity to make money) around the corner.

Once you rewire your brain to make smart money decisions you will become a lot more financially successful. Eventually, you will look around at all the dumb money around you and almost feel bad for them. You will develop a different level of clarity, and your point of view will be completely different. There are many ways your point of view will change, but you will have to experience it in order to fully understand how things change. That's the nature of quality. It's like teaching a kindergartener how to add or subtract. The answer is crystal clear in your mind, but you must be patient and let them figure it out on their own; otherwise, they will never learn.

A note of caution: once you attain clarity you will look back at the "old" you and all the dumb money decisions you have made in the past and you might get frustrated or upset. Some people might be upset at their parents or guardians for creating a dumb money environment. I strongly urge you to drop those negative feelings (there is no R.O.I. for them) and move forward. The faster you learn how to forgive yourself (and others, if applicable) and not harbor any resentment or negativity about anything, the better off you are. The faster you do that, the more open you will be to rejecting the mental baggage you acquired in the past, and the easier it will be to focus on new/ better smart money decisions that will allow you to attract money into your life and live life on your terms.

This will come when you start doing smart things and taking smart actions, not just practicing smart thinking. Walking around harboring negative feelings toward yourself and/or others is like drinking poison and hoping the other person dies. Life is too short; I teach members of the smart money circle to savor every moment and retrain your brain to enjoy the present, look forward, expect positive things to happen, and be grateful.

Remember, you can't control what happens to you in life, but you can control your attitude and how you react to things. I recommend choosing to be happy in every situation you are in. If it seems bad, either get out of the situation choose to be happy until you can exit (trust me, it beats the alternative). I spoke about this before, but really focus on your mental state. Become an optimist. Really dive deep, get rid of the negativity, and adopt an optimistic attitude of gratitude.

At first, this may sound trivial, but I can tell you that it is exceptionally powerful. The bottom line is that even if you don't have all the technical knowledge needed to make informed decisions, if you are in a positive state and you make objective decisions based upon an objective assessment of the information available to you at the moment, you'll see more opportunities than if you walk around in a negative state thinking the market (or the world) is out to get you.

STOP TRYING TO PREDICT MARKET ACTION (INSTEAD LEARN TO EXPECT IT)

People love forecasts and predictions. All the big Wall Street firms publish their predictions every year. They are almost always wrong. Not only are they wrong, most of them update their predictions when the market moves away from them (up or down), and they are still wrong by the end of the year! Why do they keep doing this, you may ask? Well, there are several reasons and they all have to do with the fact that the "crowd" wants to defer responsibility and blindly accept some authoritative figure's prediction(s). In other words, it's good for business and they are giving the kids candy. They are feeding the dumb money beast.

DEVELOPING YOUR OWN WAY FORWARD

When you finish this book, I hope you'll walk away feeling empowered, ready to develop your own strategy or use the strategy I've laid out here, and that you are eager to adopt the philosophy of the smart money circle. You'll be missing one critical component for success, however, and frustratingly, it's the one thing I can't really teach you in a book. It has to do with the idea of "quality" we've explored on a number of occasions. Just as I can't tell you what chocolate tastes like, I can't teach you how to gain a sense of how the market behaves—you're going to have to do that on your own.

I've compared the turbulence in the market to the turbulence a pilot experiences in the air. While a computer simulator can help a pilot understand the essentials of flying an aircraft, the subtle qualities that separate a bad pilot from a great pilot can only be experienced through (sometimes harrowing) real-life experiences. Luckily traders have an opportunity to learn the qualities of the market without taking extraordinary risks.

Previously, I warned that you should not start trading until you understand yourself, you understand the market, you understand risk/reward, and you understand your well-tested trading strategy. I also said that, if you're not sure what to do in the market, staying in a cash position is often a very smart thing to do—or find someone who does know what they are doing and hire them to manage your money.

If you haven't already developed a feel for the market, don't try to develop one by putting real money in the market and making a bunch of random (and lousy) oversized trades. I encourage you to do what I did: start small or start a paper trading account. Establish an imaginary value for your portfolio. If you can't make money with $10,000, how do you possibly think you will make money with $100,000 or $1,000,000? Decide what trading frequency you want to use: daily, weekly, monthly. Then watch the market. Start following a handful of stocks. Look for the patterns I've described during our exploration of technical analysis. When you think you've found a winner, set your risk tolerance and make your first "trade." Decide how much you are going to risk if you are wrong, and don't forget to set your stop-loss. Then watch and see how you do.

Give yourself time. If you're anything like me, you'll lose a lot of "small" money (or fake money, if you are paper trading) at first. However, over time, you'll start to see patterns you recognize (like the taste of chocolate), and you'll develop a feel for when to act. You'll learn to get over your losses. Once you've demonstrated that you can win consistently over time, in different market conditions, then you're ready to start risking some real capital. Still, go slow. Increase your trading capital in small units. In order to trade "size," it is imperative that you learn how to think in percentages, not in dollars. I have yet to meet anyone who is emotionally attached to 10%, but $100,000 is a real nice car.

I dedicated a whole chapter to developing your strategy, and I referenced using the scientific method to develop and test your trading strategy. Now that we've come all this way together, it's worth reinforcing how the scientific method works:

Step 1: Ask a Question

Step 2: Do Background Research

Step 3: Construct a Hypothesis

Step 4: Test Your Hypothesis by Doing an Experiment

Step 5: Analyze Your Data and Draw a Conclusion

Step 6: Communicate Your Results

Here's how I make the scientific method work for me: I create a hypothesis (have a view), test it, then expect things to happen (win or lose). The most important part of this process is that it is flexible, and I always let the market guide me. If my results are successful, I win; if not, I already know how much I'm going to lose before I enter and adjust accordingly (I might tighten my stop so I lose less than I initially planned, but I *never* widen it, because widening my stop means that I would lose more than I initially planned if the stop is triggered). If you want to take it a step further, you can create a trading "system" by backtesting strategies with modern software and get specific results over multiple market cycles.

TRADE IN THE NOW

Successful people learn from the past, prepare for the future, but live in the now. They do this by shutting out the noise in their lives and hyperfocusing on the present moment and the very next (and smartest) decision. It's very easy to get caught up in the past and carry that shock, or mental baggage, into the present, but that is very destructive. When something is over, it is over. Learn from it, then put it behind you and move on and hunt for the next opportunity. The key for a strong trader is to remain present and trade in the now.

In the market, your trading past does not matter. The market does not care about your actions, even though you do. Resist the temptation to dwell on them. Your job is to trade in the now and learn how to position yourself so you can be in harmony with the market and be prepared for the future. The key is to shift your focus to "expect" things to happen (remember, the market can only go up, down, or sideways after you enter). Plan for the worst, but be ready for the best. Do not try to predict the future. If you do, you may get psychologically married to your predictions (ego) and that will create a cognitive bias and negatively impact your decision-making. The best thing to do is to develop an informed outlook, always respect risk, keep watching the data, and always be prepared to change your view when market conditions change.

Remember, most of your trades will not work, and that's okay. The quicker you accept and learn to expect that, the better off you will be. Don't get stuck in the past, stay aligned with what is happening right now—and always ask yourself, What's the next best decision?

Welcome to the smart money circle.

CHAPTER 15

Welcome to the Smart Money Circle

If you've made it this far, I assume that you're interested in trying your hand at trading and living life on a whole new level. I've warned you that most people don't have what it takes to make money actively trading in the market, and fewer still can consistently beat the market. That's why I strongly recommend that most people invest in the stock market for the long-term by buying and holding exchange-traded funds that track the major indices. This way they can ride the Great American Tailwind. If you want to trade and do what is necessary to win, the results can be truly breathtaking.

I've also told you that in order for you to beat the market it is important that you understand what makes you tick, discover your strengths and weaknesses, and improve your relationship with yourself and with money. It is also important to dive deep and study the market, understand how it behaves, and really understand the extremely important relationship between risk and reward.

I encouraged you to develop your own strategy and to test your strategy with a small amount of money (or a paper trading account) before you risk "real" money.

You know now that the one constant in the market (and in life) is human nature. Markets rise and fall, but human nature always stays the same. Human nature causes people to make emotional, irrational decisions in life (and in the market)—that's the dumb money beast at play.

We also know that the smart money superhero is infinitely stronger than the dumb money beast and to bring out our smart money superhero we just have to control our mind so our mind does not control us.

There are many ways to do that (many of which are outlined in this book), and some of the easiest are: consciously adopt an optimistic outlook on life, focus on solutions (not problems), be brave and unafraid of some hard work, work smart, and be willing to grow (which may cause a little short-term pain at first but will give you a tremendous amount of long-term pleasure). Only then can we rewire our minds, rise above the short-term limitations of human nature, and plot our own course to thrive!

In order to do all that we must commit to always doing the right thing (which may not be the thing we want to do—or feel like doing—but we do the right thing anyway) over and over again. Anyone who does all this can enjoy financial freedom and can live life at a whole new level.

After you make the commitment to doing the right thing, you want to set lofty goals and create a plan to accomplish those goals. Those are more powerful tools in the smart money super hero's toolbox.

More ways you can control your mind (a.k.a. beat Shmelf) are to become very disciplined, stay focused, and make objective, unemotional, decisions—especially when you are under pressure.

Keep doing the intellectual sit-ups every day (even when it is hard) and get out of your smart money superhero's way (don't self-sabotage). Once you learn how to control your mind, you will control your life, and just about every aspect of your life will greatly improve.

You may have realized by now that the smart money mindset is not just about being successful in the market; it's about being successful in life. If you want to know whether you're truly ready to start trading real money in the market, take a step back and look at your life. Are you making smart money decisions in your day-to-day life? Do you have great relationships with yourself and other people? Are you getting enough sleep? How's your diet? Do you exercise regularly? What's your relationship with money? Do you have a nice 12- to 24-month emergency fund set aside, or did you spend that money on a vacation or a new car? If you're not making smart money decisions in life, you're not going to make smart money decisions in the market, and you'll be destined to lose a lot of money. Fair warning.

But if you can look in the mirror, surrender your biases, drop your ego, see yourself as others may see you—and can still honestly say that you're living a smart money lifestyle, then I'll take you at your word. Now it's time to graduate from your small account, learn how to stack the odds of success in your favor, and learn how to have your money work for you as a smart money trader.

START SMALL AND SCALE SLOWLY

People often ask me how much money they need to start trading in the market. On the basic level, there is no right or wrong answer; you are free to start with as much or as little as you want. Most people mistakenly tell themselves, "If I only had more money in my account, I would do great."

That is a complete fallacy. The truth is, the amount of money you have in your account has no bearing on your results. In fact, having more money in your account is worse than having a little when you don't know what you are doing.

The quality of your decisions is what matters. If you make lousy decisions your results will be lousy, and if you make great decisions your results will be great.

The quality of your decisions does not magically improve if you just had more money in the bank. In fact, more money will show up when you improve the quality of your decisions, not the other way around. Your physical capital (money in the bank) is a direct result of your mental capital (the quality of your decisions and your mental outlook).

Once you have money in the market, you want to focus on percentages, not dollars. We've already discussed how the best traders never risk more than 1% of their portfolio on a single idea. Does it matter if 1% is one dollar or one million dollars? It does not. Money scales. Likewise, it's impossible to judge gains in terms of dollars. If you exit a trade with a $1,000 profit, is that good? If it was a million-dollar trade, then no, it's not very good. If it was a $500 trade, that's good. It's the percentage of gain that matters, not the dollars.

Moreover, if you focus on percentages rather than dollars, it will help you scale as you find success on Wall Street. If you're not used to dealing with big money and all of a sudden you start risking $100,000 on a trade, you might freak out a little bit—but if you're still risking only 1%, the same as you always have, the psychological pressure is off. Likewise, if you're like most people and you grew up with the "filthy rich" myth, you might be uncomfortable realizing a $100,000 gain in the market, but if that same profit was expressed as a 1% return on your investment, you might feel at peace with it. Part of being in the smart money circle is using your biases to your advantage—and controlling them so they don't control you.

I strongly urge everyone to start trading with one share (or the smallest unit possible in other markets) until you have demonstrated actual results over a decent amount of time (I'll let you decide how to define that).

My good friend Mike Lamothe likes the saying "trading is a marathon, not a sprint." Be honest with yourself and don't rush it. Make no mistake about it, trading capital markets is difficult, and there is no hurry to learn everything overnight (in fact, it is impossible to do that).

If you take your time and undertrade, trust me, your portfolio will thank me (and you) later. Don't trade with more money than you're comfortable with. Trading with real money is different from trading a paper trading account, and in the beginning, you'll still have a lot to learn.

Now that I've said this, here's a reality of the market: you cannot live off an undercapitalized account. If you plan on quitting your job and becoming a full-time trader, you had better have a couple of years of living expenses or other streams of income, so you know you can get through the lean years—and there will be tough years. While I encourage traders to think in percentages rather than dollars, if a 10% annual return on your portfolio is not enough for you to live on, you'd do much better if you still have another source of income.

If you "need" to make money in the market, you're operating from a position of weakness, and you're pretty much setting yourself up to fail. In the market, you are trading risk for potential reward. If you are risking the very money you need to live on—the money that puts food on your table—then you are risking too much.

Start slow. Don't risk money that you need to pay for food with. Don't rely on the market to provide your basic livelihood until you figure it out. The market is where the smart money goes to compound and build their wealth, not to make a living.

THE LEARNING CYCLE

If you've ever tried to be really good at something difficult—like the guitar, or golf, or calculus—then you've encountered what I call "the learning cycle."

Here is how it works: at first you learn a lot, and you make big strides, but then inevitably, your growth plateaus, and you feel like all your hard work is getting you nowhere. This is where many people quit, but the smart money knows that the plateau is just a kind of mental wall, and knows how to get past a mental wall—over it or through it. If you keep at it, you'll break through and experience another exciting period of growth, until you reach a new plateau—a new mental wall. The cycle repeats itself until you decide to quit or you've reached your goal.

To break through the plateau, it helps to think of your brain as a mental sponge. Instead of absorbing water, it absorbs knowledge. Every time you learn something new, you immerse your brain in a pitcher of new knowledge, just like you would immerse a sponge into a pitcher of water. It's impossible for the sponge to absorb all the water in one shot, but it can be done if you keep squeezing out and reapplying the sponge until the task is complete. It's a simple process but it takes patience and time. The dumb money isn't willing to tolerate this painstaking process. They would rather be intellectually lazy, take the easy way out, create drama, create excuses, or literally do anything else than tackle the task at hand, they would even prefer to watch endless hours of television on the couch and eat snacks than do the intellectual sit-ups (the one thing that will actually help them).

Use the learning cycle to your advantage. Every time you plateau—or hit a wall—your brain needs a break before you are ready to dive deeper and learn more. Once you understand this cycle, you can learn to anticipate that much-needed break, pivot before you hit the wall, balance your life with other priorities, then tackle it again with a fresh well-rested set of eyes and ears. It may be only a few minutes, it may be a few hours, it may be a few days, but if you keep pushing yourself intellectually, you will excel in ways you can't even imagine.

Another very helpful shortcut here is to push yourself physically. Your mind and body are linked and whenever you are down or hit a wall, stop and change your state by exercising hard—sweat for 20 minutes or more. Then come back to the intellectual task and you will be in a much better state and have a better chance at success in whatever you are doing.

THE TRADER'S HIERARCHY OF SUCCESS

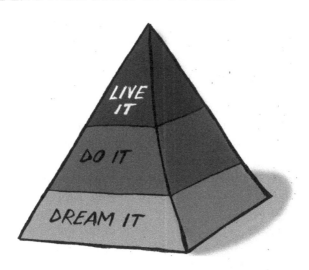

Many people want to succeed as a trader but very few people do. After spending a couple of decades working with and studying thousands of traders, I observed several patterns (some constructive and some destructive) that exist in nearly everyone. Great traders are not born with that skill; it is something that is developed. We all are constantly growing and learning on our journey, and I've developed the Trader's Hierarchy to illustrate the path traders follow to truly activate their potential.

My Trader's Hierarchy is heavily influenced by Maslow's hierarchy of needs. In case you don't remember, Maslow observed that people can't focus on self-fulfillment and self-actualization without having first satisfied basic needs such as food and shelter. Likewise, I believe you cannot become a great trader unless you first dare to dream that you can be one, and then start making smart money decisions. The three phases of the Trader's Hierarchy are Dream It, Do It, and Live It.

Phase 1: Dream It

Most people are attracted to trading because of the legendary stories of wealth and success that we have all heard about from the titans of Wall Street. Every year, the top 10 fund managers make billions of dollars in fees and profits—just by doing their job—which is more than nearly any other profession on Earth. No wonder so many people are attracted to this business. Even for those who don't desire to become billionaires, the financial freedom symbolized by even a fraction of that wealth is a lofty dream.

Most people can only dream of finding success in the market. The dreamer only looks longingly at the prize—like a child gazing through the window display at a toy store—but they make no serious practical plans for reaching their potential. The trader stuck in the dream phase often avoids reality, dismisses facts, statistics, curses their bad luck, and blames others for their failures: this is how most people start their journey on Wall Street, and it is where most people get stuck.

Inevitably, reality hits, and the dreamer starts losing real money. Each subsequent blow causes emotional wounds. *What happened to the dream of easy money on Wall Street? This can't be happening to me! I'm too smart for this not to work!* Instead of taking the time to push through and learn the skills necessary to make it (which is painful in the short-term but pleasurable in the long-term) they look for an easy way out.

The good news is that trading is a skill that you can learn. Over time, as you get more experience with risking your money, you will find that being able to consistently take money out of the market is not an easy feat, and you'll either quit or you'll get serious about putting in the work required to build the smart money mindset.

Phase 2: Do It

There is no substitute for action. A trader trades. You've got to get your hands dirty and put real money on the line and become comfortable with taking risks. Everything I told you about paper trading is just not the same as real trading. I tell people to paper trade so they don't lose their money while they are establishing a feel for the market, but paper trading cannot simulate the emotions and anxiety that can be associated with trading with real money.

If you can remember every lesson I've tried to convey in this book, great—but it's not enough. There is a huge difference between knowing what to do and actually doing it. This phenomenon plagues most people on Wall Street. In today's world, anyone can learn the basics of trading and investing. Learning the basics is easy, but consistently making money in the market is hard.

After years of reading all the classic books about fundamental and technical analysis and working with countless people (both professionals and amateurs), I realized first-hand that there was a large unspokengap between what was being taught and what was being practiced. After learning the basics, most people know what to do, but very few people know how to do it. Knowing how to do it requires a great deal of discipline that most people simply do not have. In order to get to the next phase, you must not just know what to do—you must do it consistently.

At the beginning of this phase, you'll be working to find your winning approach. You'll learn how to take a loss in stride. You'll learn how to manage risk, cut your losers, and let your winners fly. Once you find a winning approach, the key is to learn how to implement it effectively in all market environments. The people who are able to move from the Dream It phase to the Do It phase envision their success, believe it, create a plan, and then relentlessly execute that plan.

Phase 3: Live It

Here's the funny thing about success: you don't always know when you've accomplished it. Success comes when you learn how to set a goal, build a plan and execute it, and then ultimately realize your goal. More specifically, success comes when you're able to do this over and over, consistently and reliably. One win doesn't make you a great trader. It takes lots of wins over time to become a great trader, but here's the catch: there is no finish line. No one tells you when you've won. You'll just look back one day, see what you've accomplished, and realize that you're living the dream.

Here's the crazy thing: some people freak out at this phase because they cannot believe what they've accomplished. They suffer from imposter syndrome, which means they feel like they don't deserve the success they have achieved. It's akin to a kid who has been trying to learn how to ride a bike; she's fallen dozens of times; she's become accustomed to her parent's hand helping her balance the seat; but at some point, she looks around and discovers the hand is gone and she's riding on her own—and the surprise of it all makes her crash. When I first started making consistent gains in the stock market, I admitted to select friends and family that I couldn't believe it, and then I crashed, too. I started with no money and in my late twenties I was making $10,000 a week trading and I literally couldn't believe it. So I subconsciously sabotaged myself, lost all my money, and started from scratch, again.

Remember, the skills necessary to consistently make money on Wall Street have very little to do with your IQ or formal education. In fact, the only requisite to being successful on Wall Street is the ability to do the right thing—make smart, objective, and unemotional decisions (especially when you are under pressure) over and over again.

I call this final stage the "Live It" phase because success is not a result; it is a habit. If someone is able to lose 50 pounds through diet and exercise, they can't just claim victory and go back to their old ways of eating junk food and never exercising. They have to maintain the discipline that allowed them to reach their goal to claim success. They have to incorporate it into their lifestyle. It is very easy to get distracted and fall off the horse (bike). Staying in the Dream It phase is done one day at a time. The good news is that if you fall out, you can always work your way back in.

SEVEN TRADING PERSONALITIES

Here's another helpful nugget of wisdom that will help you accelerate your journey to becoming a walking, talking, money machine. After studying uber-successful traders and analyzing my own growth and the evolution of countless others, I've identified several different trading personalities. Many of these common personalities represent behaviors that make it difficult to become successful in the market. As you develop your style and establish your discipline as a trader, knowing where others fail can keep you on the path to success.

The Scaredy Cat: Fear-Based Trader

Scaredy Cats are timid and constantly operating from a position of fear. They do not have any confidence in anything they do and they are almost always afraid. They do not believe in themselves, they do not believe in their strategy, they do not understand that losing money is an unavoidable part of the process, and they are emotionally traumatized by all the losses they have encountered over the years. To the untrained mind, losing money is painful. To the trained mind, it is inevitable. If you fear losses, it means you still have an emotional attachment to your money. It likely also means that you're not properly mitigating your risk. If you find yourself in this position, check your stop orders, make sure you have a clear understanding of what your risk is, and if you feel uncomfortable with how much you have at play in the market, convert some of your assets into cash until you feel more confident. See a therapist, find out what the root issue is, and address it. It usually stems from your relationship with money or something from your childhood. The good news is that once you find the issue, you can resolve it just by changing your outlook.

The Cowboy: Aggressive and Fails

Cowboys are superaggressive and usually end up blowing up and going bankrupt. You can only have so many high-noon showdowns before your luck runs out and someone gets the draw on you. The Cowboy does not acknowledge risk; rather is focused on a quick win. They get bulled up (Wall Street parlance for overconfident) over an idea and are more than happy to go "all-in" or even borrow money (go on margin) to accumulate their position. When Cowboys lose, they lose big. The solution here is simple: respect risk. Never risk too much money on one idea—no matter how excited you are about it. Remember, if you lose 20% of your portfolio on one idea, you need a 25% gain to break even. If you lose half your portfolio, you'll need to double your money to get back to square one.

Curb your enthusiasm before entering a trade. I'm a huge fan of Larry David and his show *Curb Your Enthusiasm*. In fact, my wife calls me the Larry David of finance—for many reasons! I am bringing this up because whenever you feel happy in a winning trade or pull out the calculator to figure out how much money you are going to make, that is usually the time to exit because the trade is about to go against you. I am reminded of a great line from Nicolas Cage's movie *Lord of War*. At the climax of his success (before he fell), he said, "I suffered the curse of invincibility." Whenever you feel like you are invincible, that's normally when things reverse. I recommend that you stay in a positive state, but separate your emotions from your trading. Treat every trade evenly. When you remove your emotions from the decision-making process it increases your long-term odds of success.

The Professor: Paralysis by Analysis

The Professor loves to analyze, read, and formulate fancy opinions (some of which are smart; others, not so much), but when push comes to shove, they can't pull the trigger and actually trade. You can be the smartest guy in the world, but if you can't place trades when the pressure is on, your "intelligence" is worth zero dollars in the market and that is not good. If you think you are the Professor, consider placing all your orders as stop orders, and do that at night or on the weekend when the market is closed—then walk away and let the market handle the rest. If a stock is trading at $95 and you want to buy it if it goes above $97, all you have to do is place a buy stop at $97 and find something—anything—to take your mind off of it. If your order is filled, then you can place a protective sell stop below the market to exit at any price you want.

You can even enter both orders at the same time and make the protective sell stop a contingent order—meaning it is only activated if your buy stop is triggered. Another solution here is to hire someone to manage your money for you or help you execute your trades. Almost all the big shops have an army of PhDs who come up with brilliant ideas and an army of traders who then execute those trades. Anyone can learn how to do both of these, but be cognizant of the fact that they are two completely separate skill sets that you need to acquire.

The Machine Gun: Rapid-Fire Trader

The Machine Gun loves to trade and compulsively makes trades in a manic fashion all day, every day. Machine Guns rarely makes good trades, and they certainly have a hard time letting their winners fly. They are addicted to the rush they get from trading, so they buy and sell all day long. I have yet to meet someone who can trade like this and consistently make money. Instead, this person is usually in a negative (usually angry) state and trades in a borderline zombie or extremely manic fashion. While it is happening, they are almost unaware of their actions. If you find yourself making machine-gun-like rapid-fire trades, and if you get a thrill from trading, the solution is to stop. Right now. Convert to cash, step away, and spend some time finding your way back to the smart money mindset. The market will be there when you're ready to trade responsibly. It's hard enough to consistently take money out of the market; there is no need for you to make it harder by being sloppy and trading like a lunatic.

The Artist: Lost Touch with Reality

The Artist is much too creative and likes to think way out in the fifth dimension about crazy unrealistic "what-if" probabilities that will most likely never materialize. The Artist may subscribe to one or more conspiracy theories. Perhaps they believe in a "plunge protection team" that will never let the market fall (even though the market has experienced numerous extreme bear markets in the past) or they believe that the market is rigged or out to get them. Do some people have an edge in the market? Absolutely, but that doesn't mean you can't develop your own edge—and *win*! The market is so complicated (remember our discussion on chaos theory) that no one person fully understands every single factor that impacts it. The good news is that you don't have to! This is why I focus on the "what" (is happening) and not the "why" (it is happening). Price is primary, everything else is secondary. If you find yourself drifting out into the fifth dimension, stop, come back down to Earth, and try to make objective, unemotional decisions based on the facts that are in front of you.

The Passive Trader: Watching from the Sidelines

The Passive Trader watches the stock market from the sidelines. Perhaps they've taken one too many hits playing the game. The pain from past losses becomes too great to bear. So, instead of taking a position, they do nothing and just stand and watch on the sidelines. Now, to be clear, it's okay, at times, to exercise patience and be on the sidelines, but you should not reside there; otherwise, you will not make money. Understand that you're going to get hit again and get back in the game anyway. You can start slow; trade one share until you build your confidence back and are comfortable risking more. After some time passes and you start seeing gains, you'll remember that success is on the other side of pain, and you can start to slowly increase your stake until you are trading at your previous level. If you never get comfortable, that is okay; find a good investment advisor and ride the Great American Tailwind.

The Smart Money Trader

Smart Money Traders have learned how to consistently take money out of the market. They understand how to balance risk and reward. They practice defense first. They take care of their mind, spirit, and body. They are committed to always doing the right thing, to always making objective, unemotional decisions based on a market-proven strategy, and bringing out the smart money superhero inside of them. They're not daunted by temporary drawbacks. They know that profits are a function of time. I'm hoping you're getting this by now. . . .

The smart money understands, practices, and embodies both the spirit and the law of opulence. The smart money is happy and optimistic. They operate in a state of gratitude. They give attention, they help others, they have amazing relationships with everything and everyone around them. They are extremely bullish (optimistic) about their future. They stay focused and know how to filter out the noise and distractions. They are concerned only with information that helps them work toward their goals and remain in a positive state.

Smart money is purpose-driven. They live their lives deliberately. They enjoy serving the greater good and helping others. They know there is more than enough to go around and give generously. They know what they want, and they know how to get it. Life happens for them, not to them.

The smart money stays flexible and they are prepared to adapt to new circumstances; they are willing to change their strategy when the facts change. They focus on the moment but always have a plan for the future. Dumb money focuses on the past and worries about the future.

Smart money makes solutions, not excuses. The dumb money focuses on problems. The smart money stays focused on the goal and is constantly hunting for the next win. The smart money shares knowledge and celebrates the success of others. They give more than they take.

Smart money knows how to think accurately and speak clearly. They make rational, not emotional, decisions. They know how to motivate themselves and others, and they take bold action when action is required. They are brave, take calculated risks, and make smart decisions.

Smart money is humble, respects others, loves to learn, and always tries to do the right thing.

A smart money trader is a champion and lives like a champion. Perhaps the person I described here seems too good to be true. Perhaps you cannot believe such a person exists. That person does exist. That person exists inside of you right now. That person just needs a path to shine. Perhaps the right way to say it is that smart money strives to have all these traits. Smart money works to demonstrate these characteristics. Success isn't a finish line; it's a road we walk. We might stray from the path from time to time, but hopefully, we can always find our way back.

PARTING THOUGHTS

We've explored a lot of topics in this book, but we encountered a number of themes that kept popping up. As you begin your journey, here are some parting thoughts to help you remember what you've learned so far.

Always Respect Risk

Respecting risk is the first rule of trading. This is a great quote that reiterates this powerful concept:

> *Rule No.1: Never lose money.*
> *Rule No. 2: Never forget rule No. 1.*
>
> —Warren Buffett

Proper risk management is the most important element for finding success in the markets. Regardless of your investment approach, the size of your account, or what markets you trade, in the end, every investor and every trader is in the business of managing risk. The only way you can (legally) make money in this business is to risk your capital, so your entire job boils down to managing the relationship between risk and your expected reward.

Your job is to manage your risk better than anyone else. If you master that one facet of trading, you will have a huge advantage over 99% of your competition. Successful speculators know how to always define their risk.

Warren Buffett also talked about focusing on the things that could hurt you and eliminating them. It's helpful to ask yourself, what can go wrong? Then eliminate those things. If you can't do that, mitigate the risk as much as possible.

In the market, never risk more than you are comfortable losing, and always know that any handful of trades does not define you. The biggest and most successful funds in the world do not risk more than 1% of their portfolio per idea (and most risk less than that). Why? because you will lose more often than you win. The trick is to keep your losses small and let your winners fly.

Always Look Forward

Markets look forward, economic and earnings data look backward. Markets are a forward-looking mechanism. If you go back and study history, you will see that markets top out and bottom before major economic events. There are countless examples. A slew of housing stocks topped out in 2005 and began falling over the next few years. The housing market topped out a few years later and crashed in 2008. Then in late 2011, housing stocks bottomed (I presented this bullish case on CNBC in mid-2012), and that was followed by a huge recovery in the housing market that lasted years. Tech stocks topped out in 2000 and plunged before bottoming in October 2002. Then they started to rally and really blasted off in 2003, which was followed by a huge credit and housing boom from 2002 to 2007. These are just a few examples, but the list goes on and on.

Prepare for the worst; expect the best. Since no one knows what is going to happen at any point in the future, all we can do is make the best decision with the information that we have at any particular time and adjust as needed when the facts change. If we always prepare for the worst we will be protected and be there to prosper when the sun inevitably shines in our direction. I wake up every day saying that today is going to be a great day.

I really mean it but, unfortunately, life is not always fun and games. So when life, or the market, gaps down, learn to be prepared so you can react rationally to whatever hiccups are thrown your way.

Don't Force It

You only need a handful of really good decisions each year to create life-changing wealth. Great trades do not show up every day. Billionaire hedge fund manager David Tepper uses the term "trading windows," which means we only get a few good periods each year to trade and the rest of the time the market is choppy (in most years). I have yet to see someone consistently make *great* decisions when they are really angry or super-frustrated. Pay attention to your state. Change your state if needed to get in a powerful state when you are trading, and if and when something negative happens, control how you react to it. Don't let "it" control you.

It is also important to keep in mind that profits are a function of time. Timing and patience are necessary components of being successful in the market (and in life). Take time to understand how the market trends, and learn to "listen" to the market by getting and staying in harmony with the trend. If something is not working, take the cue and get out of the way. Wait for a better environment. Remember, choppy periods happen in the market and you do not always have to be trading. Take time off when things are not working. Keep building your watchlists and observe the market from afar; you don't have to be actively trading when the market is not rewarding your actions. Be patient and don't force it. Remember, always keep your losses small and never fight the tape.

Avoid Tickicitis

Another helpful tactic to remember is to create your plan, then step back and trade your plan. Plan your trades when the market is closed. Then trade your plan when the market is open. Some people stare at the screen all day and frantically follow every tick. That approach doesn't work for me because it is overkill and prevents me from seeing the forest because all I'm looking at are the leaves on the trees (the leaves are intraday action, the trees are the daily activities, and the forest can be seen on a weekly, monthly, quarterly, or annual basis). If you stare at the screen all day you will make emotional, not rational, decisions. You will watch your balance move up and down with every tick, and you will start to make emotional decisions and not be able to trade your plan. Choose a time frame for monitoring the market and making trades that works for you.

I work best on a weekly and monthly basis. Some people work daily, others work quarterly or annually. Whatever time frame you choose to work with, stick with it; otherwise, you'll start making unforced errors. Another thing to keep in mind is to be prepared for all possible scenarios. Don't be stunned when a stock moves up or down in a very big way. How many times have you said, "I can't believe that just happened"? Well, believe it. Take action. Because it did just happen and move on. Find your next winner.

Anticipate, Don't Predict

There are only three ways any asset can move: up, down, or sideways. People have an innate desire to know the future, but the future is unknown and no one in the history of the world has been able to accurately and consistently predict it. I've learned to anticipate the future instead of predicting it. Expect success and protect yourself and learn from the inevitable setbacks that occur.

This way you can make objective, unemotional trading decisions and you can set your order(s) and walk away knowing that your stops are in place and your risk is properly mitigated. Prediction is based on hope. Anticipation implies preparation, and I'm reminded of the old adage "If you don't prepare to win, you are preparing to lose."

Profits Are a Function of Time

Know that profits are a function of time. This is true even if you are a high-frequency trader. Remember, Jesse Livermore said, "The big money is made by sitting." That means that once you sink your teeth into a good trend, sit back and let it grow! Do your best to be patient with your winners, not your losers. Most people do the opposite. This doesn't mean that you have to buy and hope (I mean buy and hold), just that your plan should have an element that forces you out of losers and allows you to ride your winners. So many new traders, when they make a little profit on a trade, freak out and sell early so they can capture the gain, fearing the stock might go back down. If you don't let your winners win, you won't be able to afford your inevitable losing trades.

Date Your Positions, Don't Marry Them

The smart money is dispassionate about the assets they trade. If you fall in love with an idea, you'll end up making irrational trading decisions. When a position goes south, it's important that you get out as soon as the predetermined stop level is hit. If you hang on to an asset out of some irrational loyalty, it could undo your entire trading strategy. Let your losers go and let the winners fly. Remember the old Wall Street adage, "Be patient with winners, not your losers." My friend Jim Roppel likes to say, "give your stocks every chance in the world to succeed. Don't get stopped out on every minor wiggle and jiggle." What he means is to be very patient with your winners, expect they are going to pull back (wiggle and jiggle), and don't get freaked out, panic, and prematurely sell when they do pull back. As long as the stock is acting well, you want to own it through four to six strong quarters, if not longer. Remember what Jesse Livermore said 100 years ago about the big money being made by "sitting." Once you sink your teeth into a monster stock, get out of your own way. Learn to sit and you will enjoy amazing success in this business.

Stay Focused and Avoid Style Drift

Style drift occurs when someone is constantly changing their investment style. Remember, there are no hard rules for trading. There is nothing you can do that will guarantee a trade to be a winner or a loser. You can stack the odds in your favor but, by definition, every trader will experience winning trades and losing trades.

The natural inclination for most people, including legendary traders, is to bail on their system during drawdowns (losing periods). The best traders are the ones who do their homework in advance, develop a set of rules with a positive expectancy (discretionary and/or quant), and then loyally follow their system—during good times and bad.

If you give up on your system during bad times you will never succeed and will always be searching for the "holy grail"—a perfect system that simply doesn't exist. Remember, losing is inevitable; successful traders incorporate this fact into their process and follow their system, even during drawdowns.

Now, if something happens that completely changes the way your rules perform, then clearly you should leave your system and adopt a new one. Do not blindly follow a system just because you believe it works—or you think other people are using it and making money. That could just be the product of good marketing on behalf of the person who invented that so-called system. Avoid style drift when possible, but also make sure you can make money with the system you are using. Once you find a winning system, winning is not as much about the system as it is about your ability to follow it.

Reduce Your Unforced Errors

Another very helpful tactic to develop is to reduce the number of unforced errors you make at any given time. An unforced error is defined as "a mistake that is attributed to one's own failure rather than to the skill or effort of one's opponent." In professional tennis (another performance-based business), they literally count the number of unforced errors each player makes in every match.

Simple logic should tell you that the players with the lowest number of unforced errors do much better than the players who are constantly putting up unforced errors. The same is true for any performance-based business. Think about how much better you will perform if you can reduce the number of mistakes you make at any given time. Another advantage is that doing this gives you an edge over your competition, because most people think about all the positive actions needed to be successful, when in fact, after you reach a certain point, it is mostly from what we don't do that really matters. Put simply, stop doing dumb stuff! You can improve your entire life by stopping your bad habits, thoughts, and actions.

Take Responsibility for Everything

A very important part of being successful in life (and in markets) is to take responsibility for everything. It's a universal truth that anyone who takes responsibility for their life tends to live a better life than people who don't. Just because you take responsibility does not mean you will not encounter problems; it just means that you will be stronger and have a much better chance to be fulfilled and happy. This is especially true in markets. The market is not out to get you, in fact, it does not even know you. Avoid the urge to take things personally or play the victim. Be humble and take responsibility.

Focus on the What, Not the Why

The news doesn't matter; what matters is how the market reacts to the news. I learned to trade based on what I see happening in the market rather than why I think the market is behaving in a certain way. Price action is front and center to my approach. The only thing that matters in the market is the difference between what you paid for an asset and what you sell it for. My credo is: always keep your losses small and never argue with the tape. It's very easy to get caught up in your head about why something is happening but it's only a distraction from what's actually happening.

Live in the Now and Always Look Forward

The market is a forward-looking apparatus. The current price of an asset is based on expectations for the future. All your profits (and losses) in the market will be realized in the future. Your past trades do not matter and should not influence your current and future decisions. It's much easier said than done, but take some time to let go of that emotional (negative) baggage and view every trade as a brand-new trade.

Moreover, stock charts are extremely powerful and will help you identify technical patterns that can inform your decision-making, but stock charts, economic forecasts, and earnings data are all backward-looking indicators and the market looks forward. Most people do not understand that reality and are stuck looking backward, not forward.

You can't drive your car on the highway while looking in the rearview mirror; it's worth a glance every now and again, but keep your eyes on the road, looking forward. If you get into a car accident, does that mean you will never drive again? No! You learn from it. You deal with it. You let some time pass, then you get back in the driver's seat and drive again. The same is true with losing trades and future trades. Control them and learn from them; otherwise, they will control you.

Create and Tell a New Empowering Story

Become the hero in your own story. Anyone who is willing to put in the work can learn to be a successful trader in the market. Nobody is born a great trader; people learn how to become great traders. There are child prodigies with natural-born talents who play chess or piano like a virtuoso, but I've yet to meet an eight-year-old who can consistently beat the market. As you learn to become a trader, you can adopt the smart money characteristics that define what makes a good trader. You have the power to rise above your own human nature, to become awake, and to take charge of your life. Your future is your story to create, live, and tell. Create an empowering and very powerful story that you are proud of. Take control. Live life to the fullest!

You are not the same person you were in the past. We have acknowledged that everyone begins life in the dumb money circle. That's not you anymore; you don't have to be "trapped" in the same old story you told yourself as a kid. Break through those mental walls, become your own smart money superhero, and write a new narrative.

Keep It Simple

The military has a saying: Keep It Simple, Stupid. People have a remarkable ability to complicate things. From the very beginning of this book, I've stressed that success in the markets is simple but it is not easy. Just like doing sit-ups is simple, succeeding is not easy for the untrained mind. The beauty is that anyone can become wildly successful in this business if they follow this simple recipe: make rational (not emotional) decisions, always respect risk, keep your losses small, and let your winners fly.

I've given you a relatively simple strategy (my A.M.P.D. investment system) to explore and incorporate into your own trading plan. Your own human nature will do whatever it can to make things more complicated than they need to be. The key to mastering the markets is learning to master yourself. There are only three decisions to make as a trader: buy, sell, or hold. Find a healthy mindset, focus only on the facts that matter, ignore the dumb money beast inside of you (and all around you—other people's lousy opinions), and learn to make objective, unemotional fact-based decisions on the information available to you. Always ask yourself: Is this smart?

The Market Is Speaking—Are You Listening?

Now that you understand all this, it is time for you to start listening to the market. Learn how to understand stock charts, watch for patterns, study price and volume, study important inflection points, ask yourself what emotions are being expressed at this time (if the stock is up big or down big) and what the dumb money is thinking, feeling, and doing right now, and really get a good honest feeling for how the market behaves.

Become acquainted with the quality of the market—its taste, its color, its temperature. Learn how it moves. Discover trendlines. Watch resistance and support work to create recognizable patterns on charts. As a trader, your job now is to look for great ideas ("smart money setups," as I call them), opportunities—publicly traded assets that are poised to move (hopefully in your direction) that give you asymmetric returns (risk 1 to make 10, 20, or 100). Don't chase a stock. If you missed it, that's okay, move on. Ask yourself whether you are entering early or late to the trend. Do you have a clear edge? Are you making emotional decisions or rational ones? Are you following your plan? What is the smart money doing and thinking right now and what is the dumb money doing and thinking right now?

If you need some help getting started, go out and get it! Time is your most valuable asset and information is your most valuable commodity. The largest firms on Wall Street pay tens of millions of dollars for good ideas and market research. They have an army of PhDs and Ivy League grads who have one job: research the market and find actionable ideas. You should too! There are a host of research services that publish market data designed to showcase actionable ideas. I've already told you about my service: FindLeadingStocks .com, and I'd be happy for you to come and join us. Or find someone else who suits your style. However you do it, listen to the market, learn its rhythms, and follow its lead.

If I can do it, you can do it! Trust me, I've created this approach and purposely made it so simple anyone can follow it and change their life!

Find your smart money superhero, be brave, do the right thing. I want you to get to the point where you can share your knowledge and smart money mental outlook with others. I want you to become a smart money ambassador. Believe in yourself.

You can do it!

Focus on what matters. Love life. Live life to the fullest.

Remember, money is a by-product of your actions. Go out there, have fun, create amazing relationships with people, and create a beautiful future for yourself and your loved ones. There's nothing stopping you but your former self. Bring out your smart money superhero.

Remember, let your winners run, always keep your losses small, and never fight the tape.

To your success!

Adam Sarhan

Epilogue: It's Time to Become Rich

You know now that beating the market is an elite endeavor. Many try; few succeed. But we've discovered that success in the market is 99% psychology and 1% mechanics. That means that if you can master your mental state, slay the dumb money beast, become a smart money superhero, and learn to make rational, unemotional decisions, then you are on your way to becoming a successful trader.

Now it's time to be honest with yourself. If you haven't mastered your mental state and you still find yourself making decisions based on fear, or greed, or some other emotion, and if you know you haven't broken through your mental walls—then, please, don't start trading with big money yet. Start small or start with a paper trading account. Start reading charts, studying how price behaves, build a sense of the quality of the market, find opportunities, and test your ideas. Start applying the smart money lessons to the rest of your life. Focus on your priorities. Build your relationships. Invest and save as much capital as you can. The market will wait for you. It will be there when you're ready.

After you've set aside your rainy day fund (enough money to make you feel safe, so you are trading from a position of strength, not weakness), you balanced your life, you feel that you're in control of your psychology, and you've developed a proper risk-versus-reward trading strategy that works in multiple market states over time—then you'll be ready to start making your first serious trades as a speculator. To get you started, here's "Adam's Quick Trading Guide" to refresh you on the nuts and bolts of trading.

ADAM'S QUICK TRADING GUIDE

Remember, try to keep things super simple. At the very basic level, there are three key parts to every trade:

1. When you enter
2. When you exit
3. How much you risk

Once you've identified an opportunity and decided to take a risk, these are the only three variables that matter. Everything else is noise. Placing a trade is known as "executing a trade" and when your order is filled your broker will say you are "filled." Many people use digital trading apps to buy and sell from their phones; it's amazing technology, but it is nice to develop a relationship with a broker(s) you can trust as you start to execute bigger and bigger trades.

Of course, the goal of every trade should be the same: exit with a profit. But we have learned that most trades lose money, and that's okay—providing you keep your losses small and let your winners run.

Before you pull the trigger and execute a trade, here are some questions you should ask yourself:

1. *What am I buying?* Do you have a solid understanding of the type of asset you are putting your money into?
2. *Is this the very best idea I can find?* (If not, wait and don't force it.) Put your money where it can get the best return on investment.
3. *Am I buying early or late?* Is the market/stock extended? If you've already missed the proper entry point, wait for the next opportunity.
4. *What is my edge?* If you act right now, will you have an advantage over other investors? What do you see that they don't?
5. *What is the dumb money thinking/doing right now?* It's often best to do the opposite.
6. *What is the smart money thinking/doing right now?* Don't blindly follow market gurus; make sure any move you make fits your strategy. Make sure you are buying right after a digestion period is over in a pre-existing or new trend.
7. *Am I aligned with the market (long in an uptrend, short in a downtrend)?* Stay in harmony with the market and never fight the tape!

8. *Is this an easy (comfortable) or hard (uncomfortable) trade?* The market is counterintuitive and that means making the right choice at the right time can feel scary.

9. *What is the Fed doing and how will that impact my trade?* For technical traders, price is primary, but it's foolish to ignore obvious outside forces that could affect a stock's price in the near future.

10. *Would Adam place this trade? If not, why?* My trading strategy doesn't have to be your trading strategy, but now that you (hopefully) understand how my strategy works, feel free to use it as a litmus test. If you couldn't articulate to me why the trade would fit your strategy, maybe you haven't thought it all the way through.

ENTRIES AND EXITS: BUY AND SELL GUIDELINES

Keep your entries and exits simple. I am going to repeat this point because it is so important: keep things simple. People tend to complicate things they don't understand. It makes them feel smarter and gives them comfort but often hurts their performance.

After sitting down with billionaire investors and reading just about every successful investor/trader's story, I've learned that the all-stars keep things simple. Peter Lynch and Warren Buffett buy undervalued companies and hold them for a very long-time.

Legendary investor William O'Neil loves to buy disruptive growth stocks that enjoy monstrous sales and earnings growth, that are breaking out of sound digestion areas (a.k.a. bases) on massive volume, and that have very strong relative strength. Carl Icahn loves buying undervalued stocks and he loves to be an activist investor and turn a company around. He fixes their board and adds value in other strategic ways. Wilbur Ross and David Tepper love investing in distressed assets.

John Templeton started his investment firm during the depression and became famous by investing during "the point of maximum pessimism."

Others, such as George Soros, Paul Tudor Jones, and Ray Dalio, made their fortunes from understanding the inputs that occur before the market moves and making prescient macro calls. The one thing all these people have in common: their investment thesis is simple and can be easily described in one sentence. Make yours simple. Here's my one-sentence trading strategy: enter early and ride trends up and down. In bull markets, buy the bounce after the dip and in bear markets short the decline after the bounce.

BUY THE BOUNCE AFTER THE DIP

Here is my three-step method for buying the bounce after the dip. Remember in Chapter 5, I showed you some common chart patterns for stocks that may be ready to breakout, and I showed you how to recognize trendlines and how to identify areas of support and resistance. A classic breakout strategy suggests buying after a stock's price goes above resistance, but I told you my problem with that is that most breakouts fail, and you're likely to get stopped out for a loss. As a result, many people are told to buy the dip, but the problem with this logic is that you never know how deep the dip will go before it rebounds (if it ever does). The stock could plummet below support and take you down with it if you took a long position. The dip you are buying could be the end of the bull run and could be the beginning of a bear market or a huge decline. Why would you just arbitrarily buy the dip? I don't worry about buying at the bottom and selling at the top; instead, I try to capture the bulk of a move. To do this, I identify an early entry point for a possible breakout and buy after the dip, after the price has bounced off of support.

The first step is to go hunting and look for ideal setups. The easiest way for most people to do this is to look for and identify leading stocks (find stocks that are trading at or near a 52-week high and/or are outperforming the S&P 500 or their industry peers that show strong relative strength and in digestion areas). This takes time and practice. Remember, you'll have to develop a feel for how the market moves. It has an indescribable quality like the color red or the taste of chocolate. You've really got to commit time to reading stock charts and tracking your success at identifying breakout setups. Do the work. You will win.

Step 2 is to wait and look for these stocks to pull back and bounce off an important inflection point/area of support (a prior chart high, simple 50-day moving average line, trendline, or some other important area of logical support). Let me stop here for a minute and talk about an extremely important element successful people have learned to do: exercise patience. Patience is an extremely important and often underused virtue on Wall Street. Most unsuccessful people want instant results and are always chasing the last hot thing (looking backward at what has already happened). Remember, the market is a forward-looking mechanism. Also, successful people know that profits are a function of time and have learned how to rewire their brains to resist the urge to buy or the urge for constant action, and instead, they can wait for the ideal setup to emerge before risking their money. If you've ever been fishing, you know that if you yank the rod the moment you feel a nibble, you can rip the hook right out of the fish's mouth; you have to wait to let the hook set before you reel the fish in. If you've ever done it, you know there's a certain quality to knowing when to act, and that is hard to describe but difficult to forget once you know it.

Step 3 is to step in and buy the bounce after the dip. Once you identify your targets and wait for the stock to pull in to support, then you can be prepared and anticipate a bounce off support. There are many ways to do this, but one easy one is to draw trendlines by simply connecting prior highs on a chart. Trendlines can be drawn on just about any time frame but the key here is to draw a downward-sloping trendline and buy the stock as it moves above the downtrend line. Not only will this method allow you to buy the bounce after the dip, it will also give you a clear low-risk (that is key) entry and exit point—because once you get in, you can place a protective stop (exit) just below support and usually only risk low single-digit percent change from entry on that position. If or when the uptrend resumes (the ideal scenario), and your position becomes profitable, you can move the stop to breakeven and then keep moving it higher to lock in gains as the uptrend resumes. When done properly, this method will put serious points on the board for you. In bear markets, you can reverse this process and short failed rallies in a downtrend.

EXITS: BUY AND SELL GUIDELINES

There are only three scenarios for every exit:

1. Exit for a gain
2. Exit for a loss
3. Exit for breakeven

That's it. There is no other possible scenario. Most people get so wrapped up in deciding when to enter a trade that they forget all about where they're going to exit. Successful traders and investors know that every great stock eventually needs to be sold. Otherwise, it will be dead money for years (if not decades) and the opportunity cost of owning a stock that hasn't moved for decades is enormous. Now let's analyze the three scenarios.

Scenario 1: Exit for Gain

If you are long (you own the stock), you will be profitable if you exit above your entry price. The opposite is true when you short a stock (you profit when the stock falls). For my approach, I want to give the stock the benefit of the doubt as long as it is acting well and paying me to do so (meaning, my position is profitable). Remember the old Wall Street adage: stocks take the stairs up and the elevator down. So I want to hold the stock as long as it is trading and acting well. What I mean by that is I look at how the stock is trading on the chart as it settles into a new pattern after a breakout, and I watch to see how it behaves. Does it respect support? If so, where is near-term support? Where would I want to exit to lock in a decent gain? Where will the stock experience technical damage? Do I want to own the stock if it falls below support or a certain price? Then, once I define support, I place my sell stop just below that level. A few areas of support are: lows of the current base (trading range), upward trendline(s), moving average(s), prior chart highs, or recent weekly lows, just to name a few. The opposite is true when I am short: I exit above resistance (highs of current trading range, downward trendlines, prior weekly lows, or recent weekly highs). By placing sell stop orders, I'm deciding on my exit points in advance based upon my risk tolerance. When I exit a position, it's almost always because the market triggered my stop order. I rarely actively "decide" to sell. Selling is a decision I make in advance.

Scenario 2: Exit for Breakeven

If I own a stock for a few weeks and it is not moving, and other areas of the market are moving, I will likely choke my position and raise my exit to breakeven. This way the market will force my hand and free up that capital so I can make other trades that have a better chance of profiting. Remember, there is an opportunity cost to having your money parked in a position. If that money could be making more profit in a different position, you're missing out on that opportunity. The other scenario is that when my position is up over 5%, I will raise my exit to breakeven (most of the time). I really don't like to lose, and the more "wins" or breakeven I have, the better. If you position your sell stop too close to support, you risk getting "sucker stopped" if the stock price experiences a blip downward before continuing an upward trend.

Scenario 3: Exit for a Loss

As previously mentioned, before I enter a position, I know where I am going to exit if I turn out to be wrong. This way I know exactly how much of my portfolio I am going to lose on a losing trade, allowing me tight controls for managing my risk. I've told you a number of times that most trades fail, and so in order to be profitable, you have to be strict about sticking to your risk-managed stops. When it comes to limiting your risk and bailing out of a position, there are two things to consider:

1. How much of your portfolio you are willing to risk per idea (from entry to exit). Typically, I don't lose more than 1% of my portfolio on any given idea (long or short) from entry to exit, and many big institutions risk less than that.

2. What percentage below your entry price you are going to exit, if you are wrong. As you know, I have a very low tolerance for losing money. If I enter right, I can set a relatively close stop below support, and exit for a loss of under 5%. The lowest I'm willing to go is 10% below my entry price. Even if 10% is less than my 1% portfolio risk tolerance, I know that to recover from a 10% loss, I need the stock to make an 11.8% gain—which essentially means I'll have to beat the market just to get back to even. Why would I try to make that money back by sticking with a loser? I'm better off cashing out and looking for a better idea.

DRAWDOWNS

This lovely word describes a period when your portfolio loses value. Nobody likes losing money but it is inevitable, and even the best traders in the world experience drawdowns. The key to survival on Wall Street is how to manage a drawdown. Most novice traders close their eyes, ignore reality, and they just pretend the drawdown is a fluke. It's the wrong approach.

Their default setting is to make up excuses or try to justify their drawdown and blame outside forces and do everything but the one thing that is needed—and that is to take full responsibility for what happens to them. Additionally, they also enter the negative spiral that consumes almost every novice trader. They begin with a mistaken belief regarding what the market should do, they take action, they lose money, and then they lose confidence and enter a negative state. This failure loop continues with a few brief (usually minor) wins along the way.

Here's how to avoid the death spiral: First, remember, drawdowns are inevitable so instead of entering a negative state, learn to expect them and stay positive. Second, you may want to reduce the risk you are taking as you enter a drawdown. For example, instead of risking 1% of your portfolio per trade, you may want to risk 0.75%, and if the drawdown continues you may want to reduce your risk to 0.50%, or down to 0.25%, until you can get back on track. There are no set rules for how and when to reduce your trading level; you have to figure out what works best for you. The key is to learn how to manage these inevitable drawdowns (back off, trade less, take smaller positions), until the drawdown ends.

Once again, doing the opposite of what feels natural to you is paramount to getting ahead in the market. Most unsuccessful people cringe when they are in a drawdown and pull their money out. Once again (I'm sure you've noticed a common theme by now), successful investors do the exact opposite and step in to buy the drawdown (meaning they add money to the strategy when it is temporarily down, hopefully buying stocks poised to rebound). The key is not to increase your risk tolerance because there's no way to know how deep the drawdown will be.

If your strategy has a positive expectation, then buying dips (drawdown) in an uptrend will yield much better results than buying the rips (after the rally). A helpful exercise would be to constantly plot your equity curve (that is just a fancy term that means the value of your portfolio) and look at it like any other chart. My good friend, business partner, and all around angel from Heaven, Fred, taught me to trade your equity curve. Meaning, add money when you are in a drawdown, not when you are at new equity highs, and be mindful of a big run in your equity curve because that is usually followed by a drawdown. Adjust your position size and trade your equity curve accordingly. Hopefully, over time, your equity curve will be constantly moving higher.

ADAM'S SMART MONEY SECRETS

Before I send you out into the world to become a smart money superhero, I want to share the 15 smart money secrets that have guided me this far in my trading career:

1. **Always respect risk.** It's the first rule of trading. If you risk too much, you're almost certain to lose the bulk of your trading money. No matter how good you think an idea is, never violate this rule.

2. **Human nature never changes, but human behavior does.** Individuals have the ability to understand when human nature is affecting their mental state and their behavior, and they have the power to willfully rise above that influence.

3. **Set lofty goals.** You and your family deserve the best. At the very beginning of this book, I told you that you deserve to be rich and live

life on your terms. I meant it. Write your goals down, and then let all your decisions be guided by those goals.

4. **Make great decisions.** Rational decisions allow you to focus on your long-term goals while emotional decisions only serve to feed your petty short-term desires. Learn to make rational, unemotional decisions.

5. **Master the learning curve** by understanding that periods of growth are followed by frustrating plateaus. Don't get discouraged, put in the work, break through the mental walls, and you'll soon start making great strides upward. Be prepared to repeat this cycle over and over until you reach your goal.

6. **Embrace and learn from failure.** Most people are afraid of failure so they stop trying new things and they stop growing. Most of our efforts fail; the key is to minimize the cost of failure and maximize the benefit of winning. That way we only have to win a little to win a lot.

7. **Live in and embrace the present moment.** Right now is all that matters. This moment is extremely powerful. Embrace it to the fullest. Avoid living in the past or worrying too much about the future. Learn from the past. Prepare for the future. Live in the moment.

8. **Identify and destroy your mental walls.** You are probably your own biggest obstacle to achieving the success you deserve. Get out of your head. Get out of your own way. Recognize your cognitive biases and mental walls and break through.

9. **Master arbitrage.** If you want to change, you must associate with things that are changing in your direction. Look for the highest return on your investment regardless if you are investing money, time, energy, or love.

10. **Think in probabilities, not in possibilities.** Possibilities are often vague, and they're too much like dreams, and you have no way to know if they'll ever come true. Probabilities are more likely to materialize. You can build an investment strategy around probabilities, while possibilities are fueled by blind hope.

11. **Value, like beauty, is subjective, and in the eye of the beholder.** Warren Buffett says, "Price is what you pay. Value is what you get." If you learn to identify undervalued assets, you can stand to make tidy profits.

12. **Think clearly and act with a purpose.** Work to eliminate your cognitive biases so you can see the work clearly, and make all your decisions confidently with a focus on your long-term goals.

13. **Always do the right thing.** Maintaining a positive mental state is a start, but it's not enough. Translate your positive thoughts into positive actions, do the right thing, and positive results will come.

14. **Find the smart money superhero inside of you.** Being a smart money superhero is not just about taking money out of the market. It's about being the best person you can be: the best spouse, the best parent, the best friend.

15. **Slay the dumb money beast and enter the smart money circle.** Once you've arrived in the smart money circle, remember that it takes effort to stay there. Every once in a while, you may stumble and fall out of it, but once you know something is possible—no matter how difficult it is—you'll know you have the strength and courage to do it again. Now go out there and thrive!

Bibliography

BOOKS

"A Look at Bear and Bull Markets Through History" by Thomas Franck on CNBC, March 14, 2020, https://www.cnbc.com/2020/03/14/a-look-at-bear-and-bull-markets-through-history.html.

Confusion of Confusions by Joseph de la Vega, 1688.

"Different Consequences to Your Decisions," *Principles: Life and Work* by Ray Dalio, September 19, 2017.

The Dow Theory by Robert Rhea, 1932.

The E-Myth Revisited: Why Most Small Businesses Don't Work and What to Do About It by Michael E. Gerber, October 14, 2004.

Extraordinary Popular Delusions and the Madness of Crowds by Charles Mackay, all volumes—complete and unabridged, November 1, 2016.

How to Trade in Stocks by Jesse Livermore, with added material by Richard Smitten, March 10, 2006.

Indiana Jones, https://en.wikipedia.org/wiki/Indiana_Jones

Market Wizards: 12-CD Set (Wiley Trading Audio), August 27, 2012.

The Miracle of Mindfulness: An Introduction to the Practice of Meditation by Thich Nhat Hanh, May 1, 1999.

One Up on Wall Street: How to Use What You Already Know to Make Money in the Market by Peter Lynch, April 3, 2000.

The Power of Now: A Guide to Spiritual Enlightenment by Eckhart Tolle, August 29, 2004.

The Law of Success by Napolean Hill, https://en.wikipedia.org/wiki/The_Law_of_Success.

Reminiscences of a Stock Operator by Edwin Lefèvre and Roger Lowenstein, January 17, 2006.

The Secret by Rhonda Byrne, November 28, 2006.

The Slight Edge: Turning Simple Disciplines into Massive Success and Happiness by Jeff Olson and John David Mann, November 4, 2013.

Stan Weinstein's Secrets for Profiting in Bull and Bear Markets by Stan Weinstein, January 22, 1988.

Superhero definition: https://en.wikipedia.org/wiki/Superhero.

"They," Chapter III of *The Psychology of the Stock Market* by G. C. Selden, 2012, reprinted from the 1919 edition.

MOVIES

Coming to America (1988). Directed by John Landis; written by Eddie Murphy (story) and David Sheffield (screenplay).

Lawrence of Arabia (1962). Directed by David Lean; written by Robert Bolt and Michael Wilson.

Lord of War (2005). Directed and written by Andrew Niccol.

Moneyball (2011). Directed by Bennett Miller; written by Steven Zaillian and Aaron Sorkin.

Princess Bride (1987). Directed by Rob Reiner; written by William Goldman.

Trading Places (1983). Directed by John Landis; writtern by Timothy Harris and Herschel Weingrod.

Index